e-Marketing

Without a doubt, new technologies, and notably the Internet, have had a profound and lasting impact on the marketing function. A paradigm shift has occurred which will forever change the way marketers and marketing managers work. This doesn't mean, however, that 'old' marketing tools are no longer relevant.

In this brand new textbook, Cor Molenaar summarizes classic concepts and current developments to create a new, integrated marketing model, in which all components are part of a customer-oriented approach. Molenaar highlights the influence of the application of IT and the Internet within marketing and reveals how this can affect the form, focus and business model of an organization.

Supplemented by practical examples throughout, *e-Marketing* is an essential read for all marketing and business administration students.

Cor Molenaar is Professor of e-Marketing and Distance Selling at Rotterdam School of Management (Erasmus University, The Netherlands) and is the founder and director of eXQuo Consultancy.

e-Marketing

Applications of information technology
and the Internet within marketing

Cor Molenaar

Routledge
Taylor & Francis Group

LONDON AND NEW YORK

First published 2012
by Routledge
2 Park Square, Milton Park, Abingdon, Oxon OX14 4RN

Simultaneously published in the USA and Canada
by Routledge
711 Third Avenue, New York, NY 10017

Routledge is an imprint of the Taylor & Francis Group, an informa business

British Library Cataloguing in Publication Data
A catalogue record for this book is available from the British Library

Library of Congress Cataloging-in-Publication Data
Molenaar, Cor.
  e-Marketing / Cor Molenaar.
    p. cm.
  Includes bibliographical references and index. 1. Internet marketing.
  I. Title.
HF5415.1265.M649 2011
658.8'72—dc22   2011007005

ISBN: 978–0–415–67727–1 (hbk)
ISBN: 978–0–415–67728–8 (pbk)
ISBN: 978–0–203–80560–2 (ebk)

Typeset in Times New Roman
by Keystroke, Station Road, Codsall, Wolverhampton

Printed and bound in Great Britain by
TJ International Ltd, Padstow, Cornwall

Contents

Figures

Tables

Boxes

Preface

In recent years there have been many developments that have influenced organizations and markets. The most important development undoubtedly is the application and acceptance of the Internet by companies, consumers and governments. This application of the Internet has made markets highly transparent and has enabled relationships to form that were previously inconceivable. What's more, the Internet is a truly international development, the impact of which reaches far beyond national borders; purchases are no longer limited to the action radius of customers and markets can no longer be protected.

It is in part due to the Internet that markets have become so dynamic; there is now an unprecedented volume of supply, a focus on customers, direct communication with customers and a seemingly unlimited supply of products and services. It is clear that these changes have also had an effect on marketing. No longer is it possible for marketing to restrict itself to communication and a relationship with markets; marketing now has to focus on individual customers. Furthermore, marketing has to monitor and guide the organization's external contacts with both customers and suppliers. This change results from the change in markets and the different purchasing behaviour of customers (exploring, finding information and sometimes buying on the Internet).

The technology, too, has to be integrated within marketing activities. In the 1980s this involved marketing information systems and database marketing. In the 1990s it included call centres and customer relationship management (CRM) systems, and since the turn of the century the Internet as well. This enables marketing activities to be carried out not only more efficiently but also differently. It is precisely for this reason that the potential of the application of IT and the Internet has to be determined integrally within the marketing function. But that is not all. As a result of the closer customer relationships and the possibility of communicating more directly, the role of marketing within an organization is also likely to change. The influence of the application of IT and the Internet within marketing must therefore also be examined across the entire organization. This can lead to changes in the form of the organization, in its focus and in its marketing orientations. The business model may well have to be modified as well, in order to remain successful in the market. The issues involved in the application of IT and the Internet are not restricted to certain areas, such as communication or sales, but have a wider impact. As a result, marketing has to be redefined and tested once again. Marketing can no longer be regarded as a separate business function: it influences all other business functions if the customer relationship forms the basis of marketing. The choice of the application of e-marketing and the subsequent choice of the manner in which relationships are maintained determine the position of marketing within the organization (the 'marketing orientation').

e-Marketing is a form of marketing in which the application of IT and the Internet enables the marketing instruments and activities to be focused on recognizable and defined relationships. This means that e-marketing involves identifiable relationships, whereas with classical marketing the relationship with the markets or the submarket is essential. This distinction is so fundamental that there is a completely specific application issue, as well as a possible change in various organization disciplines and the organizational structure.

This book will examine the influence and the possibilities of e-marketing. As the past forms the basis for the present as well as for the future, this is done within a historical framework. The subareas of e-marketing – marketing, information technology and the Internet – are discussed separately within this context. Lastly, the developments are integrated within an organization's possible marketing orientation. This marketing orientation lies at the foundation of the application of e-marketing and of the marketing strategy that is to be applied. This makes it possible to identify, analyse and, if desired, apply future developments. A special look at social media, as part of marketing, will complete the book.

Within business there is a great demand for specialists who are able to size up and apply the influence of new technologies. No longer is it sufficient to have technical staff who are able to make a certain application possible, but the application also has to fit in with the marketing strategy. This book provides a theoretical background, giving students a theoretical foundation in order to be able to place the developments in this larger framework and thereby also to determine the marketing strategy. In addition to providing an understanding of the possibilities of marketing (Part 1), it also gives an insight into the applications of IT (Part 2) and the possibilities offered by the Internet (Part 3). Integrated in this arises the field of e-marketing (Part 4), whereby it is possible to apply e-marketing as a facility within marketing activities, as well as also integrally within the marketing function. For this a choice has to be made for the strategy that is to be followed. This is the basis for the marketing orientations (Part 5), whereby a specific interpretation of the marketing instruments and activities determines the focus of an organization and the manner in which relationships are given shape.

This book is aimed at students at Bachelor's level and Master's students of marketing and business administration. Also students who are following a technical course will be able to use this book in order to place the applications of IT and the Internet within the business function of marketing. In addition to the rudiments of these disciplines the changes brought about by the Internet and IT will be explained. This makes this book topical and enables it to cater for people in education, but also in business life. Managers responsible for e-marketing and Internet applications will use this book as a reference and for decision-making. In order to increase the direct applicability of this knowledge many practical examples are used and extra attention is given to the accessibility and practical application of the subject matter. I do of course welcome any suggestions, from students, lecturers as well as people from the field.

The history and technical information for the companies and software/hardware developments mentioned throughout the text can be found freely available on websites such as Wikipedia.

Prof Dr C.N.A. Molenaar
cor@cormolenaar.nl
www.cormolenaar.nl
www.hetnieuwewinkelen.com

Introduction

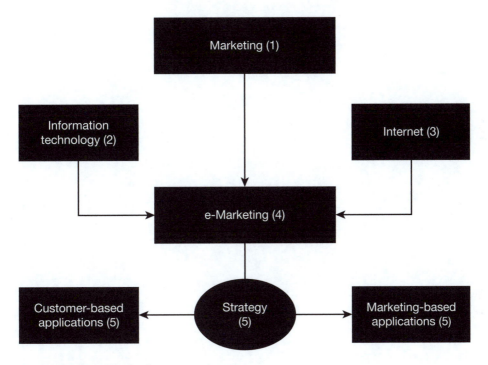

Figure 0.1 Outline of the book

e-Marketing is the application of information technology (IT) and the Internet within the marketing function. This enables the supply of products and services to be better geared towards the needs and wishes of individual customers. What characterizes e-marketing is the identifiable relationships with customers, the outside-in approach, whereby the needs and wishes of customers determine the supply. This is only possible if there is a close relationship with the customers and a direct communication supported by knowledge of the customers' wishes and the possibilities of the organization. The various applications of IT and communication technology (such as the Internet, mobile telecommunication and scanning/ automatic identification) support the objectives of e-marketing – namely, building and maintaining a relationship with an identified customer.

This book examines the development of marketing (Part 1) which leads to identifiable relationships; the development of IT (Part 2) which leads to specific function support and customer-oriented information management; and the development of the Internet (Part 3) which leads to general acceptance of the medium by businesses and private individuals. These three developments are integrated within the marketing function, e-marketing (Part 4) and change the marketing function both on an operational and on a strategic level.

In addition, organizations will also be modified (Part 5) in response to market developments. These changes in markets (dynamics) in particular will lead to a greater focus on individual customer relationships. This will require a strategic change to the organization's focus and the marketing orientation. The past leads to the situation in the present and forms the basis for developments in the future.

Part 1

Developments of marketing

An historical outline

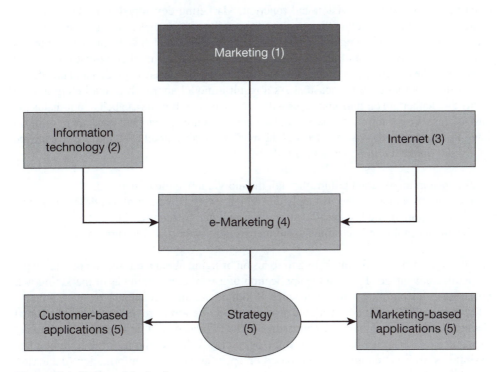

Figure P1.1 Outline of the book

Marketing has been an important business function for decades. It helps to give form to the relationship with the market and the target groups, competitive advantages are realized and more insight is gained into the needs of potential customers. In the last few decades, however, market conditions have changed immensely. There is greater prosperity, society has become multicultural, the various age groups have their own distinctive behaviour and due to greater mobility shopping can now be done everywhere, far from home. What's more, the application of information technology (IT) has also led to changes.

Since the 1980s IT has become important, initially through adding efficiency in the business processes, and later for efficiency in direct communications. Since the 1990s, however, IT has become integrated within marketing communication (telephone, Internet and databases), and it now contributes to greater insights into the purchasing behaviour of customers and the effectiveness of marketing activities. Under pressure from IT companies, specific systems have been installed in businesses that can support and initiate contacts with customers (CRM applications). As a result, IT has become essential within marketing. But marketing, too, has become an integral part of business processes and organization functions.

All these developments in markets and within businesses have changed the application of marketing as a strategy, vision and function. Marketing developed from the economic sciences, and within marketing there is a need to predict effects, make the results measurable and work with economic models. Within the sales paradigm, which is the original paradigm of marketing, activities can be controlled by the suppliers and marketing instruments are defined. But the effectiveness of the marketing efforts is not so easy to predict and the effects of the efforts not so easy to measure. As a result a model approach to marketing is only possible under certain circumstances, as will be shown later. It is human behaviour that is the cause of this. What's more, the market and the market conditions are not constant or uniform either. Particularly in the last few decades the market and the market conditions have changed rapidly and markedly, in part as a result of:

- fragmentation of target groups through the individualization of demand;
- technological innovations in supply and a high level/degree of product differentiation;
- globalization, in the last decades strongly stimulated by the use of the Internet; and
- the greater mobility of customers and increased prosperity and leisure time.

It is no longer sufficient for marketing to focus on bringing about a transaction or realizing a competitive advantage. Through the application of e-marketing the focus of marketing will shift towards the building and maintenance of individual, direct relationships.

The changes of the last decades have proven to be an iterative process that has had a direct effect on customers and market circumstances. The influence of IT and recently the Internet has worked as a catalyst, but this is just the beginning. e-Marketing uses the technological possibilities of direct communication based on specific individual information (database). This will lead to another application of marketing instruments, marketing activities and the place of marketing within an organization.

1 Marketing and strategy

Marketing is the noun of the verb 'to market', which means bringing products and services to the market. It is a commercial discipline, giving form to the relationship with the market, particularly the relationship with customers, both current and potential. Marketing developed from the sales issues faced by businesses. In the early days of the Industrial Revolution mechanization enabled mass production and there was no longer a distinction between the various products. These products (initially), which were produced for an unknown customer, had to be 'sold' to that unknown customer. The origins of marketing can therefore be found in the 1930s when production became increasingly more important. During the Industrial Revolution factories were built in order to process raw materials (such as cotton in England) or to produce machines. Particularly in the first decades of the twentieth century, factories were set up for the manufacture of consumer goods. This production went hand in hand with a specialization of labour and an increasing prosperity.

1.1 The product concept

Initially, marketing was based on products and had a product orientation. The focus was aimed at the production process and physical products, not on the potential customers. With further mechanization (see later Fordism) and increasing prosperity as well as an increasing specialization of the workforce (in which one was not able to meet one's entire needs independently), the demand for products increased, but so did the supply of uniform products (or identical products). This was an interplay that was yet further stimulated by the increase in transport possibilities (train and car), which increased the sales area. The relationship between customer and supplier, however, also became increasingly diffused (compared with customization). Intermediaries such as shopkeepers and wholesalers (the distribution chain) appeared on the scene, whereas prior to that there had been direct contact between consumer and producer (Figure 1.1). In this period (the early decades of the twentieth century) the emphasis was on expanding the production possibilities and improving the efficiency of production and distribution. In terms of marketing this is referred to as the 'product concept', and the emphasis lies in improving the quality of the product.

1.2 The sales concept

In the further development of mass production, the focus on the creation of sales also increased. The focus shifted from manufacturing a good-quality product to the sale of this product. We refer here to a 'selling concept', a sales-oriented philosophy. In this concept the emphasis is on the efficiency of the sales. It is not explicitly the wishes and desires of the

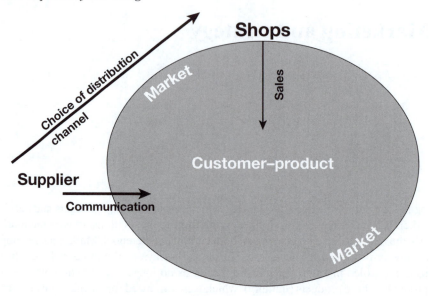

Figure 1.1 Classical approach of the market

customers that are central here; rather, that the product can be effectively manufactured, distributed and sold to an unidentified consumer. It was not until after 1950, when prosperity increased greatly, that the focus shifted towards the needs of the market to which the production and sales could be geared. In addition, increasingly more attention was given to the needs of the market, submarkets (target groups) and eventually also individuals. This concentrated focus on market needs was made possible by the development of increasingly better technologies that enabled the analysis and monitoring of this demand (market research and market analyses, but also later scanning).

1.3 Changes in the market

Markets became increasingly more mature, with articulate customers who knew what they wanted. This resulted in a decrease of the initial growth of the market and the supplier having to focus increasingly on replacement demand and the specific needs of certain segments in the market.

Distribution is also an important factor in this shift in focus. As a result of improvements in the distribution network (rail, hauliers and motorways) it became increasingly easy to quickly send goods to other countries. Soon even more links arose in the distribution process, such as wholesalers, importers and dealers, who managed to efficiently reach a large market. The standardization of regulations through economic collaborations such as the ECSC, later the EEC and EU, stimulated international trade. This is actually the basis of the marketing concept, whereby 'to market' lies at its very heart, a focus of marketing on exchange and transactions. Three elements are important in this marketing approach:

1. *An orientation towards the customer*: the market or the target group. The wishes and desires of this group determine the supply and the exchange factors (marketing mix).

2. *An integrated approach*: combining the supply, the marketing and the organization. In fact all relevant functions, instruments and decisions need to be integrated in order to be able to approach customers effectively.
3. *A pursuit of profit*: The exchange transaction also has to be profitable.

1.4 Relationship focus

Eventually the focus of marketing did not stay on exchange but rather on the further evaluation of relationships. Particularly in the 1980s when direct marketing made its breakthrough as a communication discipline within marketing and in the 1990s when communication technology acquired a place within marketing (such as the telephone and databases), the focus of marketing activities started to be very much directed at communicating with individual market parties. The application of IT and later e-marketing were important driving forces behind this. This shift from unidentified relationships to identified relationships is essential, as this requires a strategic approach to marketing. There needs to be a database with contacts, customer details as well as a direct relationship and communication. The marketing function as a consequence could no longer be isolated within the marketing department, but IT, too, became important. In addition, many more reports were written and analyses carried out in order to determine the effectiveness of the marketing efforts. This led in the 1990s to the development of CRM, customer relationship management. At the same time the focus also increasingly shifted from the financial function to more profitable customers along with profitable markets and products (Figure 1.2).

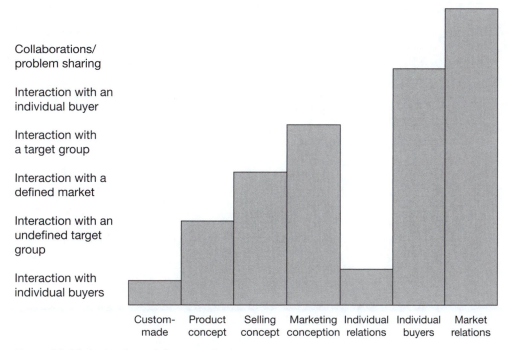

Figure 1.2 Marketing focus and communication

Summary

- The focus of marketing shifted from having a sales focus, in which the realization of a transaction was the objective, to a relationship focus.
- Within the sales paradigm this is a shift from a transaction moment to an identified relationship.
- Realizing a transaction was still the objective, but because the relationship was important, continuity and trust were also important factors.
- It became crucial to know and communicate directly with customers.

2 Marketing as a concept

The concept of strategic marketing is important in a competitive market. It is fierce competition that leads to an organization having to always think about the strategy to follow, and the focus and relationship with market parties – the customers in particular. An organization has to not only identify changes in the market, but also interpret and respond to them. This is only possible if there is a good interaction with the market parties, which allows the signals of change to be picked up immediately. This is possible through a close relationship with the distribution channel and suppliers. Within the organization there has to be a system of communication and knowledge management that can bring the communication directly to the decision maker. This internal adjustment is important for effective decision-making. But also externally we have to look at the mutual relationships in the market, the relationship within the distribution channel, the relationship with customers and the differential advantage of products, services and in the competitive position.

2.1 The sales paradigm

As marketing arose from an issue concerning sales, it is logical that the activities and instruments of marketing fit within a sales paradigm. An organization looks at the market from its own perspective and determines the distribution channels; this is an inside-out approach, on the basis of which the competitive advantage is determined, the product is modified and the price or promotion is adjusted. The organization can determine these criteria itself, which in turn enables it to create a distinction from other suppliers. The focus can, however, change within this paradigm. Over the years the focus has shifted from a strong product focus to one aimed at direct communication and individual relationships. The fundamentals, however, have not changed: there is still a strong transaction orientation which focuses on bringing about transactions. Sales and market share are still important indicators for determining the success of marketing efforts. The marketing instruments are still determined on the basis of market circumstances, such as the collective demand, competitive advantage and desired sales and profit per product.

2.2 Strategic marketing concept

The shift from product orientation to sales orientation and then to a strategic marketing concept is a radical change. This resulted in a split between sales and marketing. Sales can be regarded as more of an operational activity – the realization of the transaction – whereas marketing is more concerned with creating the necessary conditions. The strategic objective of marketing is to position the product or service in the market in such a way that a positive association arises, a 'top-of-mind' position and good preconditions for being able to realize the sale. In doing so, one must look not only at the actual product, but also at the market, the target group, distributors, the communication and the competition.

The focus of marketing has expanded within the concept of strategic marketing, and as a result it has also become more important to an organization strategically. What is more, the need to apply information technology to maintain the relationship with the market and business contacts has increased tremendously. In addition to the classic marketing approach, the e-marketing strategy has to embrace the application of information technology and the Internet.

The strategic marketing concept involves:

- a tenable competitive advantage;
- the long-term interests of the customers (i.e. a continuous relationship with the buyers);
- a good market positioning within the defined market (here one has to consider the values associated with a product or an organization and the value as perceived by external relations);
- a continuous process of actions that promote the relationship (this may be aimed at the defined market, but may also be aimed at the individual buyers); and
- a good supply of information within the organization concerning market changes and customer preferences.

Initially the strategic marketing concept was intended to provide the organization (or products) with a tenable competitive advantage by creating distinctive product values, a positive perception among business relations, good market positioning and a continuous relationship with customers. These values led to the creation of a positive image and a 'preferred buying concept' in the eyes of potential customers, whereby a customer expressed a preference for certain products on the basis of experience, perception or expectations. This led to good customer relations and often also to better pricing (for the supplier); the customer was more inclined to buy the product or to buy from the organization. Consider, for example, the value of a product brand. Customers recognize the product and trust it. Because of the advertising efforts imaginary values are also attributed to the product, for which a higher price is paid compared with brandless products. Marketing efforts are aimed at acquiring this advantage. The integral efforts of the marketing and the organization should contribute to this objective (competitive advantage) but only limited use of information technology is necessary. For the communication, in the early days mass communication to the market or to a target group was used. Direct communication was not aimed at individuals but at the house (location oriented), using direct mail (sometimes only with an address and no name), door-to-door distribution and flyers.

With the arrival of database marketing at the end of the 1980s it also became possible to direct communications to a single individual. As a result, the focus of strategic marketing shifted to the maintenance of relationships within these sales paradigms. Address information was used and, if possible, purchase information in order to inform customers about new products, additional products or extra services. This was the start of direct mail and, later, telemarketing. In addition to the advantages of direct contact there was also the advantage of efficiency. Promotions could be carried out in a highly targeted manner and in a way that would provide the best chance of success. These activities related to marketing communication and already at an early stage made use of information and communication technology.

2.3 Changes in the strategic marketing concept

In today's world it is no longer enough to focus merely on the competitive advantage based on products. The strategic marketing concept developed in markets that were less dynamic and also better defined than they are today. Now, because of the dynamics of the market the competitive positions are less clear. What is more, as a result of the Internet the action radius of customers has expanded enormously and knowledge has increased. It is becoming increasingly difficult to be truly distinctive and to get customers to commit themselves to a product, brand or shop. In addition, target groups are subject to change, and customers are no longer predictable, though they can still be influenced. Following the advent of the Internet, developments followed one another at a high rate and continue to do so. Customers are well informed of these changes and are more aware than previously. It is sufficient to quickly 'google'.

Clearly, the strategic marketing concept is more important for marketing than ever before; distinctive supply and competitive advantage influence the buying process and buying preferences, and it is through a close relationship with customers that more knowledge can be gained on the needs of customers and their changing wishes. Today, continuous communication is possible via the Internet, and customers' individual demands, needs and wishes have to be analysed better than ever before. At the same time the speed at which organizations need to respond to changes is faster than previously and the time available to do this is shorter. The use of IT is therefore of strategic importance; the information supply and the interaction with identifiable relationships (such as customers) are based on the use of IT.

In the current buying process the 'window of opportunity' is very short, from several minutes for an impulse purchase to several days for a 'shopping good'. A quick response to questions from the customer is essential. But also assessing the potential needs (latent demand) in order to communicate at the right moment has become increasingly important. This relationship can best be built and maintained through the use of databases and communication technology, with the Internet as an important component.

There is a strong correlation between the dynamics of the market and the adoption of technology by customers and organizations, and marketing relationships are becoming increasingly important. Marketing, as in 'going to the market', was originally based on being able to clearly communicate product values, controlling the distribution channel and effectively carrying out the communication strategy. These are a set of externally oriented activities, which gave marketing a distinct operational character. Because of the change of focus in the marketing concept, from a sales concept to an emphasis on identifiable relationships, attention has shifted towards building and maintaining continuous relationships (Table 2.1). The new technology, the Internet in particular, supports this change.

2.4 From market approach to direct communication

Business, as in 'doing business', has always been focused on personal contacts. Interaction forms the basis of business, but is also at the same time a source of information. Information can be gained about the customers' wishes, the competition and the possibilities of the supply. Previously the relationship was largely based on trust and wanting to give the other business one's custom, but as a result of the developments in the twentieth century discussed above, trading increasingly became the basis of the business: the ability to purchase and to sell. As organizations grew in size and distribution channels developed, personal relationships were increasingly replaced by relationships with products or organizations. Here, too, trust and wanting to give another one's custom formed the basis of doing business, but trading

Table 2.1 The evolution of marketing as a concept

Period (approximate)	Marketing	Focus	Application
Pre-1930	Production concept	Product	Personal contacts, also a great deal of customization
	Product concept	Efficiency, quality and availability	
1930–1950	Sales concept	Transactions	Distribution channel and personal contact
			Advertising, mass media, product characteristics
1950–1980	Marketing concept	Bringing and stimulating transactions	Mass media supplemented by direct marketing, loyalty concepts
	Strategic marketing concept	Strong focus on competitive advantage and repeat purchases	
1980–2008	Integral marketing concept	Communication and direct contacts	Interactivity, direct contacts and moment-specific communication such as location-based
2008 to present	Relationship concept		Integration of location-based and the Internet

also became more rational, and price became an increasingly important element. As a result this increased the pressure to make production cheaper, to introduce more mechanization and to optimize processes. But this was at the expense of the personal relationship, making the communication with the market ('market communication') increasingly important. This communication was not a true form of communication, as this would require an interaction. Market communication consisted of conveying the values of the products and the organization via mass media to a defined market, in order to influence people's perceptions and promote customer loyalty. For items that required some explanation (such as computers in those days, or complex financial products such as mortgages and pensions), personal contact was still desired.

The marketing communication of manufacturers was focused on selling the product as effectively as possible, with product information and product values. Advertisements and commercial messages were therefore predominately informative, but a direct response was not possible. A distinction arose between making products and selling through a distribution channel on the one hand, and the customer contact with a sales point within the distribution channel on the other. The personal customer relationship was part of the sales approach at the distribution point, and manufacturers communicated the product values and competitive advantages compared with other suppliers. Marketing was mainly applied by manufacturers, and a direct relationship was not necessarily an important component.

In the 1980s this changed, and consideration of the relationships within marketing rapidly gained momentum, largely prompted by the advent of automated systems. In 1980 Siemens introduced the first laser printer: a so-called 'line printer' for computer output, which for the first time allowed the personalization of letters. Now letters could contain variable and fixed texts. A name and address could, for example, be added to a standard text, as well as personal

Figure 2.1 The changing face of retail

messages such as gender, purchasing frequency or past purchases. As far as the recipient was concerned, this was a personal letter. All he or she had to do was complete and return the reply coupon in order to buy the product. This form of direct communication was referred to as direct marketing, and was quickly taken up, particularly by magazines (subscription sales) and mail-order companies (direct sales).

It soon became apparent that not only could the response (or non-response) to the letter produce more information about the customer (and the target group), but the results and success of the communication activities could also be assessed. As the personal computer became widely used in offices, direct marketing was applied increasingly frequently. A database of customer details (at least the names and addresses) connected to a printer was enough. This form of direct communication required the organization to know and communicate with the customers and prospects, and information was gained on the response behaviour. The unidentified relationships of marketing and those within the strategic marketing concept became 'identified relationships', however limited they were – often no more than the name and address details. In the case of businesses, added to the name and address were details such as a contact person and an indication of the customer value (sales or turnover figures). In the world of advertising, at this point specialist agencies started to focus on direct communication. Direct marketing agencies were usually part of or allied to a larger advertising agency.

This gives us a good picture of the position of direct marketing at the time (the 1980s), as part of the discipline of marketing communication. However, the realization soon began to grow that automation might well become an important tool in marketing communication. As a result the manufacturers' distribution model as described above was also evaluated. Manufacturers became increasingly interested in individual customers and the communication with these customers, and savings schemes and loyalty programmes were a first attempt to realize a direct contact.

In the early 1990s direct marketing was complemented by direct communication making use of the telephone – telemarketing. This enabled direct contact with customers or potential customers. Initially people and companies were telephoned en masse by telemarketing agencies with the purpose of selling (teleselling) or conducting research (tele research). This *outbound telemarketing* became increasingly more advanced but also led to growing irritation. Consumers in particular found it annoying that they were called with commercial messages at popular times, such as between six and nine o'clock in the evening. Eventually this led to restrictive legislation, but also to changes within companies. The Do Not Call Me Register, with which consumers could register if they did not wish to be phoned for commercial purposes, became popular very quickly.

The telephone is now increasingly being used for 'inbound' calls, whereby customers phone companies for services or support, and it has become a tool for direct communication along with flyers and letters. And the latest addition has been the Internet which makes many different forms of direct communication possible, such as FAQs, chatting, email and twittering. All this is part of e-marketing and should therefore also be part of an organization's e-marketing strategy (Figure 2.2).

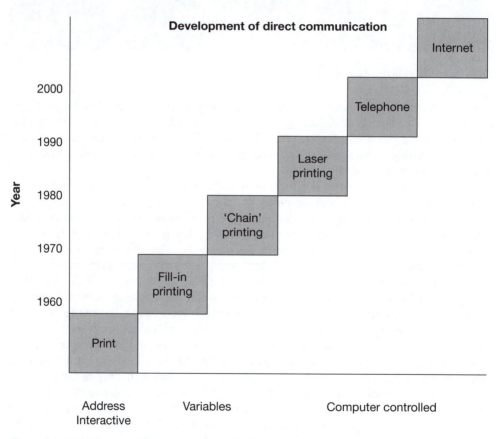

Figure 2.2 Development of direct communication

Box 2.1 3.6 million people do not wish to be telephoned

THE HAGUE – Since October 2009 one million people have registered with the Do Not Call Me Register. Telephone salespeople are no longer allowed to bother them. The total number of people who have blocked their phone number from telemarketers is now 3.6 million.

This was announced by the Ministry of Economic Affairs last Thursday. Prior to 1 October, some 2.6 million consumers had already registered with the existing Infofilter.

Companies are no longer permitted to call telephone numbers registered in the Do Not Call Me Register to phone private individuals. What's more, sales staff now always have to ask whether they may ring again and whether the consumer wishes to have their number included in the Do Not Call Me Register. If the consumer wishes to have their number included, the salesperson has to arrange for this immediately.

Source: *De Gelderlander*, 24 December 2009

Summary

- The marketing concept has changed from a product concept to a sales concept, and then eventually to a strategic marketing concept.
- The focus of marketing has changed. It is no longer based on merely the company's product or service but also on the market conditions.
- Within the strategic marketing concept competitive advantage is important as this will lead to buyers' preference.
- As a result of the use of information technology and the Internet, an integral marketing concept has increasingly developed whereby in addition to the product characteristics all other facets of an organization are important, such as the proposition, image and the delivery (ordered today, delivered tomorrow).
- The future focus of marketing will be on building and maintaining continuous identified relationships on the basis of customers' wishes and preferences. This interaction will become an important condition for the relationship with customers. Therefore, it is no longer just about effecting a transaction but also about realizing a tenable relationship with customers and relevant market parties.

3 Marketing as an activity

Change can come about through the use of new techniques such as mechanization and automation; but it can also come about because a need for change is felt. Both of these circumstances arose at the start of the 1980s. At that time there was a recession in Europe with high unemployment and a reduction in disposable income. As a result, a need to adapt arose among companies in the areas of organization as well as sales and marketing. Effectiveness and efficiency became increasingly important. The application of automation and change in processes formed part of this adaptation drive. The marketing function, too, was analysed further and more effective sales and communication techniques were sought. The change in the market made adaptations to marketing activities necessary.

The consumer in the 1980s was different from that of previous decades: he or she was more outspoken, more individual and spent money more freely. These aspects helped to create a good foundation for building relationships, not just with a market or a target group, but a personal one with the individual customer. Within the existing marketing paradigm, which was focused on transactions, a shift took place to a focus on relationships and direct communication.

The development towards direct, identified relationships in marketing arose from:

- increased interest in direct distribution and direct communication as a consequence of the efficiency of these activities, but also because of the possibilities offered by this technology;
- market fragmentation and the possibility of dividing the market into identifiable groups (target groups) (demand from customers became increasingly more personal and determined by the moment; the classic target groups eroded away);
- the buyers' relationships with brands that developed (customers began to attach increasing value to the imaginary values of a product);
- product innovations and differentiation which led to target groups becoming ever smaller, as well as an ever shorter product life cycle; and
- the application of information technology in general.

3.1 Direct distribution and communication

New distribution techniques that were aimed at lower costs, and therefore also lower prices, formed the basis for a greater effectiveness and efficiency. Mail-order companies and insurance firms were highly active and adopted these new techniques very quickly. The application of direct mail led to an intensification of the market approach and to direct sales to potential customers. In addition, the professionalization of the (direct) communication agencies led to increased effectiveness. As the costs and return of a direct marketing campaign were easy to work out, the result was easy to determine quite accurately. On the basis of responses (direct sales) it could be calculated immediately whether a promotion had been profitable and with which articles. This led to improved insights into the success of marketing activities, as well as into the profitability of customers and customer groups.

This effectiveness in distribution and communication was not initially such a great change in the marketing concept. It was merely an adjustment within the sales paradigm. The truly big change did not take place until customers also adopted the new technologies and began using them en masse; this only occurred after 2005.

3.2 Market fragmentation

Another trend noted in the 1980s was a marked increase in the pressure on leisure time. The number of double-income earners rose, which resulted in more people having less time to shop. As a consequence convenience became more important. Home deliveries and advice on the telephone (for example, insurance companies selling by direct marketing without agents, such as Direct Writers) helped to save time, which consumers began to value more and more. At the same time, consumers started to display increasingly divergent behaviour. The uniformity of buyers' behaviour of the 1950s and 1960s faded away and a variation in buying preference was observed which depended on the place of residence, profession, family composition, income and, for example, gender as well. Following the emergence of subcultures in the 1960s (such as the *nozems* and the *Provo* counter-culture in the Netherlands, the skinheads in the UK and the hoods in the United States), youths became increasingly outspoken and also wanted to show themselves to be different in other areas. This group of youngsters from the 1960s subsequently became the breadwinners of the 1980s, but their behaviour remained radically different from that of the generations before them. The openness to change and recalcitrant behaviour of the 1960s as well as the need to be different from others and other generations remained as the cohort got older, which led to a stronger individualization of purchasing behaviour. This revealed itself for the first time in the 1980s (Table 3.1).

Old market segmentation models that were based on objective characteristics in order to predict the behaviour of groups (the target groups) increasingly lost value. Objective characteristics no longer led to a uniform (buyer) behaviour, and the actual buying behaviour became the basis of the trend. The characteristics of the actual buying behaviour could afterwards be used to determine the identical behaviour of groups. This was not to do with objectively recognizable criteria but behaviour-based criteria (for example, which product combinations were bought at which time, in which shop and for what amount). The predefined target groups made way for behaviourally defined target groups (behaviour based), or post defined target groups. Inevitably, this more complex behaviour requires more analysis, which can therefore only be done well by using information technology tools. Behaviour is generation based and is no longer based upon age group alone.

3.3 Brand loyalty

Because of an increase in the supply of more or less comparable articles it became increasingly difficult for suppliers to realize a competitive advantage. As a result it became necessary to communicate more and more the imaginary values of the product. Such values included convenience, trust, familiarity and brand values. Testimonials were an example of creating trust by using customer references or recommendations from well-known people. These days

Table 3.1 Overview of generations, environmental factors and behavioural factors

Born	Adolescence	Environment	Behaviour profile
1945–1955	1960s	Changes, positive, no war, emergence of the youth subculture	Open to change, somewhat arrogant, self-confident
1955–1965	1970s	Negative, recession, oil crisis, Vietnam War, high inflation	Uncertain, short-term focus, jump at any opportunities that arise, not hesitant
1965–1975	1980s	New selfishness, individualism (Thatcher, Reagan), reward performance	Selfish, looking after one's own interests, making one's own choices, independent
1975–1985	1990s	Changes through technology, highly focused on communication (mobile telephone, Internet), economic growth	Restless, much communication, adopt new technology, social
1985–1995	2000s	Uncertainty, large transparency, restless, rapid changes, international unrest (Iraq, Afghanistan) recession, financial crisis	'Remote' generation, know and do everything, short concentration span, want to be entertained, many 'casual' relationships

weblogs and guestbooks on Internet sites are used frequently. Brands were also often sold on the basis of the imaginary values that were attributed to the product (Table 3.2). Originally products were assigned brands in order to create trust. In this way the brand was able to set itself apart from the brandless products and so capitalize on the suspicion of consumers. But this changed as a result of:

- mechanization and later automation – consumers became increasingly convinced that bad articles were no longer being sold;
- legislation to protect consumers – under pressure from consumer organizations, such as Consumer Watchdog (USA) and Which? in the UK, legislation was repeatedly modified and the consumer was given more and more protection;
- shops that wanted to gain the trust of the buyers – exchange, money back and other guarantees removed potential uncertainties; and
- manufacturers offering ever more guarantees with the product, including a repair service as well as an exchange guarantee. The guarantee period became longer and longer, up to several years. This greatly increased the trust in the product.

As we have seen, it was actually marketing that had to make a distinction between various, often similar products. Marketing had to realize a competitive advantage. By applying automation in the production process, it became increasingly easy to make various product

Table 3.2 Top brands 2010

Brand	Value of the brand (US$ billion in round figures)
Coca-Cola	67
Microsoft	57
IBM	56
General Electric	49
Intel	32
Nokia	30
Toyota	28
Disney	27.5
McDonalds	27.4
Mercedes	22

Source: Business Week

types with small differences but also in small quantities. It was difficult to communicate these various product types individually. And so other methods were sought for communicating these individually en masse.

One method was to communicate a group of products, so that all the distinct types did not have to capture a market position separately (an efficiency advantage). The brand could function as a communication icon onto which many different product types could be attached. Umbrella brands are an example of this.

But as a result of the adaptations among suppliers and in legislation, consumer trust increased as well. As all (bona fide) shops and manufacturers offered such certainties to the buyers the competitive advantage no longer existed and it was replaced by competitive equality. For the brand, based on the product or the manufacturer, there was now no distinction as a result of the automatic production process. And trust on the basis of the brand was no longer sufficient either for a competitive advantage. Other values became more important (an extra perception in the eyes of the customer). These imaginary values were built up based on marketing activities such as marketing communication, or product characteristics such as name, packaging, design and colour.

Marketing communication, however, was still based on communication to a target group or the market (undefined relationships). As product innovations quickly succeeded one another (through automation, for example) and due to the various product characteristics and types, direct communication turned out to be a better means of communication. This enabled a highly personal response to customers' needs and preferences. As the customers were known, it was also possible to communicate new products and innovations directly to them. Not only was this form of communication more effective, but a direct response was also possible. Early introductions and effectively reaching the most promising prospects turned out to be successful. The Internet has helped to make marketing activities even more focused and personal. The communication can take place through a website, but this is usually still very static. Much better options are weblogs, emails or other developments, such as Twitter and social media. These enable very small target groups (even one-to-one communication) to be reached. The concept of a 'long tail', whereby in addition to a few popular articles, many articles are sold in small numbers, applies to communication as well. Larger groups of consumers are reached via mass media or the traditional media, and personal communication in small groups is achieved with new media. This allows the communication to be kept to a minimum. Usually a limited number of messages will take place through the traditional media and an unlimited number via targeted media. Often the traditional media is used to develop brand awareness, to build up imaginary values or to generate traffic to the site (or shop).

Summary

- Marketing as an activity was largely focused on the sales paradigm in the early days, which led to a relationship with markets and target groups.
- Market share was an important instrument for measuring the success of marketing activities.
- Communication was primarily based on product properties.
- Because of the fragmentation of target groups and the application of information technology, it became increasingly important as well as increasingly easy to target the communication towards individuals and identified relationships.
- As a result, marketing activities changed from trying to make the product distinctive from the competition to building and maintaining relationships with customers.

4   Marketing instruments

Traditional marketing refers to the following marketing instruments: price, place, product and promotion. These instruments are intended to position (that is, to market) a product or service in the market and to enable clear and unambiguous communication to that market. The *price* is usually determined by the cost price and the possible market price; the *place* of sale is a distribution policy with sales outlets; the *product* is an entity with value, as well as physical and virtual properties; and the *promotion* is usually mass communication using mass media and generic product-based promotional activities. This approach was defined in the 1950s and elaborated upon by, for example, Philip Kotler in his book *Principles of Marketing*. The marketing strategy is based on the definition of these marketing instruments, and the relationship between the products (or business) and market (or target group) forms the guiding principle.

With e-marketing, however, there is a specific application of the marketing instruments, as the focus is not on the market or the target groups. Instead the focus is on the identified relationship. This enables the marketing instruments to be used in a highly personal and individual manner: a customer-based price, a customized product (certainly in the case of services or by adding service elements to a physical product), a preferred sales outlet, Internet, telephone or physical place (multi-channel approach) and targeted promotions based on behaviour. Although this does not reduce the value of the marketing instruments, it does mean that their application depends on individual customers and the degree to which an organization is willing and able to respond to personal wishes.

In the traditional approach to marketing, instruments are adapted to the market situation, whereas in the e-marketing approach they are adapted to the individual relationships.

4.1 Product innovations

As a result of product innovations fashion has become increasingly important in recent years. The sensitivity to fashion has led to product life cycles becoming shorter, with new product variants coming on the scene more quickly. In order to be able to communicate quickly about these new products, a direct relationship is, of course, advisable. Attention is no longer sought through the (mass) media, which is a rather slow process. Instead, direct communication is used. The differences between what is on offer today and other products or previous product generations can be communicated very directly and in a highly targeted fashion. The application of technology is the main cause for the realization of product innovations, but direct communication can also help to achieve large sales quickly (until eclipsed by the latest innovations).

Efficient production technology has also made it possible to produce many product variations in small numbers at low cost. Each product variation appeals to a relatively small group

Figure 4.1 Changes in shopping behaviour from location-based to the Internet

of consumers who have to be approached. The mass media is not effective for this. Target group media (such as magazines) have a much too long 'lead time', so direct communication is the most suitable method for communicating product variations or product changes. Good target group selection, identifiable relationships and the use of communication technologies such as the Internet, mobile applications, laser printers and the telephone are ideally suited communication to these smaller groups.

4.2 Price differentiation

Each product area can be priced separately. This makes it easier to better match the product to the target group. The price no longer has to be fixed, but can be based on specific product characteristics as described above. The price can also vary according to the distribution channel (direct sales, Internet and shops). The customer then chooses his or her preferred channel, with all the advantages and limitations that come with it.

Also, by determining specific customer values, a more personal price can be realized. This can be done by giving discounts to loyal customers, which some supermarkets do with their loyalty cards, or by offering other specific advantages to customers such as services (for example, with loyalty programmes). The price as a fixed component of a product is therefore no longer the only possibility; a more personal price strategy, linked to personal services, leads to more binding with customers.

4.3 Promotions

Promotions have also become more personal. Direct media, letters, telephone and email have become the fundamentals of communication. If personal details are also used then we speak of direct communication. This is no longer product-related but person- and behaviour-related. The use of loyalty systems and the registration of purchases and behaviour on the Internet make it possible to communicate certain benefits based on a customer's recorded purchasing behaviour, but also through reference to other participants. This could be by referring to other participants within a similar loyalty system, but also through the application of affiliate marketing on the Internet by referring to other suppliers. This has led to the reduced efficiency of the price in favour of other benefits such as customer knowledge and personal service.

Box 4.1 How to get loyal customers

But as shoppers need supermarkets over Christmas, so supermarkets need shoppers. This year the battle for shoppers' loyalty between the UK's large grocers is fiercer than ever. Tesco might be the UK market leader by a country mile (it is also the third largest supermarket in the world), but rivals Asda, J. Sainsbury, Wm Morrison, The Co-op, Waitrose and Marks & Spencer are all in better shape than they have been for a long time. City analysts calculate that there is more promotional activity than ever before as the chains vie for loyalty.

Tesco, for its part, has been offering double Clubcard points to shoppers and recently sent out its February money-off vouchers early. Sir Terry says that promotions are 'part and parcel' of what supermarkets do, but he concedes that the level of promotion is high and will come down next year.

'I think there will be fewer promotions next year because high–low promotions reach their natural peak and then you get diminishing marginal benefit. And so I think it is past its peak,' he says.

Source: *Daily Telegraph*, 26 December 2009

4.4 Place

Place as a marketing instrument is no longer a physical, location-based place. Customers now have the choice of going out to a shop or home shopping, with the Internet as the major channel. In addition, there are still the classic home shopping possibilities, such as mail-order companies, teleselling and buying via a television channel. The latter is very popular in Spanish-speaking countries and the United States. Suppliers therefore have to decide upon the best sales tactic to employ: a distribution channel with a physical shop, an Internet-only outlet, or a multi-channel strategy where various purchasing options are available. Each distribution channel has its own advantages and disadvantages, and attracts its own particular customers. These days a deliberate strategy, based on the expected preferences of customers, is part of a marketing strategy (Figures 4.2 and 4.3).

4.5 The application of information technology

Marketing started to make use of the possibilities offered by automation relatively late in the day. There are many reasons for this:

- In many companies the marketing function developed quite late. This was because the the focus was on marketing, as in 'to market', which was a sales-oriented approach with fewer possibilities for automation to be applied. The focus was mainly on mass communication, both in the printed form and through other mass media.
- The application possibilities of automation were also not that easy to fit into marketing. The operational activities are difficult to quantify and automate. What is more, marketing people often also had an aversion to technology. There is a certain fear attached to new technology.
- It took a long time for specific software to become available which could be used effectively for marketing purposes. It was not until the mid 1980s that the first specific marketing program was developed. For a long time all that was available were generic software programs, such as word processing and spreadsheets.

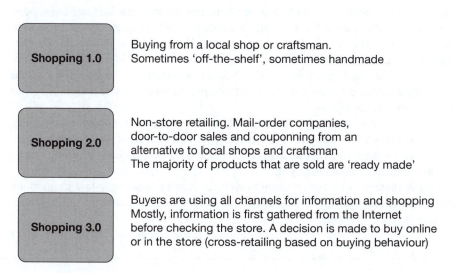

Figure 4.2 The evolution of shopping

Figure 4.3 Place is no longer static

- The computer industry also played a role. It did not have much affinity with marketing, and was totally focused on innovation and technology. Market conditions were also dominated by quick successions of product innovations. The industry did not really look at the demands of the market but was totally focused on introducing even better products, and faster.

The application of information technology finally started to gain momentum in the 1980s thanks to the rapid decrease in the cost of computers, the miniaturization of computers (mainframes became PCs) and the development of standard software at a lower price. This resulted in the increased use of information technology in offices and in business functions that were not part of the key processes of an organization (such as marketing). The standard software that became available was based on a database plus a word processing program. This combination made direct communication possible. Standard software was also developed for direct marketing and for sales ('sales information systems'). The CRM software from Siebel, which dates back to those early days, is still on the market. Sales information systems were also based on a database, linked to a word processor. This combination was used to plan sales meetings, record those meetings and plan follow-up actions. As the sales and marketing department itself was in charge of the system and also entered the data, there was initially a separate (department-related) application (not integrated within the business functions). The application for direct communication, standard letters and planning follow-up actions was an obvious one. In the dedicated software for sales support – for example, ACT! – and sales information it was also possible to keep a record of both sales and stocks. This was therefore also used for direct sales. In fact, these applications were the first integral software used within marketing; however, due to the limitations of information technology at the time its application was restricted to small organizations or to the departmental level (marketing department) of large organizations.

Because of the application of information technology within the marketing function companies became better able to develop relationships that were based on database information and interaction (automated communication cycles). The foundation for communication as it is carried out today through the Internet was laid in the 1980s with the direct marketing applications of sales information systems. The application of direct marketing can be regarded as the forerunner of e-marketing. With direct marketing, however, there was a strong emphasis on direct communication whereas with e-marketing we see an integral strategy based on customer behaviour.

Because of the use of information technology and later the Internet it became possible to also offer extra services in support of the product or the distribution channel. These included arranging the guarantee of a product, as well as extra services for customers. Companies started to provide support via a telephone helpdesk before and after the purchase. In the 1990s Philips launched a toll-free number so that potential buyers could get more information about their Philips products and request brochures directly. For the CD-I, a product that had just been launched, a separate product brochure was even developed through which the products could be bought directly from Philips. Unique at the time, this was a manufacturer supporting the distribution network through personal communication with the consumers and selling 'supplies' directly to the consumers. At the same time a database was built of interested parties and buyers (of CD-Is). This enabled further personal contacts. We see a similar method now with, for example, Nespresso: the coffee machines are sold via the shop and the supplies, the coffee capsules, have to be ordered via the Internet. Nespresso is therefore an example of the integration of the distribution channel (machines) and the Internet (sale of supplies).

4.6 The move towards direct relationships

The development of marketing showed a shift from a transaction orientation to a relationship orientation. This shift, however, took place within the existing sales paradigm; sales had to be made. Within this sales paradigm transactions remained important and the focus stayed on products and services. The increased attention to personal relationships did, however, have consequences for the execution of the marketing activities (particularly communication) (Table 4.1).

Summary

- The traditional application of marketing instruments was based on a fixed price (per market or submarket), a fixed place of sale, mass communication, generic promotions based on the product and a standard product.
- Marketing instruments were used to bring products and services onto the market (to market) and to communicate with the market. Sales were based on a distribution strategy with sales outlets.
- As a result of developments in marketing and the application of information technology, companies were increasingly better able to adjust the marketing instruments according to the individual customer's wishes.
- The undefined customers within a market or market segment became defined relationships, initially only for direct communication (direct marketing); but later, with the application of information technology and the Internet, all the marketing instruments could be customized. This meant that marketing instruments became increasingly important for building and maintaining personal relationships (Figure 4.4).

Table 4.1 Developments in markets that are important in direct relationships

Demand	Supply
1. *Interest in direct sales* Due to price advantages as a result of the convenience of home shopping	1. *Direct sales and direct communication* Increased power of distributors, limited shelf space and shop room
2. *Market fragmentation* The need for differentiation and individualism	2. *Product innovations and differentiation* Fast pace of new developments
Smaller target groups that are difficult to trace	Shorter lifespan of advertising messages
Difficult to predict the behaviour in advance	Less attention on traditional means of advertising
3. *Brand loyalty* Switch behaviour on the basis of inertia instead of commitment	Pressure on quick payback time
Brand confusion	3. *Retail trade* Declining appeal due to parking problems and opening times
Declining loyalty	
4. *Re-evaluation of leisure time* Different free time activities, more time for hobbies, friends and family	4. *Information technology* New possibilities for direct communication
Diffuse separation between work and private life (time)	New possibilities for after-sales service
	Personal communication

Figure 4.4 The use of the telephone was important for maintaining personal relationships. Later the Internet became important as well

5   Direct marketing as a form of marketing

Within the sales paradigm direct communication was regarded as an effective way of reaching the target group, both unaddressed through leaflets and door-to-door distribution, and later also addressed via labels and address databases. Automated systems made it possible to communicate in a highly personal manner. At the start, relationships were not built, as this required fully fledged interaction. The interaction within direct marketing is the response to a mailing or telephone promotion. The purpose is not to build a relationship but to bring about a transaction; the profit per transaction is still an important measurement criterion here. (Direct marketing was part of the sales paradigm and a component of the promotion and communication marketing instruments.) This changed only once the paradigm, the total concept, changed from a sales-oriented to a demand-oriented concept. This would only take place, however, if full communication was possible, as was previously the case with customization and the personal contact between manufacturer and buyer. Technology was necessary for this; initially telecommunication (telephone) and later the Internet.

The telephone made it possible for customers to be in direct contact with the manufacturer (such as in the Philips example described in Chapter 4) or a distributor (shop). The supplier was also able to record the information in a database and then use this information for personal and direct communication. This laid the foundation for a relationship and later the application of e-marketing.

5.1 Loyalty systems

Loyalty systems were the first direct application. On the basis of the registered information (such as name and address) purchase information could be stored. Buyers were rewarded for their purchase. This reward was not directly linked to a transaction but to a series of transactions. These loyalty systems were also referred to in the literature as 'frequency systems', returning buyers. Based on the generated turnover, points were awarded which could be exchanged for gifts. Here use was made of the fixed data of the customer, variable purchase details and the value of the customer expressed in turnover. Finally gifts could be chosen. The stamps issued by certain shops, as still in operation today, is an example of a classic saving scheme in which no personal details are recorded. The difference between this and the new types of 'saving schemes' lay in the registration in a database. In the old scheme stamps had to be collected and affixed onto a stamp book which could then be exchanged for cash or gifts. Now it was also possible to correspond directly on the basis of purchase data.

In the early 1990s various loyalty schemes appeared. These included Airmiles and airline loyalty programmes, such as the Flying Blue loyalty programme of KLM and Air France. These loyalty systems differed from the old saving schemes in that:

- various suppliers could collaborate in them (such as with Airmiles and Rocks);
- additional services could be combined (such as KLM); and
- personal services could also be offered (such as with KLM).

The KLM programme has points that are awarded on the basis of the tickets that are bought as well as service points that can be awarded if purchases are made from other participants, such as car rental companies or hotels. The programme also has various levels. The number of points that are awarded and saved in a particular year determines the level. Based on the level, extra service facilities can be allocated that are directly linked to the KLM product. This can include seating preference, an extra check-in counter without long queues, admission to a lounge or the possibility of a guaranteed seat to ensure there is always room on the plane for this 'golden customer'. Linking customer value to service facilities is, of course, only possible if the use of the card is registered as well. As a result, a strong preference for flying with KLM can be created due to the service level and the associated facilities. Business travellers who fly frequently value these extra services much more than any possible gifts that can be saved up for. It is therefore also possible to donate some of the points (and the possibility of gifts) to a charity.

The Airmiles savings system works through collaboration between various companies, which award points for purchases. All these points are added up in an account statement and can be exchanged for gifts. This, too, is a database with purchase information. By working together the costs of such a programme, as well as the experiences gained, can be shared among the participants. Airmiles is an independent organization in which the participants are also shareholders. As a result they all have a share in the profit and can determine the structure of the programme.

Separately from Airmiles, supermarkets like Tesco have introduced loyalty cards. This allows for electronic registration of purchases made. Discounts are awarded immediately on the 'bonus items' in the shop. It is also possible to distribute flyers in a highly targeted manner, based on the purchase behaviour not only of customers in a particular area but also sometimes of individual households. This integration of identified customers, purchase behaviour and the value of a customer leads to more insights into how best to approach customers. A mass approach therefore becomes more individual with the actual purchase behaviour at the heart of it.

The history of direct marketing is summarized in Table 5.1.

Table 5.1 Developments in direct marketing activities

Period (approximate)	*Direct marketing activities*	*Focus*
Pre-1970	Direct distribution: mail order	Bringing about transaction
1970–1990	Direct distribution: mail order, insurances, publishers	Direct communication leading to transactions
1990–2008	Direct communication	
	Behaviour-driven communication	Continuous transactions, relationship based

5.2 Integral concept

The move towards direct relationships involves the development of an integral concept for specific applications: the mail-order system whereby the direct communication, direct distribution, low price perception as well as targeted promotion all form part of the total concept aimed at a known relationship. Marketing is interwoven within the total concept and based on direct relationships. It is therefore logical that it was the mail-order sector that was the first to use information technology within marketing, as marketing formed an integral part of its operational process. It was also necessary to register customer information for communication and deliveries. The mail-order sector also used analysis techniques to measure the effectiveness of advertising efforts. These included the effectiveness of promotions and brochures, the yield per page of catalogues and the effectiveness of the position of each product in a catalogue.

Techniques developed by the mail-order sector in the 1960s and 1970s are still being used today within the Internet, and are part of e-marketing. The methodology of Internet companies is similar to that employed by mail-order companies in the 1970s and 1980s; it is only the distribution and promotion channel that is different (through the Internet instead of the post). In order to measure profits not only was the transaction value determined but also the relationship value. To this end a method was used which calculated the value of a relationship on the basis of the value per transaction, the return ratio (how often a purchase was made in a certain period of time) and the variety of the purchases. This was expressed by calculating the RFM ratio (recency, frequency and monetary value). Here, recency relates to how recently a customer has purchased something. The view arose that a customer who returned regularly, spent a lot of money and bought a large variety of products was a better customer than one who did not buy so often, perhaps for smaller amounts and a limited variety of articles. This RFM model is not entirely accurate, as a customer who spends a lot and returns regularly but buys only a limited number of products is also a good customer.

Over the years, mail-order companies have amassed a great deal of experience with the RFM model, and they have also used it to effectively determine the loyalty of customers and to distinguish between good and less loyal customers. In addition, RFM analysis has been used for targeted and effective communication. Why bother a customer with sports items if he or she only buys women's clothing? Efficiency is gained by targeting the communication, and through testing more insight is gained into what customers do and do not want.

Following the development and use of RFM analysis, organizations started to look for other ways of ascribing value to customers. Traditional marketing used market segments, often determined by the marketing instruments (top of the market through higher prices, regional distribution, gender-based supply). Thanks to direct contacts and identifiable relationships it was possible to give customers a certain value. For example, customers could be described as 'loyal customers', 'marginal customers' or 'golden customers', and ascribed other characterizations that gave them a certain value. The segmentation of customers could be based on actual behaviour, such as responses to mailings and other direct communication (telephone and coupons), but also on purchasing behaviour.

The response to direct communication already indicated a particular characterization. It soon emerged that the source has a direct effect on the later responses. If there was a response to a telemarketing promotion, for example, the later purchases were fewer than when people had responded to a coupon in a women's magazine. Using sophisticated CHAID (Chi Square Automatic Interaction Detection) analyses, response trees were constructed from which the customer value and the expected response could be calculated (Figure 5.1). This manner of segmentation was promotion-oriented and in theory complex as each customer could have a different customer value depending on the source code and the follow-up actions and response.

By using the actual purchasing behaviour the customer value could be shared within a group on the basis of recognizable characteristics. Customers were divided into turnover groups. A large amount of turnover per customer led to the classification of 'golden customers', and when the turnover decreased this would result in a reduction of the customer value. As it is always possible to define a top 20 per cent customer group, of course, a pyramid is formed. Thanks to this characterization by customer group, facilities can also be

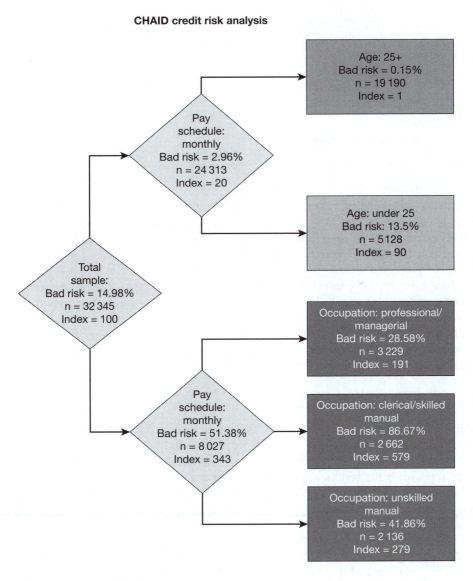

CHAID credit risk analysis

Figure 5.1 Example of CHAID analysis

Characteristics

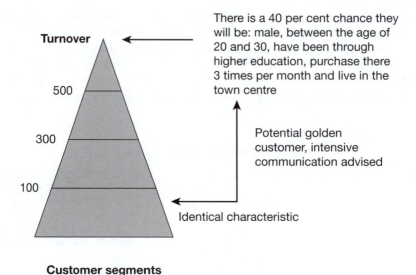

Turnover

500

300

100

There is a 40 per cent chance they will be: male, between the age of 20 and 30, have been through higher education, purchase there 3 times per month and live in the town centre

Potential golden customer, intensive communication advised

Identical characteristic

Customer segments

Figure 5.2 Customer segmentation as a basis for targeted communication

assigned to each customer group. VIP customers were given better service and a different selection of products than other customers. A department store, for instance, will allow its VIP customers into the shop one day earlier to see and buy the reduced-price items in its clear-out sales, and airlines introduced separate check-in counters for their good customers (frequent flyers) and separate lounges depending on the customer value.

These segmentation clusters were analysed further according to specific characteristics, which were then also searched for in other clusters in order to make these customers special as well so that they would buy more and consequently also become VIP customers. This technique is clearly only possible with automation. Automation was used to register the purchasing behaviour at an individual level, and to analyse buying behaviour and customer characteristics for the cluster analyses (Figure 5.2).

5.3 Testing in direct marketing

Mail-order companies were able to test, analyse and determine the effectiveness of every aspect of their marketing. Tests were carried out on the product range, the place in the catalogue as well as the promotional messages to determine the answer to questions such as: What produces better results, a special sales price or a gift? And what sort of gift produces better results: a necklace or a book? Comprehensive tests were also carried out at various price levels, and the numbers of customers who would make use of these determined. By measuring the response to the various tests and making comparisons it was possible to work out which would be the most effective, and by using customer criteria it was possible to determine which type of customers would be more appropriate for a certain promotion. The response was estimated in advance and a cut-off rate determined. Based on a number of different variables the company could decide which customer would receive a particular promotion and the expected response per group. It could then be decided which group of variables would receive a promotion and for which group of variables the response was too low to cover the costs. This optimization of the promotion was only possible through the application of information technology, in particular analysis software and of course direct communication.

In many ways mail-order companies differed from other suppliers in their application of marketing. For example:

- Within the business operations marketing, together with logistics and finance, was the most important discipline.
- Marketing was aimed at building and maintaining identified and individual relationships.
- Marketing communication was determined on the basis of cost/benefit analyses and targeted directly at the individual customer.
- Analyses determined the profitability per customer and per promotion, and formed the basis of follow-up promotions.

This helped to pave the way for e-marketing, and the experience of mail-order companies formed the basis of the application of the Internet as a sales and communication channel.

By 1998 the Internet had developed to such an extent that it was clear to the mail-order companies that there were great benefits to be had. They became the early adopters of this new channel. Other new entrants made immediate use of the knowledge of direct marketing and mail-order companies for the development of their own direct sales channels.

Box 5.1 Landsend

Companies such as Landsend.com were the early adopters of the new media, whereby initially the telephone was used for recording orders by making use of voice response systems, automatic call dispatchers and call response systems. It was possible to key in the order number on the telephone after which the computer repeated the order number before the order was confirmed. At the end of the 1990s the Internet was also already intensively used for processing orders as well as for providing access to digital catalogues. Landsend.com was one of the first mail-order companies that developed a separate Internet strategy alongside the traditional mail-order strategy.

In 1996 shop.org in the United States, alongside similar organizations in England and the Netherlands, came together to form an interest group for direct sales through the Internet. This helped with the professionalization of e-marketing and brought together traditional mail-order companies with newer web-based shops. In addition to representing the interests of their members, these organizations became important discussion partners for consumer organizations and governments. The introduction of certified home shopping guarantees, as introduced in the Netherlands in 2009, has reinforced their position further.

Mail-order/direct-distribution companies and traditional marketing companies are compared in Table 5.2.

Table 5.2 Marketing of mail order versus traditional marketing

Mail-order company/direct distribution	Traditional marketing
Part of the core process	Separate function
Aimed at individual relationships, identifiable	Targeted markets and target groups
Measurable promotions and relationships	Measurability limited to market share and sales results
In addition to the traditional marketing instruments also customer value as an instrument	Four important marketing instruments
IT integral part of the marketing activities	IT initially limited to market research. Not until the application of database marketing (1990) and later the Internet (2000) was IT applied more often
The application of the Internet is a logical evolution	The application of the Internet is still often regarded as a means of (mass) communication

Summary

- Marketing instruments are less rigid than they first appear.
- With a sales focus (the sales paradigm) the organization is able to determine and apply the marketing instruments itself. This makes it possible to respond to changes in the market and competitive positions.
- A competitive advantage can be achieved by communicating product values and realizing a preference for the product. Through the application of information technology and later the Internet, companies became increasingly better able to identify customers and to give them a personal value.
- As a result, striving for constant and uninterrupted relationships became important.
- New concepts, such as loyalty programmes and new supply propositions such as mail-order companies, could then help to create a buying preference.
- Marketing instruments had an ever more supportive role in the individual relationship and were no longer used just for creating a competitive advantage (Figure 5.3).

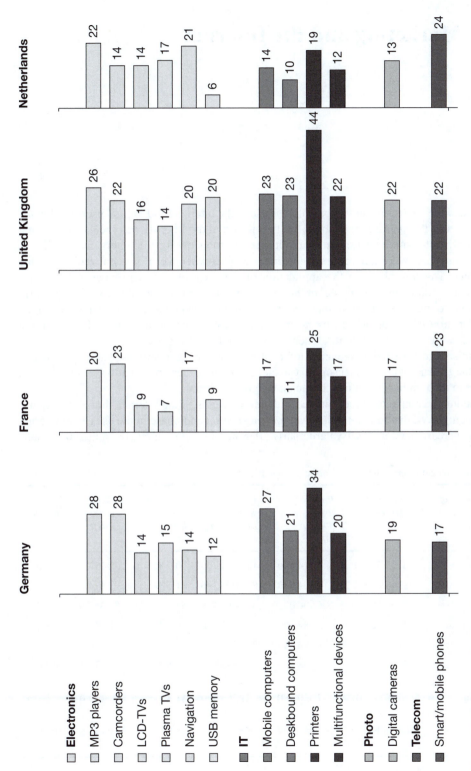

Figure 5.3 Percentage of online sales compared to total sales per product group

Source: GFK Amstelveen, basis 2009

6   Marketing and the Internet

The end of the 1990s saw an explosion in the use of the Internet (360 million users worldwide by the end of the year 2000) (Table 6.1). In this period the Internet was increasingly being used for direct communication, although it was still too slow for true interactivity. What is more, companies were not yet ready for direct contact whenever it was convenient for the customer. The first phase in the application of the Internet was only what was called a 'presence', with companies being on the Internet with a limited website. It was particularly important to make information about your company or product available online. A limited mail function was possible but by no means yet always part of a website. In truth these websites were, in fact, just digital brochures suitable for a mass medium.

At this stage advertising agencies and companies allied to advertising agencies pounced upon the Internet with enthusiasm. It was not surprising, therefore, that these sites looked similar to the familiar brochures, but in an electronic format.

In addition, companies experimented with new concepts on the Internet, though marketing was not involved that much in this development. The second phase in the use of the Internet saw an increase in interactivity. Particularly after the 'dot com' bubble burst in 2001, result-

Table 6.1 World Internet usage and population statistics

World region	Population (2010 est.)	Internet users 31 Dec. 2000	Internet users Latest data	Penetration (% population)	Growth 2000–2010	Users % of table
Africa	1 013 779 050	4 514 400	110 931 700	10.9 %	2 357.3	5.6
Asia	3 834 792 852	114 304 000	825 094 396	21.5 %	621.8	42.0
Europe	813 319 511	105 096 093	475 069 448	58.4 %	352.0	24.2
Middle East	212 336 924	3 284 800	63 240 946	29.8 %	1 825.3	3.2
North America	344 124 450	108 096 800	266 224 500	77.4 %	146.3	13.5
Latin America/ Caribbean	592 556 972	18 068 919	204 689 836	34.5 %	1 032.8	10.4
Oceania/ Australia	34 700 201	7 620 480	21 263 990	61.3 %	179.0	1.1
WORLD TOTAL	6 845 609 960	360 985 492	1 966 514 816	28.7 %	444.8	100.0

Source: www.internetworldstats.com 2010

oriented strategies began to be increasingly used. And in this arena marketing activity and marketing communication became an integral part of the website. Direct deliveries also became part of the sites.

The real breakthrough for the Internet, however, was not until 2008 when the recession made it necessary for companies to reconsider their business models. It was not just efficiency that lay at the heart of this, but also changes in the market. Customers began to buy in different ways and were less loyal. What's more (the supply from abroad had become so large that any competitive advantages based on product or price turned out to be no longer feasible.) It was no longer necessary to shop nearby; one could buy everything on the Internet and the purchases were delivered to the home. Buyers began to express their wishes as a result of the amount of information on the Internet and the convenience provided by search engines such as Google, Yahoo and later Bing.

Thanks to the Internet, customers knew exactly what was available to buy, how much it cost and what the benefits were. National borders no longer played a role. Domestic suppliers were being confronted with foreign competition without it actually being active in the home market. Foreign suppliers could be found on the Internet just as easily as the domestic suppliers.

6.1 Building relationships

The market changed as a result of:

- well-informed customers;
- the vigorous growth of buying on the Internet, also from foreign suppliers;
- the extra services (home delivery) that Internet suppliers could provide;
- the lower costs of the web-based shops, but also of foreign suppliers, making the prices on the Internet frequently lower than those in physical shops;
- the direct communication possibilities such as email, call centres and FAQs; and
- the ability to analyse the viewing, clicking and purchasing behaviour of Internet buyers.

Box 6.1 International sales

In 2008, due to the recession, the British pound fell to a level of near parity with the euro. In addition, the British economy and retail trade were severely hit by the recession and suppliers began to offer large discounts. This made British products more attractive for buyers with euros. British suppliers sent the products at minimal shipping costs to the euro zone which led to unfair competition. The English language was not a problem for most residents of the euro zone. The UK had advantages in other areas as well, such as good logistical systems, delivery within two days, reliable and well-known suppliers, good payment systems with a credit card and good legislation. In the book sector the UK also had the advantage that there was no fixed book price. English-language books are significantly cheaper than their foreign-language translations. Due to the rise of the e-book reader it has, however, become easier to download books digitally. For English-language e-books the average price is 9.99 euros, a fraction of the price if you pay for a translation or the English version from a supplier outside of the UK. At present this market is still somewhat limited, though it is experiencing strong growth as well as being indicative of the new market relationships.

The real breakthrough for building relationships via the Internet came only after 2008. This was the start of the Internet era that would lead to great changes in marketing: changes in the market, such as those described above, changes in the buying process with customers and companies, and the integration of technology within the marketing function. The focus did shift from a sales orientation to a demand-based paradigm for companies active in dynamic markets. These are rapidly changing market circumstances where changes in supply and buying behaviour follow on from one another quickly. The focus would no longer be on creating a competitive advantage by making products distinctive, by creating imaginary values or through a distinctive price or distribution strategy. The focus would lie with the relationship, the needs of the relationship and the buying and orientation behaviour of the relationship. In order to be able to compete effectively, the use of the Internet as an integral part of a company's infrastructure would be essential.

Changes in the market resulting from the application of information technology are summarized in Table 6.2.

Table 6.2 Changes in the market through the application of IT

Period (approximate)	Marketing	Orientation	Information technology
Pre 1930	Production concept Product concept	Product, product characteristics and product application	Limited application of mechanization
1930–1950	Sales concept	Transactions and product values	Mechanization of processes and production. For transaction processing, administration and market research. Limited application with communication
1950–1980	Marketing concept	Communication to the market, product values (brands), transactions	Loyalty concepts. Application with direct communication
1980–2008	Strategic marketing concept	Target groups, buyers' behaviour and needs. Realizing competitive advantages and building relationships	Application of the Internet and CRM
2008 to present	Integral marketing concept Relationship concept	Relationship development interactivity based on individual customer needs and wishes	Interactivity and the Internet. Tracking and tracing, location-based services, 'near field communication' and development of communities and 'social networks' as communication platform

6.2 Market strategy and information technology

In the 1980s Michael Porter was regarded as one of the most important strategists in the world. In his books *Competitive Advantages* and *Competitive Strategy* he described the ways in which an organization could realize competitive advantages. One of his models was based on the forces within a market that determine the market circumstances and the competitive edge of an organization. This vision fits in with the strategic marketing concept as described above (Figure 6.1).

Porter's model is practicable in stable markets protected by physical restrictions. This allows suppliers and customers to have a good insight into the market relationships and the supply. With the application of IT and the Internet, however, this situation has changed: markets are less protected, and customers have a much better insight into the supply in markets that were previously separate (for example, the supply in other countries) and can now also buy directly.

The organizations are still focused on sales, and often make use of traditional distribution channels and physical sales outlets. In the last few decades market conditions changed dramatically. For example:

* There are more and frequently successive product announcements.
* New entrants in the market, also from abroad, result in blurring of borders.
* There is the increasing impact of technology, both in the organization and at product level.

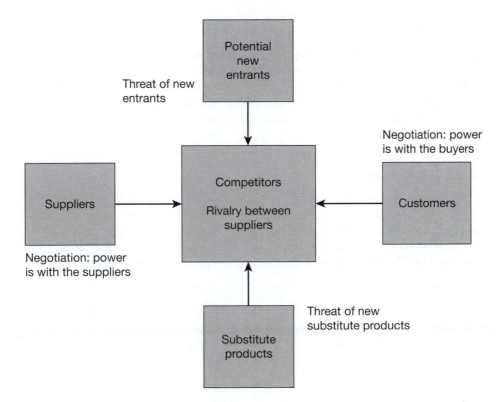

Figure 6.1 Five forces model of Michael Porter

- In addition, the management has access to more and greater detailed information on the organization and the market, thereby increasing the effectiveness of the organization's control.
- Customers no longer buy just from physical sales outlets or local and national suppliers, but increasingly use Internet sites of suppliers that are not based in their own country.

The focus of the organization is looking increasingly beyond the organization and beyond the old market boundaries. The relationship with suppliers is defined in more detail, as well as the relationship with customers. There is a growing need to reinforce the relationship with customers. Initially the focus was on a product relationship, which was given form by strong brands and good quality; however, at the end of the 1980s and in the early 1990s, technology was being increasingly integrated into the relationship with suppliers (as with electronic data interchange (EDI)) and customers. Database marketing and telemarketing are examples of this. Because of the direct communication with customers and a segmentation of customers, the communication was intensified. Very quickly we also saw the introduction of loyalty systems such as Airmiles (1994), airline programmes and all sorts of customer card programmes for retailers. The customer relationship was regarded as an important tool in realizing a competitive advantage. Switching costs (emotional and in monetary terms) had to be increased, so that customers actually no longer wanted to, or could, leave. The new boundaries of the market were no longer determined physically but on the basis of customer relationships, customer values and buying preference.

There were three forms of binding for customers: financial, social and structural binding.

6.2.1 Financial binding

Financial binding results from a low price per product, but can also consist of savings programmes in the form of loyalty points. As a result, customers do not wish to leave as they believe they have a 'good deal'. The problem with financial binding is the durability. Financial binding through lower prices is difficult to defend, as new suppliers constantly come onto the scene with even lower prices or discounts.

Box 6.2 Price battles

During the 2003 price war of the supermarkets in the Netherlands there was a fierce battle for customers. Customers naturally went for the bargains, but as soon as items returned to the normal price level they went back to their regular supermarket. Customers also went shopping at various supermarkets to buy the cheapest items at the various shops. Some customers, however, actually did change supermarket.

With a savings programme the binding is greater, depending on the savings objective and the speed at which one can save. And so it is also fairly normal to take part in various loyalty programmes. After all, you do not want to rob your own purse. Overall, the eventual effect of customer binding is quite low.

6.2.2 Social binding

Social binding can be seen, for example, with brands. Customers perceive a difference and feel emotionally connected with a brand. These days there are various 'social media' sites with brand fans. Here customers can register as a fan of a particular brand and talk with other fans about their brand! Similarly, football clubs have hundreds of thousands of fans who feel emotionally connected with the club. Through good times and bad, a fan always stays loyal to his or her club. As that also goes for product brands it is difficult to break through this unless a new product comes along that is much more attractive, trendier or more appealing, and with which the customer can identify. Loyalty systems attempt to realize a social binding, which is stronger than a financial binding.

Airmiles has a social binding function in addition to financial binding. Although it was originally thought of as a bit of a hype, the scheme has been around for more than 20 years now, and has a certain emotional value for many savers. As a loyalty system Airmiles is the first that people mention when asked and is often considered the best. With objective measurements, however, the results can look completely different. As described in Part 3, on the Internet a form of emotional binding can develop. This combines the 'top-of-mind' position, positive associations, habituation, convenience and trust, and large Internet suppliers, such as Amazon.com, Google.com or Yahoo.com, have succeeded in winning such a position.

6.2.3 Structural binding

The last type of distinctive binding is structural binding. Here the binding is very strong but is also often given shape through contracts. Supplier contracts, framework contracts and long-term contracts are examples of structural binding. You only consider switching supplier once a contract has expired. Subscribers have a similar structural binding. They can't stop just like that, but have to wait till the end of a contract period.

Microsoft has a strong structural binding with its customers due to the integrated Windows concept, the operation system linked to specific applications such as the Office suite and Explorer.

The current legislation ensures that structural binding is increasingly subject to regulations to the benefit of the customer. For suppliers this means that they have to look for other forms of structural binding. One possibility is to offer extra services via the Internet that can only be used after logging in. Customers therefore have to be registered in order to be able to use this service. For each case it can be checked who is allowed to register and whether costs will be charged for this. In this way newspapers can offer extra services to their subscribers. Another possibility is a product concept with supplies or add-ons. For this, the main product has to be bought in order to be able to make use of the add-ons and vice versa. In the 1980s software was often based on a single type (or make) of computer (in the pre-Windows/ Microsoft period). In those days if you bought a certain make of computer you also had to buy the specific, and often expensive, software. Apple employed this strategy for a long time, and it is only in the last few years that it has become more open by also supporting modified Windows programs.

With Senseo there was also a structural binding between users and the coffee brand Douwe Egberts. This binding was based on the patent on the capsules. Senseo had defended the patent on the coffee capsules for a long time; after all, that was where the profit was made. Now the same is happening with, for example, Nespresso. For a Nespresso machine the Nespresso capsules have to be ordered separately (via the Internet). This creates a structural binding. If a significant market position is realized with the main machine as well (the coffee machines or the Apple computer in these examples) then a tenable competitive advantage arises.

A new business model can also be formulated whereby the profit is primarily generated through the add-ons or supplies, and not with the main machine. The main machine can therefore be sold below the cost price; the profit after all comes from the supplies (software or capsules in this case). Competition for the main machine is therefore always favourable because of the low purchase price.

6.3 Suppliers

The relationship between supplier and customer or organization has also changed in the course of the years. Initially, sales were ad hoc supplies whereby a seller would try to realize a sale. Later, the aim was to get customers to sign long-term contracts. Particularly in the 1990s the objective was a close relationship with co-makership and strategic alliances. In the last few years the collaboration has become even closer. This has come about through companies coordinating each other's Internet strategy, participating in each other's business models through outsourcing, and by deciding who is responsible. In the supply chain the information can be shared, and the responsibility for the items determined. The manufacturer can, for example, give the goods in consignments or take on the responsibility for the entire stock (both at physical shops and at webshops). This concept is called VMI (vendor-managed inventories). The supplier takes care of the stock, which is possible because the supplier knows what the shop's sales are.

Of course automated systems are an important precondition for this to work. Developments in the supply chain mean the relationship between the final link (retailer) and manufacturer is becoming increasingly close through sharing information and collaborating in business models once again.

Automation and the application of the Internet contributes to the ability to form closer relationships with suppliers by linking the purchasing system and by admitting suppliers to warehouse management systems, or by giving customers a log-in code via the Internet. In Parts 2 and 3 we will examine this in more detail.

Other factors that have an influence on the market relationships are substitute products and new entrants. Substitute products are sometimes 'imitation' products that do and look the same, but can also be products that take over another product's function. This can occur through another use of another technology. Take, for example, the coffee machines that have practically driven coffee percolators from the market or computers that have made typewriters redundant. We also see fierce competition between photocopiers and printers. Why make a copy these days when it is just as quick to make a printout?

In addition, an increasing number of new entrants are coming onto the market. Because of the Internet this will happen even more frequently. No longer does a company necessarily know who its competitors are or where they come from. Today companies have to compete with international, frequently unfamiliar, competitors. By purchasing via the Internet, borders disappear, but it also becomes very easy for suppliers to approach other markets by using a language mode.

All these developments have caused a turbulence in the markets that requires new strategies and new business models. It is becoming more difficult to acquire a competitive advantage, and close relationships with suppliers and customers are more frequently fundamental to business models. e-Marketing has to form an integral part of any organization's strategy if it is to be successful within these new market circumstances. In Part 4 we will take a closer look at this.

Summary

- Porter's model lists the influences on a market and where competitive advantages can be achieved based on the traditional supply paradigm.
- Through the application of information technology and the Internet, not only can a closer relationship with customers and suppliers be achieved, but also the dynamics in the markets will increase. The boundaries of markets will blur, customers will just as easily buy abroad as from home markets and customers are very well informed about the supply in other markets (and the associated prices).
- A regular check and, if necessary, modification of the strategy and an intensive application of information technology (and the Internet) is required in order to acquire and maintain a stable market position. This position will be increasingly determined by the strength of customer relationships and by customer preference.
- The focus is shifting from competitive advantage based on the product and the services on offer, to competitive advantage through closer customer relationships. The role of the Internet and information technology is essential in this.
- Marketing continues to change from a business function that defines and implements the relationship with the 'market' to a business function that stimulates and manages customer contacts.
- In particular, the application of the Internet and information technology makes it possible to change the focus of the marketing function. e-Marketing can support the execution of marketing activities; however, it is also e-marketing that will lead to this change in focus.

Part 2

Impact of information technology on marketing

A buyer's perspective

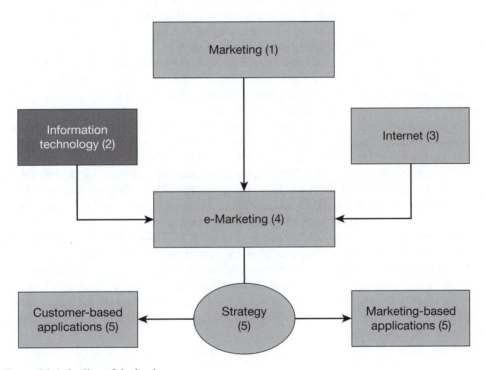

Figure P2.1 Outline of the book

In the 1930s mechanization began to take true form within the production process. Mass products and identical production were the result of this and made sales and marketing necessary. After mechanization came automation. Initially this was only intended to make processes more efficient, but it was later used to also realize greater effectiveness in the business operations. Automation seamlessly followed on from mechanization.

Table P2.1 Evolution of the functional use of automation (IT)

Application focus	Mechanization efficiency	Automation, IT/ effectiveness	Internet communication/ connectivity
Mechanization	Pre-Fordism (1930)		
	Fordism (1940)		
Automation/IT	Post-Fordism (1960)	Data processing (1960)	
		IT (1980)	
Internet		Integration (2000)	Pre-Internet era (1990)
			Internet era (2008)

The difference between automation and mechanization lay not only in the application of a different technology. The objective was also different. With mechanization the objective was to produce more efficiently, whereas automation focused on a more effective use of the tools for an organization. The focus of automation shifted from production and production-related activities (data processing) to information, and finally to the integration of the tools that support an operational function. This was also a change in viewpoint from making existing activities more efficient to determining how functions can be fulfilled and better performed through the application of technologies.

The Internet also began as an addition to information technology (IT). The transfer of data between various people, computers as well as organizations became much easier as a result. It also became easier to make use of other sources of information. There was a change in the use of the Internet at the end of the 1990s when consumers also started to use the Internet on a large scale and when the user-friendliness increased. Initially the Internet was an addition to the existing systems; it was only later that the Internet became the basis for systems as well as for how organizations and consumers acted. Behaviour and activities were modified on the basis Internet use (which therefore varied a great deal between various people and organizations). This era dawned around 2008, the year of the worldwide recession.

As the application of automation (and later the Internet) became more function-oriented and was used increasingly often between organizations, marketing also started to become more involved with automation. First for making processes efficient, then for making activities more effective, and later for guiding and managing market relationships (including customers and suppliers).

7   The development of mechanization

As we discussed in Part 1, marketing only became involved with information technology (IT) quite late; the large-scale application of IT did not take place until the 1990s. Initially it was associated with data processing and the management of vast quantities of information. The first automation companies (in the 1960s and 1970s) worked on this data processing using mainframes (IBM was market leader). The first applications of IT in marketing also involved data processing and were used by market research companies in the 1970s. It was only when IT was database driven and focused on the provision of information that it also began to be applied within marketing increasingly often (mid 1980s). Then when the focus in marketing shifted from bringing products to the market to building and maintaining relationships, a process developed that was mutually influential. The development of automation, however, originally began in the 1930s with mechanization. This formed the basis of the marketing function.

7.1 Mechanization

During the global depression of the 1930s there was a surplus of workers, who were often poorly educated. However, this time also saw the beginnings of a growing prosperity, although still somewhat modest. Various technologies discovered at the end of the nineteenth century were launched onto the market. This contributed to a sense of change. These discoveries included those in the area of mobility, such as the car and the aeroplane, as well as those in the area of telecommunications, such as the telephone, telex and the radio. These 'innovations' had to be incorporated into a new paradigm. Handiwork and customization were not logical methods for these products and they had a wide range of applications. Factories were set up for the production of consumer goods using new machines. These machines were invented in order to be able to produce more quickly, and with a constant quality. The product, however, was always the same. It was not efficient to have many product variations, which is why for example all Model T Fords were made in black (uniform production led to efficiency). Efficiency and mechanization had to lead to mass production at low costs. Man was part of the machine and carried out the activities that could not (yet) be mechanized.

This mass production resulted in a sales problem, certainly in the 1930s during the depression. Sales became increasingly important. A sales person no longer waited in the workshop or shop for a customer to walk in. Sellers now went out to look for customers. Colportage and the travelling salesman were born. These early years of mechanization are also called the early days of Fordism, which can be divided into three periods: pre-Fordism from 1920 to 1940, Fordism from 1940 to 1960 and post-Fordism from 1960 to 1990 (Table 7.2).

Table 7.1 Marketing and technology developments 1930–1990

	Marketing	Technology
1990	Emergence of direct communication	Automation of processes and functions
	Uniformity in supply	Workplace support automation of production, robotization
	Decreased impact of advertising	
After Fordism	Reorientation of the role and function of marketing	*Basis*: efficiency and effectiveness. Central automation, automation of activities, process activities
	Concentration in retail, franchise formulas, international retail chains	Mechanization and labour are replaced by automation
	Emergence of shopping centres and increasing power of consumers	
	Emergence of target groups with their own characteristics and wishes	
1960	Mass supply and mass consumption	Mechanization. Introduction of machines and process-oriented robots. Far-reaching mass production and standardization
	Emergence of mass media and advertising	
Fordism	Emergence of large retail department stores	
	Strong need for growth and integration	
1940	Strong local supply and first self-service	
	America as shining example in Europe	
1930	Mass production leads to sales problems	Machines for efficient production and constant quality. Uniform products
	Travelling salesmen, distribution strategy and sales become increasingly important	Production for unknown demand

7.2 Fordism

Fordism was named after Henry Ford, a great proponent of efficient production. He wished to have uniformity in production, efficiency and mass production. In fulfilling his wish he made a definite step from craft production to mass production. Mass production, however, also goes hand in hand with mass consumption, as well as with how we work, how we buy and what we buy. In the pre-Fordism period it was this application of mechanization that was important, involving the ability to be able to produce efficiently and with constant quality. Initially this was intended for complex products, such as cars, but later it began to be applied to consumer goods as well. Mass production became important for mass consumption.

After the Second World War production capacity was no longer needed for 'war production' and could be switched to the production of consumer goods. The foundations had been laid in the War years and in the War industry, but immediately after the War the technology was used for consumer goods. America led the way in this because it had more experience with mass production and because it had the prosperity necessary for mass consumption.

This shift from handiwork to mechanization and mass production was a fundamental switch that formed the basis for the focus on sales (and the marketing efforts) of the twentieth century. The pre-Fordism period was followed by the Fordism period. This was a changeover period to consumer goods (after the years of depression and war). It became important not only to produce efficiently but also to reach customers. In America an advertising industry developed which used the mass media to sell products. It was not only the products' properties that were being communicated but also the values associated with their use. Potential buyers were informed about the benefits of the products and their amazing results. Advertising became the selling of dreams.

Mechanization then became automation and vice versa. Mass production became increasingly important for stimulating prosperity, but greater efficiency was also necessary in order to be able to guide and control organizations, and this involved data processing. This typified another change: a generic demand and direct availability of products. All products were similar (mass production), made for an average demand and were available immediately. The consumer no longer had to wait until the product was made by the craftsman. Products were made en masse for an unknown demand. This meant that there was a build-up of stocks at various levels of the supply chain. As a result, selling these stocks became problematic and so marketing was born.

Marketing communication became increasingly professional. It began to respond more to the needs of the market and sections of the market. In order to realize this, market research became essential. The measuring of consumers' wishes produced a great deal of information that had to be processed and interpreted and the computer was the ideal tool for this. The demand economy of the pre-Fordism period (one-off production and customization) evolved in the course of this period into a supply economy, based on vast quantities, uniform wishes of the target group and fixed prices. Consequently consumption became important, and consumerism was fed by an ample supply, seductive advertising and increased prosperity.

7.3 Mechanization and automation: post-Fordism

The sales issue, as described above, led to the emergence of advertising and marketing for selling products and the need to emphasize the distinction (if any) between the various products. Products became increasingly similar; the distinction was realized through the experiences and perceptions of the consumer. The increased prosperity and progress in production efficiency led to a wave of new products and a steadily growing demand. The sales-oriented economy of the post-Fordism period (1960–1990) led to economies of scale in various areas, both in production and in demand. There was ever more bulk production and assiduous efforts were made to look for larger markets. This market expansion was also seen in a growth of market share, which was a direct consequence of successful marketing.

Mass production also changed organizations. Production was no longer the only important factor; the control of an organization and the sale of products became important as well. Problems became more complex, organizations larger and the financial requirements greater. Organizations became more professional, and in addition to a need for efficiency there also arose a need to know what was happening. The risks for the organization, as a result of the greater financial interests and the uncertainty of the demand, were magnified. This was the deciding factor for the application of automation, the computer, which gave decision-makers access to increasingly more or better information. This ushered in a new wave of economic growth and a period of development for marketing, beginning in the mid 1970s and lasting until the end of the 1980s. This period was characterized by flexibility (Japan set the tone with quick and flexible production methods), an incredible amount of information at low costs thanks to the use of the computer, the emergence of world markets and the changing demands of consumers: consumption for the sake of consumption. What is more, fashion and prosperity went hand in hand; there was an increasing sense that money had to be kept rolling. This in turn led to a further segmentation of the market and a differentiation of consumer demand.

IBM mainframe computers, such as the 360 and the 370 series, typified the post-Fordism period. The purpose of automation was to save costs and to economize on manpower.

In summary, the post-Fordism period (1960–1990) led to:

- the application of IT and the automation of data processing;
- a greater focus on the needs of the market and segments of the market (target groups);
- the start of globalization of supply and organizations; and
- a development of marketing as an important operational function for the success of an organization.

The automation in this period was a continuation of the mechanization of previous periods. Automation was applied within the organization in order to make operational processes more efficient. It was only later that automation was extended to other areas and people started to refer to it as 'information technology' (Table 7.1).

Summary

- Fordism is the application of mechanization and automation within operational processes which leads to efficiency, a constant quality, as well as identical products.
- Automation was initially aimed at data processing, for which administrative data was ideal.
- After the Second World War mechanization was mainly used for the production of consumer goods. This led to a sales problem which formed the basis for the development of marketing.
- The first application of automation within marketing involved market research.

8 The development of information technology within the organization

Mechanization formed the basis for automation, just as information technology (IT) under-pinned the Internet. These are sequential developments that influence one another in their application. Automation was also used for mechanization (industrial automation), which made more and more innovations possible in the application of mechanization. The same applies to the influence of the Internet on IT, which makes increasing use of Internet applications and structures such as 'cloud computing' and 'grid computing', as well as databases linked to Internet applications.

Automation developed in the post-Fordism period. Initially it was used for processing mass data, but later also for information management. The development of automation can be divided into three phases (see Figure 8.1):

1. the data-processing phase (1960–1980);
2. the information technology phase (1980–2000); and
3. the Internet phase.

8.1 From data processing and IT to the Internet

In the data-processing phase the application of automation was very much aimed at primary processes and at processing mass data. This allowed for greater efficiency, and therefore cost

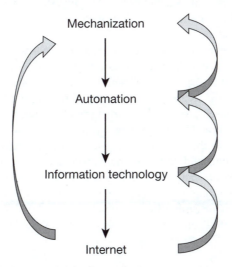

Figure 8.1 Evolution of IT, from mechanization to the Internet

savings. The activities of an organization were not modified, just made more efficient. In this period the use of automation also led to resistance from the trade unions, who considered automation to be a threat to employment. Some even pictured a gloomy scenario in which an underclass of society would arise that would no longer be able to participate in society because they were uneducated and therefore unable to find work. The machines, after all, would do the work of the worker!

After the data-processing phase people no longer referred to automation, but to 'information technology (IT)', or sometimes 'information and communication technology (ICT)', which implied that communication technology was separate from IT. The IT phase started in the early 1980s and was boosted by, for example, the new generation of computers, which became smaller, faster and cheaper. In addition, the software available was increasingly standard. During this period the relationship between the use of IT and the goal that was to be achieved for the various business functions was clearly recognized. It was therefore no longer about efficiency but about the effectiveness of the operations and the use of IT. The provision of information became the basis for the use of IT. The applications also became much more varied, and no longer focused on automation, but rather on information for the organization, including the marketing, sales and finance departments. Organizations were modified in order to become more effective and decisive. By doing so, organizations responded directly to the changes in the market conditions, the increased competition and the behaviour of the customers.

With IT the focus was initially on the provision of information to, and regarding, specific business functions. Information systems formed the basis for this. Separate information systems for each business function then increasingly made use of the same source of information. As a result, in the 1990s the focus shifted towards a generic information platform – the infrastructure – which would form the foundation for the organization. Based on this infrastructure, applications that were specific to particular functions were realized. For marketing and sales this was the CRM (customer relationship management) system. The further development of IT applications led to the integration of IT and (tele)communication technology. This allowed the application of the information supply to extend across the boundaries of departments as well as organizations. Within an organization the information supply was harmonized as well as adapted to external systems. This integration of systems (one all-encompassing information system) formed the basis for a further growth towards connectivity between systems.

In the meantime, however, the application of the Internet was in full development and information systems developed from one into the other (an amalgamation process). This integration started around the year 2000. The Internet played an important role in this. No longer could IT be regarded as a separate business function; it became an integral part of the organization. IT acquired a strong infrastructural character, a basic condition for every organization. The focus of the IT applications was no longer only internal but also external. Particularly with the use of the Internet, IT could be used to arrange all contacts between fellow workers, departments and parties in the market (including suppliers and customers). The application of networks facilitated new possibilities, such as cloud computing, grid computing and distributed data processing. These were often based on the application of the Internet as a network (for further information on this, refer to Part 3). Depending on the application and the role of IT, changes in the organization would be needed (Table 8.1).

Table 8.1 From data processing and IT to the Internet

	Data processing	IT	Integration/Internet
Application	Data processing	Information provision	Communication, connectivity
Purpose	Efficiency	Effectiveness	Decisive
Place in the organization	Head of administration/ finance	Independent responsibility, head of IT	Shared responsibility in application and technology
Role within marketing	Market research and marketing communication	Relationship management and direct communication	Integral part of operational management

8.2 Data processing

The data-processing phase lasted from approximately 1960 to early 1980. At that time there used to be a central automation department. This department managed the central computer and was responsible for the programming. In view of the great financial importance of this department (large investments in computer hardware and software) and its field of application (mainly administrative), it was the financial manager (head of administration and automation) who was responsible for this department. This remained the situation for a long time, and is sometimes still seen even now. After all, the financial department closely monitors the processing of data and management of investments. This organizational division was actually quite logical in this early phase. It was only when automation as a field of application became bigger as well as more complex that a special place within the organization became necessary.

8.2.1 Mainframes

In this phase a central computer system was used, the mainframe. It was often a stand-alone application, which means that it did not have any terminals and monitors. We would have to wait until the 1970s for these, and they then became even more popular in the 1980s. The mainframe department was the domain of the operator and the programmer. Programs were often still written on paper tape or punched cards (Figures 8.2 and 8.3). Paper tape was a strip of paper with holes that gave binary instructions to the computer. As the paper tape was highly vulnerable, particularly to breaking and tearing, and once made could not be changed, this was later replaced by punched cards, magnetic tapes and floppy disks. The first disk was an 8-inch floppy disk onto which programs could be written. Later the floppy disk was to become the information carrier for smaller computers such as the mini and microcomputer, and later the personal computer (Figures 8.4 and 8.5). By then, the size of the floppy disk had been reduced to 3¼ inches but had a greater memory capacity (up to 1 MB).

Market research data was originally punched onto cards which were read by the computer and processed. In the 1970s it also became possible for computers to read forms by designing them as multiple choice questions that could be answered by blacking in boxes using a pencil. The answer could be determined by reading the light and dark areas. The punched cards or paper tape (later magnetic tape) were then made. It was also possible to produce script that could be read automatically by computers, the so-called OCR (optical character recognition) font.

Figure 8.2 Paper tape as an input medium for computers

Figure 8.4 The original 8-inch or 5½-inch floppy disk

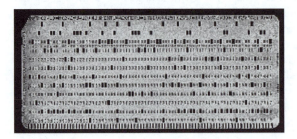

Figure 8.3 Punched card as an input medium for computers

Figure 8.5 The floppy disk for personal computers

It was consequently no longer necessary to punch in the data, a manual activity that sometimes led to errors; forms could now be entered directly. One common use was the bank payment slip, which could be read directly into the computer. The symbols needed to be clear (printed without dirt or smudges) and precision was essential for correct input. A strong focus on the input of data typified this data-processing period. High costs (and the possibility of errors) were caused by mistakes in inputting and great efforts were made to design efficient input systems in which human actions would become superfluous. Data needed to be stored on media that could not be damaged so easily. The paper tape and punched cards were therefore replaced by magnetic disks. These were solid disks as well as the previously mentioned flexible disks (floppies). As a result, computers were given an internal memory on top of their external memory. The internal memory was intended mainly for the storage of software and for the operation of the computer. The external memory was used for the variable data, input and output.

Departments had to deal with the output produced as a result of computer processing, usually in the form of vast amounts of printouts on continuous stationery (also known as tractor-feed paper). The layout largely determined the readability of these printouts. The marketing department also received these printouts with the data of market research, sales, turnover and departmental costs. The automation was very much focused on operations, which led to little involvement being exercised by, or necessary from, the higher management and company board. They were only informed about the results by the departmental management. And if there was an error or delay it was usually the computer's fault, and of course there was nothing one could do about that. 'There is a problem with the computer' or 'our computer has crashed' were common excuses in the 1970s.

A number of developments typified the 1970s:

- The internal storage capacity of computers and external data carriers increased greatly.
- The demand for computers increased worldwide, as well as at departmental level.
- Higher management became involved in automation because of the ease of application, the results and the required investments.
- The knowledge and experience of automation increased among those not technically trained.
- Computers became smaller and more affordable, enabling automation at departmental level (mini computers).
- There was an increase in computer service agencies that carried out the automation for companies or that were specialized in particular applications (such as administration).

8.2.2 Growth model

In the 1970s the attention of management shifted from a computer focus to a data focus, and then ultimately to a focus on information. This revealed a growth model in the application of automation. A similar growth model was developed by Richard Nolan, an American management consultant, who showed that the application evolved from a central computer department to a differentiated application, from a business function to an infrastructural application (Table 8.2).

The phases of Nolan's model show that during the data-processing era the application of automation evolved from a data-processing activity to the provision of information. These

Table 8.2 The initial phases of Nolan's model that indicate the development of automation within organizations

Characteristic	Initiation phase	Popularization	'Control'	Integration	Data management	Maturity
Application	Cost savings/batch processing	Island automation	Restructuring of existing applications	Reconstruction of existing applications	Organizational integration, only 50% batch	Infrastructure, networks, real-time computing, online
Attention management	On technical tools	On possible applications	On controllability	On effectiveness	On information provision	Information as strategic weapon (data resources)
Involvement	Central department, technical focus	Central department and management	Central finance, F&A manager	Departmental management with own budget	Large involvement of users	Management and users working together

phases do not yet take into account the application of the Internet. They do, however, indicate that networks had become an important component, but mainly within an organization. If an organization wishes to achieve a competitive advantage through automation, then the importance attached to the provision of information increases. The first focus is a collaboration between departments through the sharing of data. This led to internal problems concerning responsibilities and autonomy. For example, in the battle for customer data, was this information the property of the financial department or of the marketing department? In most cases the marketing department lost this battle which then in turn led to a delay in the automation of the marketing functions. In addition, the budget for non-marketing-related investments was often limited to about £1000. This was an important figure that helped to accelerate the introduction of PCs (IBM, Commodore and Amstrad) in marketing departments, as these PCs cost £999.

8.3 From data processing to information technology

The shift in focus of departments from recording data to using this data heralded the start of the IT era. No longer was recording data (data processing) an end in itself; acquiring and disseminating information now became important. As a result of these rapid technological developments, all sorts of new application possibilities arose, and the use of IT acquired an increasingly greater strategic value for an organization. This led to changes such as:

- the social acceptance of the new technological possibilities (and the limitations);
- new hardware and software, that were smaller, more flexible and mutually exchangeable (compatibility);
- a greater applicability in an organization, particularly also with those important primary processes;
- a change in information technology's place in the organization (it was no longer a department separated by technology, it had now become a facilitative centre); and
- application possibilities that went beyond the boundaries of an organization through the integration with telecommunication. As a result automation was no longer bound to an internal application, but it was possible to also use this same data externally. This led to the adoption of the term 'ICT' as an integrated concept.

These changes in turn led to major changes in the applications of IT and, also partly as a result, to a greater impact on marketing and an organization's competitive edge in the market.

The increased competitive edge was the result of the focus of an organization's management on the information provision; not only processing more data in order to achieve better efficiency, but also to add value to products and services and to increase the organization's impact in the market. Automation was deployed in order to increase an organization's ability to adapt to changes in the market (agility). As a result, IT became of strategic importance within the field of marketing. In the data-processing era there was the automation of data processing. Now the supply of information became important for decision-making at various levels throughout the organization.

During the data-processing era the hardware, software and data were of equal importance. IT is more to do with the speed of information provision, the currency and correctness of information and the accessibility of this information. Speed, currency and accessibility determine the ability to make decisions and therefore have a direct influence on competitive relationships. Marketing as a function increased in importance within the organization;

however, that is not to say that the marketing manager also became more important within the organization. Rather, other functionaries began to take marketing decisions as well which then threatened to operationalize marketing. The cause of this is the large focus on the operational activities of marketing (marketing communication), as well as the slowness of the marketing management to adopt new technologies. As a result, other disciplines were quicker to adopt marketing than marketing departments were to adopt technology. In the IT era the strategic value of marketing increased, while the place of marketing in the organization decreased in importance.

The IT era required new skills from management, different from those of the data-processing era. The management now had to be able to disseminate and interpret information. This led directly to a number of problems:

- Who owned the data?
- Who had the leading role in the collaboration between functions and departments?
- How compatible was the data?

8.3.1 Ownership of data

During these changes there was a great deal of friction around the question of the ownership of the data. The information supply was fragmented (as was the organization itself), with separate departments that had little collaboration with one another. While sharing information or making use of one another's information, it is essential to be able to collaborate. This can only be successful, however, if there is mutual trust and if the perceived value of the data is at least of the same level for all parties. This difference became all too clear when the marketing department wanted to use the customer database of the financial department. The quality of the addresses was insufficient for a mailing. Names were spelt incorrectly, contact names were missing from addresses or the contact persons were people from the financial department (who after all took care of the payments). There were also various addresses associated with a single name; these were often the invoice and the delivery address. Then there was the problem of double addresses. Sometimes in the bookkeeping system an address was created for each invoice or for each contact person. The chance, therefore, that a certain department or person would receive a letter several times was more often the rule than the exception.

8.3.2 Who had the leading role in the collaboration?

Another problem in collaboration between departments was the question of responsibility. Who was responsible for the information, and what was someone allowed to use and what not? Authorizations were too stringent, and were determined on the basis of independently operating departments. Suddenly departments had to collaborate and share data. In addition, departments were dependent upon one another in, for example, the data processing and the quality of recording this data. Conflicts arose particularly concerning this latter point, as departments differed in their views regarding the importance of quality data. This was another reason why data needed to be accurate. In the early years in particular this resulted in frustration and unwillingness from both sides. As marketing was usually dependent upon data, which was recorded at another department, this led to frustration in the marketing department. The data was sometimes out of date or the address details were incorrect. This made it difficult to make analyses and made direct communication awkward. There was no budget to do things oneself, and there was a great deal of frustration as a result.

8.3.3 Compatibility of the data

Friction also arose between the old and the new technology. The data was set down in mainframes, whilst more and more PCs were being used. The compatibility between PCs and the mainframe, and often between the PCs themselves, was very limited. This made it difficult to transfer data from one application to another. As the application had become of such strategic importance, the higher management could no longer avoid taking decisions regarding IT issues. Internal conflicts did not help either in an organization's ability to act decisively. Departments became increasingly dependent upon one another in order to be effective. In order to be able to apply the new technology optimally, it was necessary to share information. In order to realize this, change was required within the organization. This led to:

- a transition from a product-oriented organization to a market-oriented organization;
- greater insight into the customers' wishes and direct decision-making for the external functions (empowerment); and
- more insight into the effectiveness and progress of the activities.

The changes that took place due to the application of IT were quite dramatic. Based on the new possibilities and the new market relationships (in the 1980s), separate developments came about which became integrated within the application at organizational level:

- The market conditions changed because of the emergence of new entrants, a different customer behaviour, globalization and the innovation and imitation of products. The previous chapter examined these changes from a marketing perspective.
- Changes were possible because of new software techniques and a different method of developing software based on architecture. In particular, the application of relational database systems was important for the integral approach of an organization (collaboration instead of fragmentation).
- The hardware changed, producing faster systems, but also a radical miniaturization of hardware, faster chips and smaller computers that offered many possibilities to the user.

8.4 Software applications

These developments also meant that the existing automation systems would have to be assessed again on their applicability and effectiveness. So-called 'island automation', whereby each operational function had its own automation system, was not desired. There now had to be an integrated system. This integration was based on a coherent model that described the various databases. Up until then each application had had its own specific program. For the databases use was made of hierarchical databases, whereby the structure was determined in advance. Any modifications were tricky and costly. This of course hampered the transfer of data between departments. As a result, a different structure was necessary that would allow more flexibility (modifications in response to any changes) and enable different functions and departments to use the same data. A number of software applications and their use are discussed in the following subsections.

8.4.1 Relational databases

More flexibility in the use and transfer of data became possible due to a new methodology, the relational database. In contrast to the existing database systems that were based on fixed structures and fixed access software, a relational database consists of independent databases

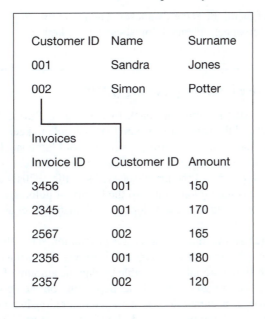

Customer ID	Name	Surname
001	Sandra	Jones
002	Simon	Potter

Invoices

Invoice ID	Customer ID	Amount
3456	001	150
2345	001	170
2567	002	165
2356	001	180
2357	002	120

Figure 8.6 A relational database

(tables) that are linked to application software. A relational database consists of three different layers: the data layer, the access layer that manages the data files (the database management system) and the user's layer, the application software (Figure 8.6).

The database shown in Figure 8.6 consists of two tables. The column 'customer ID' refers solely to the customer in the 'Customers' table with the same ID. When information is requested regarding which customer belongs to invoice 2, the information is retrieved from the 'Customers' table. In this way any change to a name would only have to be applied once. This process is called 'database normalization', and its execution is referred to as normalization. A database can be normalized to various degrees. This is referred to as 'normal forms'.

The application of this relational method forms the basis of the information provision, automation and new forms of organization. The basis was formed by the blueprints, the so-called architecture, with which the information flow and information processes could be described. This occurred across the departments throughout the organization. It also included marketing as a function; not always within the new marketing focus that developed separately (no markets but customers and relationships), but on the basis of the sales-based strategy that applied at the time. It was therefore not yet foreseen that, for example, direct distribution or direct communication was possible. Information, however, was integrated across distribution points, markets and product groups.

It is interesting to note here that it was not until the 1990s that customers and direct communication became part of the information provision. Specific application software was created that could be linked to the systems that had been developed in the 1980s. This software is now better known under the name CRM (see Chapter 9).

8.4.2 ERP

The 1980s were dominated by this adaptation, as well as the change of focus, from data processing to information provision. Each department had its own information system, but with the possibility of using the same databases. Each department actually wanted its own information system: personnel, financial, logistics and marketing.

Box 8.1   Enterprise resource planning (ERP)

The origins of the ERP system date back to the 1960s. During this period many companies experienced the need for a system that was able to keep up-to-date records of their stocks. At that time it was still possible to hold large stocks and yet remain competitive. The most important objective of these stock control systems was purely to keep a centralized control of the large stocks. As of the 1970s, however, it became clear that companies could no longer afford the luxury of holding onto large amounts of stock. This gradually led to the development of 'material requirements planning' (MRP) systems.

For the first time use was made of a master production schedule (MPS). An MPS specifies the amount of completed product that is necessary during every phase of the planning. Using a bill of material it is possible to plan the amount of raw materials and components that is necessary in every phase, depending on the necessary production time. With the help of an accurate stock system that meticulously monitors the existing stocks as well as the stocks to be delivered, the net material need can be determined. This meant a leap forward in the field of productivity.

In the early 1980s companies began to profit from the increased possibilities and the affordability of the available technology. MRP consequently evolved from a planning and control system to a system that was capable of planning almost all the resources of the company. This development was such that in 1984 Oliver Wight introduced the term MRP II: manufacturing resource planning. With MRP II the primary functions (production, marketing and finance) are integrated in the planning process with other functions such as human resource management, project management, technology and purchasing. This allowed companies to indicate the activities in detail and to take action if these activities were not in line with the desired planning. Although MRP II was a significant improvement to the previous systems, due to their dynamic developments companies needed ever more integrated systems. Constantly larger sales markets, internationalization, and integration with customers and suppliers brought about a global change in the way in which business was conducted. Quality and costs were taken for granted, whilst delivery times, flexibility and product differentiation became increasingly more important. This led to the development of the enterprise resource planning (ERP) system. The term ERP was introduced by The Gartner Group in the early 1990s.

Whilst MRP II traditionally focused on planning the internal resources of a business, ERP aimed to plan the resources of suppliers as well, based on the dynamic demands of the customers. The description of The Gartner Group states the three major characteristics of ERP systems. First of all, they are multifunctional: from financial results, via production planning, to HRM. A second characteristic is that they are integrated. This means that if data is entered in one of the functions, the information in all the related functions is also immediately modified. Thirdly, ERP systems are modular. A business can for example implement all modules while another may only use a few modules. Any combination is possible.

With good architecture it was possible to acquire various 'views' of the same database supplemented with application software for each function. The various information systems formed the basis for an organization's total information provision and ICT. This integral application was later also referred to as 'ERP' (enterprise resource planning). Within ERP, information systems were linked, the information provision was based on a planning structure (therefore not tied to a specific department) and external components of the planning of resources, such as suppliers and customers, were linked. This helped to create a basic infrastructure within the organization based on the primary process and had information provision for secondary operational functions (Table 8.3).

The ERP system was also important for the automation of the marketing function. Within the sales focus of the marketing department, marketing was only part of the information provision. Information concerning stocks, distribution channels, sales outlets and products was provided as standard. This led to information regarding turnover and planning. As a result marketing became integrated within the organization. This also immediately led to a change.

The marketing department had to take responsibility for the planning of sales. Budgeting and forecasting became part of the marketing function. Based on this forecast the marketing budget was determined, as well as the production. If the marketing department had not planned well, either high levels of stocks would arise which would then have to be sold at a

Table 8.3 Differences between data processing and IT

	Data processing	*IT*
General	Automation is a separate business function	Automation has been integrated within the organization. Large user involvement
	Automation is technically oriented	
	There are relatively few people directly involved	IT is used to improve business processes and for supporting and creating new organizational forms
	Limited management attention, limited to delegating activities and (limited) monitoring	IT determines the position that the organization assumes within the market
	Automation is applied in order to support processes	IT is no longer internally oriented but externally oriented towards contacts with the market
	The objective is efficiency in the execution of mainly primary operational functions	Applications on the basis of users' wishes. Broad application in the organization, also with secondary processes
Financial scope	Expenses	Investment
Role of application	Process support	Integral application
Significance of application	Tactical	Strategic
View of application	Traditional	Innovative
Persons involved	Little/limited	Much and aimed at users
Management attitude	Delegating to head of department	Controlled by management

(marginal) loss or there would be insufficient stocks to meet the demand. In the 1960s and 1970s the marketing department was often a support department within the organization; however, due to this change this was no longer possible. Marketing was now contributing to an organization's commercial success. This was also noticeable in the level of the marketing function and the required skills. The marketing department had to have knowledge of planning processes and economic forces, such as price elasticity and marketing strategies. Financial reporting and analyses also became increasingly important. The marketing function became more important to the organization. The need for a specific marketing module as part of an integrated information system was, in fact, a logical consequence.

8.4.3 Uniformization and registration of articles

In the 1980s there were a number of developments that had a direct influence on marketing automation. First, a need was felt to have access to information earlier and to have direct contact with customers and suppliers. The problem of automatic data transmission led to data having to be manually entered into a computer system. This resulted in a delay in the transmission and a risk of errors, making it difficult to establish links between data files. Finally, at the end of the 1980s it had become possible to standardize data transmission, enabling systems to communicate with one another. This made it possible to place orders directly, generate automatic invoices and send other documents electronically. Electronic data interchange (EDI) led to a closer relationship between the parties (agreements after all had to be made in order to allow systems to communicate with one another) and to quicker and more efficient processing of data. The risk of errors was also reduced.

Box 8.2 EDI

Software for generating and processing EDI is generally expensive, and data communication was until recently in the hands of a number of large companies. With the arrival of the Internet, EDI has also become more accessible for smaller companies, and the software has also become better and cheaper. What's more, EDI software has become available as open source.

The EDI standard describes the layout of a message that is used for the electronic data exchange between companies, with the objective of minimizing the amount of writing involved in commercial transactions. This standard is mainly used in Europe, but is increasingly being regarded and accepted as a standard worldwide.

The syntax of the data elements are defined as well as the meaning of the various elements. A definition is also given of how this data is built up in a message that is being sent.

The messages ensure that various computer programs that each have their own standards can still communicate with one another. A translation, however, also takes place at both the transmitter and recipient of the message, whereby the EDIFACT information is converted to or from the ERP program that generally works with other standards. The EDI FACT standard provides:

- a set of syntax rules to strucutre data;
- an interactive exchange protocol (I-EDI); and
- standard messages which allow multi-country and multi-industry exchanges.

8.4.4 Bar codes

A need also arose to link information at article level. With automatic data transmission it becomes essential to maintain unambiguity concerning the articles. Working with article numbers that are specific to organizations is therefore not practical and would always lead to differences. The need to also use identical numbering systems increased. In conjunction with this need efforts were made to find ways of automatically reading article codes, which would reduce the risk of errors (Figure 8.7).

Figure 8.7 A bar code based on the EAN standard coding

Tests carried out with OCR font revealed that the risk of distortion and contamination was too great. Efforts made to find another method resulted in the bar code. Through a series of light and dark patches the bar code gives a certain number code. This made it possible to scan the number.

Box 8.3 EAN

The European article numbering (EAN) was developed from the universal product code (UPC). It was introduced in 1974 and looks to become the new world standard. Practically all packaged products on shop shelves in the Netherlands and Belgium have an EAN-13-code, a series of 13 digits. The company 'EAN International' has a coordinating function and issues codes to manufacturers when they introduce new products onto the market.

When the UPC was extended into the EAN code, an extra digit was added in front of the 12 digits of the UPC. In order to make EAN compatible with UPC, the first digit of the EAN code had to be implicitly coded, which means that the EAN bar code retained the same structure as the UPC bar code. The solution was found in another coding of the L-digits. Following this new method the EAN code now has the second up to the thirteenth digit converted into bars. The first digit is as it were hidden in the bars of the second to seventh digit (the L-digits of a UPC).

The European Article Number or EAN is a bar code that is used worldwide in shops for cash till transactions and stock administration.

8.4.5 The use of data

Once the data has been recorded it has to be used. The data was initially recorded in a specific system for a single function, but in the 1980s and 1990s the data was increasingly used for various business functions. This cross-departmental use of data led not only to a different division of tasks and authorizations in the organization, but also to another (relational) database technique. This relational database technique made it possible for various functions to use a single database source. Agreements were made concerning the authorization: viewing only, making changes or total management (including deleting). Users initially were provided with a hard copy of the information, later the data was provided on a floppy disk and then finally it was also possible to deliver a subset of the data for specific use or one's own analyses. The data was then fed into a program that was developed for this specific function. This could be, for example, invoicing data that was supplied to the marketing department, which would then analyse this data according to region, sales territory, distribution channel or salesperson. The invoicing data formed the source, and the analyses the secondary application. Programs that were used for analyses were, for example, SPSS and SAS. Within these programs, models were built that were fed with the primary data. As a result there was no problem regarding the property of the data or any fear that another department could distort the data. Prior to the transmission, however, clear agreements needed to be made regarding the layout and field size.

Other software made it possible to support specific applications. Executive information systems were highly visually oriented and converted the data into tables and graphs; marketing programs, for example, converted the data into marketing entities and marketing applications, such as targets, budgets or price policy.

The information infrastructure and information logistics increasingly formed the basis of an organization. In the 1990s the various developments in the areas of IT and telecommunications, as well as developments due to the changes in the organization, grew towards one another, so that optimal use could be made of the various possibilities.

The 1980s and 1990s were dominated by information, from its recording to its use. The infrastructure was created in order to make this possible: networks, terminals, portability of data (via new data carriers) and new forms of organization. At the start of the twenty-first century the various developments came together very clearly as a result of the following:

*   *The data processing era*: recording data; first of all manually, later automatically (scanning) and then finally only once for joint use.
*   *Information technology*: first off-line information provision through printouts, later online possibilities and finally the provision of tools for generating information oneself (data retrieval systems, analysis systems and conditioned reports).
*   *Telecommunication*: first through separate networks and conditioned data transmission (indicate the layout precisely in advance) then later through open networks and more or less unconditioned transmissions such as through the Internet.
*   *Organization*: first separate departments who had their own separate responsibilities (fragmentation) and later a more function-driven organization with joint (and interactive) responsibilities.
*   *Focus*: at first efficient production, then achieving competitive advantages and later striving for a close relationship with stakeholders (such as customers) (Figure 8.8).

The applications were increasingly led by and based on the Internet. Particularly at the start of the twenty-first century it became clear that the Internet was not a network that could be

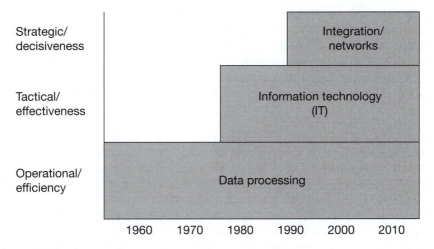

Figure 8.8 Application of IT in an historical context

regarded as separate to the information infrastructure and information provision of an organization, but that it should become an integral part of this. This led to a new development for organizations, but also for the relationship with the market players (including the customers). Part 3 will look at this in more detail.

8.5 Applications within the organization

The influence of IT on an organization is strongly determined by its dependence on information. If a company's dependency is great, then the IT will contribute directly to its competitive advantage. This is thanks to better and more accurate data as well as better and more resolute decision-making. If the dependence on information is less, then the IT will mainly be used for achieving greater efficiency (lower costs) or effectiveness (at departmental level).

8.5.1 Roles

The application of IT can play three roles for an organization:

- a support role;
- a strategic role; and
- a factory role.

Support role

In the support role automation activities are used to make existing activities more efficient, such as order processing, text processing and other forms of communication. The activities remain the same; the difference is that new tools can be used. The introduction of the PC in offices led to IT having a similar support role. The activities were no different; however, letters could now be stored automatically, analyses carried out more effectively (through spreadsheets) and more impressive presentations could be made by, for example, using PowerPoint. The first generation of software packages for the PC were also made for this support function. The spreadsheets looked very much like an 11-column folio sheet, such as those used in accountants' offices. The word processors (e.g. WordPerfect and Wordstar) had few automatic functions. The user always had to enter codes themselves. And the first data-bases (dBase 1, 2, 3 or 4) still had to be fully programmed by the user. Later there was more sophisticated software such as the Microsoft Office suite, which is an integrated application package for office applications based on Microsoft software such as Windows.

Strategic role

In the strategic role there is a widespread application of IT throughout the organization. Departments make use of one another's systems and information databases. The use of IT is of strategic importance for the organization, and there is target-oriented strategic planning of IT activities. When developing these activities various staff members from different departments are involved. The technology policy is aimed at realizing a coherent structure (architecture) of technologies, such as described earlier, on the basis of a blueprint. Information-driven companies in particular, such as mail-order companies, Internet providers and airlines, are dependent upon information technology and use it for strategic reasons:

- in order to be able to offer their services more cost effectively; and
- in order to acquire more information on their customers, on their behaviour, the purchase moment and purchasing process.

What's more, business functions are modified according to the available information and determined once more on the basis of the application of IT.

Factory role

In the factory role there is integrated use of automation in activities and processes. The systems are regarded as production factors that have to be available to a sufficient degree and deployed in a highly efficient manner. They are necessary, a basic precondition, but should also be as cost-effective as possible. Data entry, and these days also call centres, are regarded as production departments. The reason for this is that the application of IT does not lead to competitive advantages. For these applications this only applied to the first organization that used IT. It led to lower costs and a temporary competitive advantage. However, once other companies had realized similar applications there was once again competitive equality. An organization can no longer operate without IT, but this does not give it any extra advantages over the competition. It therefore has to be used as efficiently as possible (that is to say, at the lowest possible cost).

Examples of this are the various loyalty systems that came into existence. In the 1990s they were seen to result in a competitive advantage over suppliers that did not have a similar system. Once the competition responded directly to this, attempts were made to reduce the costs, while retaining the same customer benefits. An example of this is Airmiles. Initially participants in the Airmiles programmes had a wonderful competitive advantage in the market, but soon afterwards other competing programmes were introduced along with other discount cards. This all contributed to an erosion of the advantage. As a result, the costs of the programme came under pressure and a number of suppliers decided to stop issuing Airmiles.

Also in aviation a similar process developed with frequent flyer programmes. Today all large companies have their own frequent flyer programme. Only the low-cost carriers (such as Ryanair and Easyjet), which offer lower prices, do not take part. The conclusion here is that the application of IT does not lead to lasting competitive advantages, but rather to competitive equality. Not participating in the application is not an option, unless you are able to implement a new successful strategy, as has happened in the aviation industry with the low-cost carriers. As a result, there is competitive equality between the companies with a frequent flyer programme and the low-cost carriers. Customers have little preference for the suppliers within either of the groups.

8.5.2 Cycle in the application

When IT is applied in order to realize competitive advantages we can see an innovation cycle. The organization that introduces a new application onto the market has a competitive advantage. Imitations, however, usually follow quickly and so the advantage is of short duration. In the end the focus is simply on maintaining the application at as low a cost as possible (Figure 8.9).

In the 1990s it became necessary to determine the business processes once more and IT was used for this. Organizations had to modify the processes because:

• the competition also did this;
• customers wanted it;
• the costs had to be reduced due to the greater competition on the markets; and
• it was necessary to be able to respond more effectively to changes in the market.

In the first half of the 1990s there was a strong focus on business processes. Michael Hammer made it clear that 'business process reengineering' (BPR) was necessary in order to reduce costs, to be effective and for a better collaboration within the organization (see Figure 8.10). He suggested that efficiency improvements that could be achieved fully by applying IT are determined by the manner in which business processes are set up. Information provision, the manner in which activities are carried out and the mutual relationship between the activities are determined by the application of IT. The influence of IT on the organization determines to a great extent its effect on the market. If the influence of IT is limited to a specific function, then a separate application will also be made. The effect on the market would therefore be less.

The implementation of sales information systems in the 1980s did not immediately lead to big competitive advantages. The sales efforts, however, did become measurable and more efficient. And as a result this led to relatively lower sales costs. In the 1990s when the sales

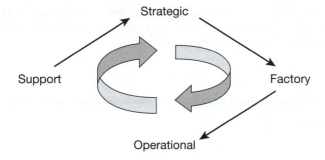

Figure 8.9 Role of the IT application

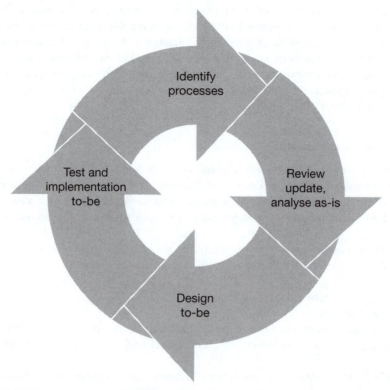

Figure 8.10 Business process reengineering cycle

information systems became part of an organization-wide CRM system, the effect was much greater. Organizations changed their business processes according to the CRM system. The commercial functions were also modified. Account management, direct communication (initially by telephone) and sales management were modified immediately according to the new possibilities. This also led to an increased dependence on IT for the organization as well as for commercial functions, including marketing.

A BPR cycle looks for a better coordination between processes and a greater optimization. This should lead to better quality and lower costs.

The application of IT increasingly determines the success of an organization. In Part 3, which deals with the impact of the Internet, we will examine this in more detail. The effect of the application of IT is also determined by the manner in which staff and functions in the organization (including the management board) adopt the technology, and the degree to which they do so. This adoption is influenced by:

- innovation;
- the management;
- the customer; and
- the competition.

Innovation

There is a negative relationship between the degree of adoption and the complexity of the application. The more complex the technology, the more difficult the application. However, as is the case with the Internet as well as with call centres, the simpler the application, the greater the adoption by the user.

The management

The degree of centralization and formalization within an organization adversely affects the adoption of new technologies in the organization. Delegated decision-making and flexible lines of control in an organization, as well as the empowerment of management and officials will greatly increase the adoption. With automation we saw the use of stand-alone PCs in departments with their own software. It was only later that a policy was developed for the entire organization, and the organization (and its functions) was adapted accordingly. For further information on this, please refer to the described development of ERP, CRM and BPR. The efforts made towards autonomy at departmental management level in the 1980s had a negative effect on the adoption of new technology. Although automation was good for the department that implemented it, it certainly did not benefit the other departments.

The customer

By implementing a marketing strategy that focuses on the customer and by adapting the communication function, the provider can influence the acceptance process (diffusion). Customers would have certain expectations and respond in certain ways, forcing organizations to adopt the new technology. This took place in the 1990s with the call centres: customers suddenly started to call the organization. Later the same thing happened with the Internet: customers sought to contact organizations directly (or buy online). An organization could do nothing other than offer the desired facilities.

The competition

If the competition has a new application (innovation), the other suppliers cannot lag behind. The greater the competition in the market, the greater the need for innovation.

Summary

- Initially the application of IT led to cost reductions.
- Through the application of IT competitive equality arose.
- IT increased the barriers to new entrants.
- Due to the influence of the market position, IT has to be applied even more within marketing.
- By applying IT integrally in relationship management with customers and suppliers, the business model also has to be modified.
- Because of the new business model, competitive relationships can change.

9   Applications of information technology within marketing

The application of information technology (IT) facilitates changes in the marketing function and supports the execution of marketing activities. Because of the change of focus of marketing brought about by changes in the market and different competitive relationships, but also by the application of IT, the pressure to apply IT within marketing has increased. Initially, IT was only used to support marketing activities (efficiency), but soon it was used to adapt these activities, such as market research and market communication. Finally, it led to more knowledge and insight into buying processes and customers. It is this that prompted a shift in the focus of marketing towards individual identified relationships, and made it possible to do this efficiently. IT was no longer aimed at the efficient execution of activities but at pro-active approaches to customers. Knowledge of the market increasingly became 'a bundling of knowledge of individual customers'.

9.1 Marketing applications within data processing

As a result of the increased competition in markets and the larger economies of scale of the sales area, in the 1970s organizations started to look for ways to achieve a competitive advantage, as described in the strategic marketing concept in Chapter 2. Marketing was a separate department that focused on the relationship with markets. This department usually consisted of market communication (including PR), distribution and product management. This did not include any process activities, which initially could be automated (marketing is not a process). For that reason the first application was for the processing of data obtained through market research. This could achieve efficiency, but also quicker insights into the results of the studies. The pace of decision-making and the appropriateness of the decisions could lead to a competitive advantage. The studies (usually quantitative) were punched and read into the computer, and statistical analyses made of the results. It was these kinds of calculations that were a typical application of automation at the time (1960s and 1970s). The market research department would interpret and translate the computer output (stacks of forms on continuous stationery, also known as tractor-feed paper) into policy advice (Figure 9.1).

The computer output was also used for printing standard letters. Blank (or pre-printed) forms on continuous stationery were used for this. The letter as standard often already had a pre-printed signature. The computer only printed the address details on the forms. This was a first step towards automated marketing communication (direct marketing). In addition, organizations started to experiment with more personal communication.

Adding variable data at the end of the letter allowed, for example, purchase data to be integrated or payment information added. This could be a giro payment form, including all

Figure 9.1 Continuous stationary for standard letters among other things

relevant details such as invoice amount, name and invoice number. Using an optical character recognition (OCR) font meant a giro payment form was created that could also be read automatically. In order to allow the addition of variables within the standard text, space had to be left blank. Using special programs, variables could be printed in a specific position in the letter. This was meticulous work: not only did the program have to specify the right position, but the operator also had to take extra care that the paper was placed in the printer correctly. The first line had to start exactly in the right place otherwise the variable data would be printed somewhere in the middle of the standard text. Determining the blank space in the letter was a precise task. For set data, such as amount or invoice number, this was simple enough; for address details, however, this was more difficult. People with a long surname often saw their name abbreviated to 20 characters, whereas people with a short surname often saw their names printed within a large blank space. Reader's Digest infamously used this technique and form of communication for a long time. In the end it was regarded as a form of authenticity – a style that was in line with the image.

Other direct marketing companies, mail-order companies in particular, were quick to use the possibilities for direct communication, as it was efficient and much more personal than the old forms of communication (for example, a standard letter in an envelope with a stuck-on label). A small number of organizations, however, still continue to use this form of communication – a pre-printed letter with a label.

9.2 Applications with information technology

The change for marketing communication came in the 1980s when laser printers and databases started to be used. And thus the marketing function started to get involved in the various possibilities of IT within marketing communication. The reasons for this were as follows:

- The marketing department wanted to communicate directly with (potential) customers. The competition became increasingly fierce and it turned out to be increasingly difficult to reach customers. The focus shifted to maintaining relationships with individual customers.
- Technology enabled personal communication through the introduction of the laser printer but also due to new computer systems and developments involving the telephone (telecommunication). It also became possible to measure marketing communication directly.

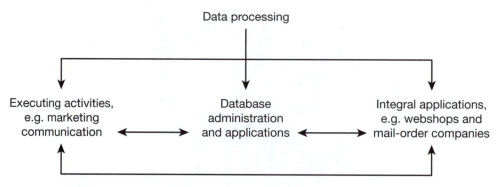

Figure 9.2 Integral application of IT in marketing

- Advertising agencies set up dedicated direct marketing departments, in order to be able to carry out not only mass communication but also 'below the line' activities.
- The PC and specific software brought automation within the field of the marketing department, in terms of both budget and applications. This resulted in knowledge and an understanding of the potential of IT.

Data processing is the foundation for database and information systems. These in turn form the basis for integral applications. Data processing and the database are essential for carrying out marketing activities, as illustrated in Figure 9.2.

9.3 Database marketing

The aim of database marketing was to acquire and retain customers. But it was also to bind customers by achieving a greater share of their wallets (Figure 9.3).

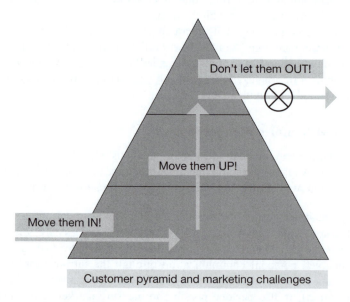

Figure 9.3 Database marketing

Database marketing was a direct marketing application whereby a database with addresses was used for direct communication, initially via direct mail. Later the database was supplemented with buying and response information. This resulted in greater knowledge about customers' behaviour and the effectiveness of the advertising. It was direct marketing that aimed to experiment and determine the success of the marketing communication activities. Direct marketing is more results-oriented than, for example, advertising; the effects of an advertising campaign are measurable objectively only to a limited extent.

The experiments with direct communication involved all sorts of mailings and the selection of addresses. Prior to the mailing, test runs were done with various types of letters. A random selection of addresses from the database was then used, which were divided among the communication messages that were to be tested. It was then examined which form of mailing generated the highest response. Tests were done on, for example, fonts, colour schemes and letter size. But the various incentives were also tested: for example, does a pen as a gift generate better results than a make-up set? The types of customer who responded were also analysed. The files were complemented with key data such as postcode, gender and customer characteristics. Loyal customers scored perhaps better than customers who bought only once in a while. It is precisely this testing that became so much easier to do with automation and formed the backbone of direct marketing (Figure 9.4).

9.3.1 Postcodes

As a component of addresses the postcode became important for database marketing. The postcode is in some countries a unique location code, but in all cases refers to a defined area. The main purpose of the postcode system was mail delivery, but sometimes special codes were assigned to streets, houses or institutions. This made it possible to link contact details to the postcode.

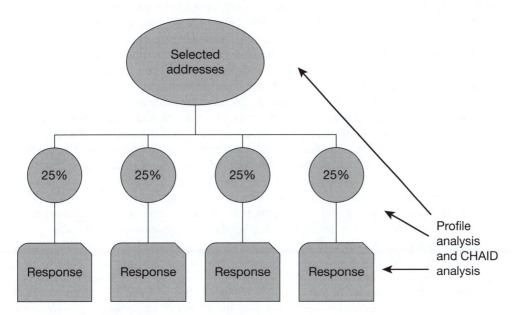

Figure 9.4 Analysis of respondents, profiles and variables

A postal code (known in various countries as a post code, postcode or ZIP code) is a series of letters and/or digits appended to a postal address for the purpose of sorting mail. Once postal codes were introduced, other applications became possible.

In February 2005, 117 of the 190 member countries of the Universal Postal Union had postal code systems. Countries that do not have national systems include Ireland and Panama. Although Hong Kong and Macau are now Special Administrative Regions of China each maintain their own long-established postal system, which does not utilize postal codes for domestic mail, and no postal codes are assigned to Hong Kong and Macau. Mails between Hong Kong, Macau and mainland China are treated as international.

Although postal codes are usually assigned to geographical areas, special codes are sometimes assigned to individual addresses or to institutions that receive large volumes of mail, such as government agencies and large commercial companies.

Source: Wikipedia postal codes

The use of postcodes in combination with name and streetcodes made it easy to take duplications out of address files. By checking whether this constructed code appeared in the files more than once, the data could be linked to just one address. This could prevent several letters being sent to a single address. The removal of duplications was at address level, not at an individual level. When various addresses were used, for example a house address and a post office box address, companies could still get two letters. Also when the postcode was incorrect, a similar problem arose. The combination of house number and postcode was adopted increasingly often as a unique code to guard against duplication, and was also used as a unique search code in address files. The code was based upon a postal area divided by grid coordinates. The code was enriched with name and address information, such as the first, third and fifth character of the street and the name. Using this code or a postcode in conjunction with PCs made it easy to maintain files. It was in fact a unique cluster code and on the basis of these codes it became possible to carry out cluster analyses.

Cluster division allowed not only for various clusters to be compared with one another, but also for areas to be broken down into smaller units (territories) and characterizations ascribed to a cluster. Based on the notion that similar people live in similar houses and display similar behaviours, areas could be compared with one another. It was possible to select good clusters, predicting good responses. In addition, the database could be expanded using area characteristics. In the 1980s databases were developed in which the unique characteristics of neighbourhoods were maintained at postcode level. These unique characteristics were linked to location, for example owner-occupied houses or rented accommodation, distance from schools and socio-economic classification, but also buying behaviour and reading behaviour, so that a lifestyle database could be constructed for marketing purposes. Databases were used to compare files both with one another and at a postcode level. This allowed for the penetration per cluster to be determined, but also for a customer segmentation to be made. This segmentation was the basis for an active approach to the customer. Examples of these databases are Acorn and Pinpoint, socio-demographic database systems to enrich addresses in one's own database or for selected direct mail.

Identical postcode clusters were given separate names, such as young neighbourhoods with families, well-educated and well-off middle-aged or retired residents. In this way postcodes could be classified and sorted further according to unique clusters. In addition to the practical use of removing the duplications and expanding the address files, these characterizations could also be used for creating customer profiles, drawing up response expectations and credit scoring. By adding more information these databases became ever more intricate. The marketing campaigns thus became more effective and this resulted in a better understanding of the customer behaviour (Table 9.1).

Table 9.1 ACORN classification

Wealthy achievers	Wealthy executives	01 – Affluent mature professionals, large houses
		02 – Affluent working families with mortgages
		03 – Villages with wealthy commuters
		04 – Well-off managers, larger houses
	Affluent greys	05 – Older affluent professionals
		06 – Farming communities
		07 – Old people, detached houses
		08 – Mature couples, smaller detached houses
	Flourishing families	09 – Larger families, prosperous suburbs
		10 – Well-off working families with mortgages
		11 – Well-off managers, detached houses
		12 – Large families and houses in rural areas
Urban prosperity	Prosperous professionals	13 – Well-off professionals, larger houses and converted flats
		14 – Older professionals in detached houses and apartments
	Educated urbanites	15 – Affluent urban professionals, flats
		16 – Prosperous young professionals, flats
		17 – Young educated workers, flats
		18 – Multi-ethnic young, converted flats
		19 – Suburban privately renting professionals
	Aspiring singles	20 – Student flats and cosmopolitan sharers
		21 – Singles and sharers, multi-ethnic areas
		22 – Low income singles, small rented flats
		23 – Student terraces
Comfortably off	Starting out	24 – Young couples, flats and terraces
		25 – White-collar singles/sharers, terraces
	Secure families	26 – Younger white-collar couples with mortgages
		27 – Middle income, home owning areas
		28 – Working families with mortgages
		29 – Mature families in suburban semis
		30 – Established home owning workers
		31 – Home owning Asian family areas
	Settled suburbia	32 – Retired home owners
		33 – Middle income, older couples
		34 – Lower income people, semis
	Prudent pensioners	35 – Elderly singles, purpose built flats
		36 – Older people, flats
Moderate means	Asian communities	37 – Crowded Asian terraces
		38 – Low income Asian families
	Post industrial families	39 – Skilled older family terraces
		40 – Young family workers
	Blue collar roots	41 – Skilled workers, semis and terraces
		42 – Home owning, terraces
		43 – Older rented terraces
Hard pressed	Struggling families	44 – Low income larger families, semis
		45 – Older people, low income, small semis
		46 – Low income, routine jobs, unemployment
		47 – Low-rise terraced estates of poorly off workers
		48 – Low incomes, high unemployment, single parents

continued overleaf

Table 9.1 continued

Burdened singles	49 – Large families, many children, poorly educated
	50 – Council flats, single elderly people
	51 – Council terraces, unemployment, many singles
	52 – Council flats, single parents, unemployment
High rise hardship	53 – Old people in high rise flats
	54 – Singles and single parents, high rise estates
Inner city adversity	55 – Multi-ethnic, purpose built estates
	56 – Multi-ethnic, crowded flats

Source: http://blogs.warwick.ac.uk

9.3.2 Sales and marketing information systems

In addition to database marketing, which was aimed at direct communication, sales and marketing information systems were also developed. These systems were able to store more data and were not only aimed at direct marketing but also served to support the sales staff. Customer cards, visitor reports and visit schedules were part of such a system. As already described in Chapter 4, these sales information systems led to a close collaboration between sales and marketing. Sales staff used these systems for operational activities, which in turn formed the basis for marketing. Planning and pipeline management were important aspects. Here the success rate per contact was determined. The intensification of the communication resulted in more contacts in the pipeline. This made it increasingly easy to plan and to adapt other business activities to the results (such as finance, production and stock control). This shift in the application of IT within marketing over the years is illustrated in Table 9.2.

9.4 Customer relationship management (CRM)

Customer relationship management (CRM) is a coherent combination of separate functions and facilities that are jointly used to approach the customer more directly and to build and retain a personal and interactive relationship. CRM involves knowing the customer or business associate in such a way that it is possible to respond to individual wishes. It can be used prior to the purchase, during the buying process and for the after-sales support. In order to use CRM effectively, knowledge has to be available about the customer and their purchasing and contact behaviour, as well as information about the customer value and the potential customer value. On the basis of this information, proactive communication is also required. It is possible to have proactive communication carried out by telephone, letter and email.

This whole strategy, in which the organization, the marketing and the provision of information have been set up in such a way that it is possible to optimally respond to the individual contacts and the individual relationship with customers, is referred to as CRM and is illustrated in Figure 9.5. Important components are the ICT, the adjustment in the organization and the focus of marketing.

At the beginning of the 1990s automation applications within marketing were mostly aimed at supporting the communication function. In particular, call centres and sales functions used various supporting applications. The sales information systems were based on a PC, although the data was also used for other files and vice versa. A stand-alone application soon resulted in all sorts of interface problems. For small organizations this dilemma was partly solved by making use of a network based upon a central server. Large organizations had larger systems that had already been used for other business functions for some time.

Table 9.2 An historical perspective of the application of IT in marketing

	1970s	*1980s*	*1990s*	*After 2000*
Application	Data processing	Sales information and sales management. Support sales process, direct communication and analyses	Commercial information provision, link to other systems and business functions	Integral application based on the Internet and network possibilities
Hardware	Mainframe	Minicomputers and personal computers	Servers and personal computers	Networks and the Internet
Integration	None, stand-alone application	Limited, only at departmental level	Part of total provision of information. ERP-based CRM applications	Fully integrated within and outside of the organization
Management	Automation department	Marketing/sales department	Marketing and IT jointly	IT and infrastructure, marketing the application
Focus	Efficiency	Function support and information	Customer contact and direct communication	New market conditions, new business models, external relationships including customers
Area of attention	Process efficiency	Selling and effectiveness of sales	Relationship management and influence of buying process and buying moment	Facilitating buying process and need for information
Applications of marketing automation	Data processing, data analyses, office automation such as word processing, desktop publishing and laser printing Sales support, data processing in batches (sales results, shop turnovers, stocks), data management	Communication support (call centres), management support (CRM), scanning, support helpdesks, applications of loyalty systems, multimedia applications, relationship management, communication systems, EDI	Data transmission Network application Internet-based applications, external communication, participation in processes, interaction with customers, tracking and tracing, new concepts, collaborations	

It was not easy to make an interface with these. Often the relational databases were not available yet and traditional, rigid programming languages such as Cobol were used. A stand-alone solution was a flexible alternative for marketing, but this also led to problems. The stand-alone application was often not supported by the central department, which led to

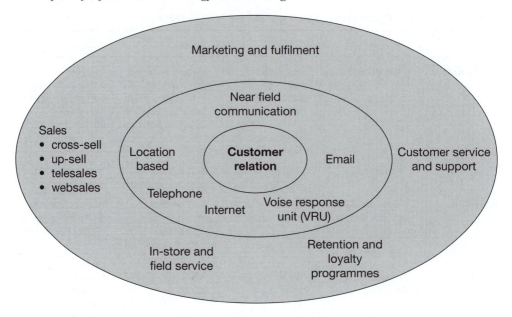

Figure 9.5 Core competences of CRM

Source: Based on Kalakota, R. and Robinson, M. (1999), *e-Business Roadmap for Success*, Addison Wesley Longman

difficulties in the event of problems with the hardware or software. In addition, it was difficult to use data from the mainframe in the stand-alone application and vice versa.

   Once the marketing department started to get used to the automation and saw the benefits it offered the positive aspects became clear. For the operational activities an immediate advantage in efficiency was achieved, while the better reporting led to an improved under-standing of the results of the promotions that were carried out. After this initial success the need for an integrated solution also increased, so that the data from other departments could also be used. This need grew at the same time as the focus of marketing was changing into an integrated, relationship-oriented concept (Figure 9.6).

9.5 Call centres

In addition to the sales supporting software (sales information systems) an increasing need for software to support the telephone traffic arose (call centres). Customers started to call or were being called and the marketing department also wanted to encourage a more personal relationship with customers (see Part 1), which stimulated more telephone contacts. The call centre agents needed more information about the customers, including their buying behaviour, what was sold or what they wanted to buy. Specific call centre software was introduced for both outbound calling and inbound calling.

9.5.1 Outbound calling

Outbound calling refers to telephone calls made by an organization or its agent to a list of contacts. It is relatively easy to plan. The system generates the telephone number and ensures that the relevant customer information is also available. The call is recorded 'automatically'

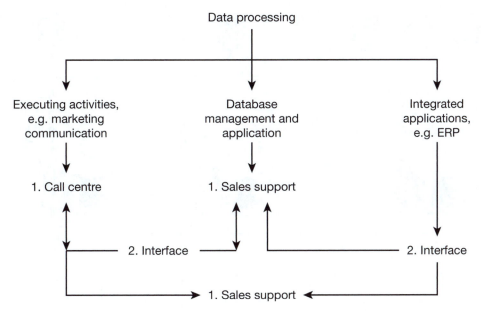

Figure 9.6 Integrated application of IT within a relationship-oriented concept

and the agent immediately makes notes on the 'customer card' of the person being called. Using comprehensive management reports it is possible to determine the effectiveness of the telephone activity immediately as well as the efficiency of the agent, how long the call lasted, how many people were phoned and the success ratio. For outbound calling a direct link with other systems, such as sales accounting, is desirable though not essential. The data can also be read as a batch in the evenings.

The first systems were often stand-alone systems. External call centres could also easily carry out these services. All one had to do was to send a file with addresses, telephone numbers and relevant details. Only later was it possible to log in directly to the client's computers. These days this is often preferred because of the linking of systems, networks and, of course, the Internet.

9.5.2 Inbound communication

For inbound calls a direct link is necessary with other systems as the questions are not known in advance. It is also not known who will call when and about what. Software for supporting inbound calls consists of several modules: call dispatcher, scripting and dynamic answering and call handling/analysis.

Figure 9.7 illustrates a contemporary call centre with call dispatchers, departments and remote telephones.

Call dispatcher

The transport of the call (the routing) is important in order to be able to provide a good service. Many calls come in at the same time and then have to be re-routed to the available agents. The call dispatcher ensures that the call is directed to the appropriate agent. The

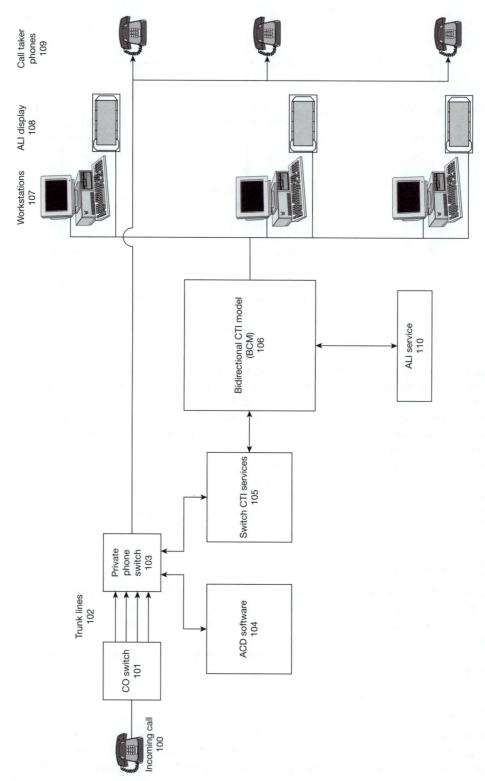

Figure 9.7 Illustrates a contemporary call centre with call dispatchers, departments and remote telephones

agents are often ascribed certain qualifications, so that a first line support and a second line support are arranged on the basis of subject. Queues are also formed, so that a priority can be given to the caller. If, for example, a customer number is entered, it is then possible to give a priority to certain callers (VIP code). These callers are given the privilege of having to wait less time than the others.

Through the call dispatcher it is also possible to arrange an overflow to other locations. If the queue is too long then an external agency, even in another country, may deal with the calls. Call centres in South Africa, for example, can in this way handle calls from clients in Germany, the UK and the Netherlands. South Africa has lower labour costs, the same time zone and, because of the country's history of immigration, it has people who are able to speak Dutch, German or English with little or no accent. This choice is made not only out of cost considerations, but also with a view to keeping the service at a high level.

Box 9.1 Call centre KPI's

Accessibility

Great Britain has the highest accessibility in the retail sector, where 98 per cent of callers are answered in their first attempt to call. In the financial sector this percentage is 95 per cent, as is the case in the entertainment and travel sector. The government scores lowest with 87 per cent, which is below that of the telecom and energy companies that score 90 per cent.

First call resolution

Impressively, 96 per cent of callers have their query resolved during the first call. Again the retail sector scored the highest with a first call resolution rate of 98 per cent, followed by the financial sector and the telecom and energy companies with 97 per cent.

The government again scores the lowest with 92 per cent, 4 per cent lower than the entertainment and travel sectors.

Waiting time

The average waiting time, including time that is spent in the IVR (interactive voice response), amounts to 1.3 minutes. Some 58 per cent of callers had to wait less than 60 seconds.

The retail sector again scores the highest: 74 per cent of callers had a waiting time of less than 1 minute. For the financial sector this percentage was 60 per cent. Telecom and energy companies scored the lowest here with 52 per cent. For the government and the entertainment and travel sectors this percentage was 53 per cent.

Source: www.klantinteractiekenniscentrum.nl

Other forms of support are also possible. Technical questions, for example, (particularly from America and the UK) are regularly dealt with through service agencies in India. Lower labour costs and well-educated and trained personnel are reasons for this, as well as the advantage of the time differences. Customers are often not aware that the service agency is actually located abroad.

In addition to this, through an ACD (automatic call dispatcher) the call itself is monitored. How long did the call last, which agent, what subject? This helps to bring about a greater efficiency in the activities. The system also registers the number of calls during the day, the length of the queue and the speed at which answers are given. In order to guarantee quality, a service level is agreed between the departmental manager and the principal. This agreement can be made both internally as well as in the relationship with an external call centre. Service levels where customers have to wait too long are not acceptable. The service level is evaluated as a percentage of the agreed maximum waiting time. For example, if the maximum waiting time for a caller is 30 seconds and the service level is 90 per cent, then 90 per cent of calls must be answered within 30 seconds.

In order to reduce the amount of time spent waiting, voice response systems are used. The call is answered by a computer, often followed by an option menu (an interactive voice response system). By indicating who you are (customer number) and why you are calling, your call can be transferred directly to the appropriate agent or department. This helps to increase the service level. Often while the caller is waiting music is played, and now and again the caller is informed of the call's progress. This system is suitable for peak periods, but is, of course, customer unfriendly for normal telephone traffic. If this happens during normal telephone traffic as a result of insufficient numbers of agents or poor planning, it can be negative for a company's image; customers often get very irritated if they have to wait too long.

Box 9.2 Performance indicators at call centres

Four categories of KPIs

Twenty of the most used KPIs (key performance indicators) are described below. They can be classified into four categories, namely the indicators that measure the 'service' (how quickly), the 'quality' (how good), the 'efficiency' (how efficient) and the 'profitability' (how effective).

Service (how quickly): 6 KPIs

- Blocking. A very important indicator. High service levels can after all be attained at the expense of accessibility ('all trunks busy'). Bandwidth and server capacity, as well as fax lines, need to be sufficiently available.
- Abandon rate. Although dependent on all sorts of partially uncontrollable factors, such as the availability of alternatives, time period, etc., this gauge is closely related to retention and revenue. 'Abandonment' does not play a role in email, but it does so in chatting.
- Self-service availability. Measuring the use of self-service is important; after all, greater use should lead to a reduction of the work pressure for the agents.
- Service level and ASA. Service levels and ASAs are also important for web chatting. For email the norms that are set regarding response time apply.
- Longest waiting time. Both for telephone and chat the current and historical longest waiting times are important. This concerns both the wait until contact is actually made and the wait, without contact, until the caller hangs up.

Quality (how good): 4 KPIs

- First call resolution. This variable is closely related to the customer's perception of the quality of the contact. Also for both chat and email the number of necessary interactions are an important indicator for the quality of the contact handling.
- Transfer rate. The number of transfers, in response to the telephone call, chat or email, provides information for improving routings and for any necessary training and skills of agents.
- Politeness. Monitoring the quality of the communication is important for every channel.
- Following procedures. Adherence to workflows, scripts, is essential for every channel in order for a channel to deal with contacts independently and consistently.

Efficiency (how efficient): 7 KPIs

- Agent utilization. The agent utilization rate is an important variable when assessing forecasts regarding workload and the quality of the staff roster. This is an important KPI for telephone and chat. Email provides possibilities for increasing the average productivity.
- Not productive. Also in multichannel environments the number of non-productive hours as a result of meetings, training courses, etc. are important for optimizing the utilization.
- Schedule efficiency and adherence. The quality of the staff roster, the amount of understaffing and overstaffing, and the actual productivity, are important control variables for telephony and chat. For email chance in the workload plays less of a role.
- Handling time and 'after call work'. 'Average handling time' and 'after call work' are less easy to identify for chat and email.
- System availability. Availability and response times of computer systems and for example IVR should be optimal and have to be monitored constantly.

Profitability (how effective): 3 KPIs

- Conversion ratios. Percentages of transactions per 100 contacts are relevant in every channel.
- Up-sell/cross-sell ratios. Percentages of transactions (deals) that are closed at a higher or lower price than for which the contacts were initially intended are increasingly measured in contact centres as a control variable.
- Costs per contact. Widely used, although there are differences between organizations in the costs that are included. This complicates benchmarking.

Source: www.klantenservicekenniscentrum.nl

9.5.3   Call handling

A call can be handled well and quickly if the agent has access to the appropriate information. With outbound calls this is the correct name and address details, along with other relevant information. A script forms the basis of the telephone call. This script is read out by the agent and the answers are entered. The advantages of this are that there is univocal communication (everybody asks the same questions), the agents can be trained very quickly (they simply read the script) and the work can be carried out by people with a relatively low level of education (standardization). The disadvantage is also clear: if the answer is different from the available answer options the agent does not know what to do.

As conversations often do not proceed as planned, a need arose for a dynamic script. Here, any question depends upon the answer given to the previous one. Initially, closed questions were used in order to make the process dynamic. Later generations of software also allowed open questions. Keywords were sought to generate the next question.

For inbound calls a script is much more difficult. Of course, for known subjects such as complaints, delays and payments, answers can be standardized. This is more difficult for a service desk. For questions concerning a delivery, a logistics system must be consulted and sometimes also the financial system. For questions concerning malfunctions, an appointment has to be planned in or a support system with FAQs has to be consulted in order to provide telephone support. Specific helpdesk software is necessary for this.

9.5.4   CRM software

In the early 1990s specific software packages came onto the market that could provide support to call centre agents, both inbound and outbound. Initially these were stand-alone systems. The external data was loaded in batches. An online interface can be awkward, and this also led to problems with the owners of the systems who did not want others to have access to the data or to be able to change the data. But the demand for more information and for direct contact with customers and business associates led to the helpdesk becoming a more integral part of marketing and of an organization's total operations. This made interfacing an important area of attention. Often the interfacing costs of a call centre application were higher than those of the system itself. The demand for an integral solution increased, both for the marketing department and for the IT department. This was the main reason that customer contacts began to be part of the total information provision within an organization. The demand for a link with the ERP (enterprise resource planning) system was so great (see Chapter 8) that the customer contact systems had to become part of this.

Specific call centre software such as Siebel provided the interfaces. Sometimes these were standard and at other times they were customized. Siebel also provided supplementary applications (such as financial systems) in order to meet the growing demand. At the same time ERP software suppliers such as SAP began building a separate module as part of the ERP suite. These developments grew towards one another. Eventually SAP's CRM software became the market leader. The customers of the ERP modules of SAP also bought the CRM module. If there was no SAP platform present, Siebel or another application was often opted for. Eventually Siebel merged with Oracle, which optimized the integration between the Oracle applications and Siebel. This marked the integration of marketing within the organization and of the marketing software within the core systems of an organization.

9.6 Marketing organization

From an organizational point of view the focus of marketing shifted strongly towards operational activities based on direct customer contacts. This led to a clear split within marketing into operations and strategy. The focus lay very much on the operation, building and maintenance of direct customer relationships. This was at the expense of the strategic acceptance of the marketing function. In many cases there was a business development manager who was part of the management team or the management board of a company, but this was not the case with the marketing manager. Automation of the marketing function has led to an operationalization of marketing due to a strong focus on the marketing activities. But just as it became important to integrate CRM within information provision and the marketing function, the Internet arrived on the scene (Figure 9.8).

The attention of the marketing department is very much focused on the customer as an entity. By linking fixed and variable data to this entity, not only can specific analyses be made (such as customer value analyses) but also the communication process can be standardized. Individual data is used for this which functions as a trigger that is able to activate certain communication messages. Examples of this are birthday cards and Christmas cards (objective triggers) or inviting customers to a meeting or event. Other triggers, however, can also be used, such as last purchase date, how long ago the last contact was made and follow-up details

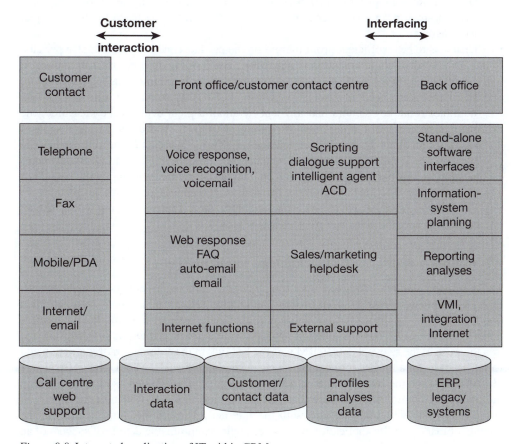

Figure 9.8 Integrated application of IT within CRM

after a contact. A communication message can be sent automatically (letter or email) or a 'call alert' generated.

Within the communication department the person who has customer contacts as part of his or her responsibilities should also be authorized to independently handle the contact. This is efficient but also reassures the customer that there is an authorized person available. Analyses of the meetings and the handling of communications – a complaint, for example – take place afterwards.

Marketing focuses increasingly on individual customer contacts. Marketing instruments and activities are also individualized. It is possible to base a price on variables other than a cost price or a market price (transaction-based costing). The price can also be based on the time of purchase or the use of the products or services (as is the case these days in the aviation industry with the price of air tickets). Personal pricing is possible through the 'customer values pyramid' and on the basis of knowledge of the customer. The communication can also be made highly personal by using knowledge of the individual customer and of previous contacts. Personal communication based on personal information leads to much better responses than a standard communication message. Market communication within marketing has now become much more personal. CRM and integrated information provision forms the basis of this. In order to be able to apply CRM successfully a number of conditions have to be met:

- There has to be a repeat buying behaviour. If a customer makes a one-off purchase then this is no reason for a supplier to maintain contact (a dilemma faced by, for example, estate agents).
- There has to be a sufficient profit margin on the products and services but also per customer. Personal communication is not cheap. The profit margin per transaction and in the repeat purchases must be sufficient in order to be able to build a lasting relationship.
- There is a logical need for association. Customers would also have to want this contact. With electronic newsletters that are sent by email a great deal can be measured: the opening percentage, the duration of reading, what is clicked on and what responses follow. Sometimes the opening percentage is just a few per cent of the addressees. The question would then have to be asked whether this newsletter is the right form of communication for this particular target group or if there is something lacking in the content of the newsletter. Too much of a sender orientation? Too much focus on sales?
- The customer details have to be correct and up to date. There is nothing worse than an incorrectly spelt name or incorrect variable data.

9.7 Evolution of information technology within marketing

The development of marketing led to a strong focus on relationships and individual contacts. IT underwent a development from process automation to information provision, and then finally to an integral infrastructure within organizations, incorporating marketing applications. This eventually led to an integral approach of marketing within the organization and of a joint use of the relevant data. CRM was the last link in the automation of marketing and forms the basis for a further application of new developments such as RFID (radio frequency identification) and the Internet. The marketing department also adapted itself to this. Within the marketing communication function, direct communication has become an important component (both with analyses and with the Internet). The Internet, too, belongs to the domain of marketing. Its application will increasingly determine the degree of success of an organization. IT has led to marketing becoming an integral part of an organization, allowing marketing to make use of the data of other departments and vice versa. The application of IT has also resulted in marketing becoming more focused on individual customers and in customer value becoming an increasingly important form of key data.

9.8 Radio frequency identification (RFID)

RFID is a 'smart' chip that makes it possible to monitor goods and people. This provides more insight into the logistics flows, and items can be monitored, making it possible to track and trace them. In addition, specific functions can be based on similar technology. There are two types of chip: an active chip and a passive chip. The difference between these chips lies in the source of energy. In the case of an active chip there is an energy source that ensures that the chip can transmit a signal that can be monitored via the mobile network. This enables goods and people to be monitored. An example of this can be seen during the Tour de France. The cyclists can see exactly where they are in the race, as well as how far ahead or behind they are. This system can also be used for items that are sent via a logistics service provider (a chip per item, per container or per lorry is possible).

A passive chip does not require a direct source of energy; the energy of the reader is used. The reader sends out a signal that is received by the chip, which is then able to send back a signal. An example of this application can be seen in runners who carry a chip on their shoe. The number is registered by stepping onto a mat. The number and owner of the number are linked via a database so that an exact time registration is possible. This is used during the crowded marathons of, for example, London and New York.

A specific application of the RFID chip is the public transport card, as in Hong Kong and London. By holding the chip close to a reader the number can be registered. This is done at the start and end of the journey, which then allows the distance travelled to be registered and the relevant costs charged. In this way RFID chips make identification possible without the need for physical contact.

The chip can be 'hidden' in a card, in a start number or in a mobile telephone, that is, in a smartphone. Smartphones enable the owners to be monitored and to have specific facilities offered to them. If the telephone has a passive chip then the owner first has to identify him- or herself (as with the public transport card). In the case of an active chip the owner can be traced within a certain area (location based) and be offered specific services (location-based services). This also makes it possible to set location restrictions, for example for an elderly person with dementia so they can be traced or restricted to their home. It can also be used to help to trace 'supporters' with a stadium ban. Dog walking services sometimes also make use of these RFID tags to monitor the dogs and find them if they have run off.

Clearly, the RFID chip will be used much more frequently in the future in a commercial environment for identification in the physical shop (direct messaging) and at the checkout (loyalty systems and customer recognition).

Summary

- Marketing has evolved from a focus on markets and transactions to a focus on relationships and individual contacts.
- Information technology was first used for process automation and later for information provision; it eventually provided an integral infrastructure for information and function supporting applications, as well as for marketing.
- By applying IT as an infrastructure a joint use of data is unavoidable.

- CRM applications are the result of the development of the focus of marketing and the application of IT.
- Marketing originally used IT for communication and analyses, and only later for a total support of the commercial processes (Internet sales).
- The application of the Internet has become part of marketing.
- Because of the Internet the focus on customers and identifiable relationships has developed rapidly.

Part 3

Impact of the Internet on marketing

From support to strategy

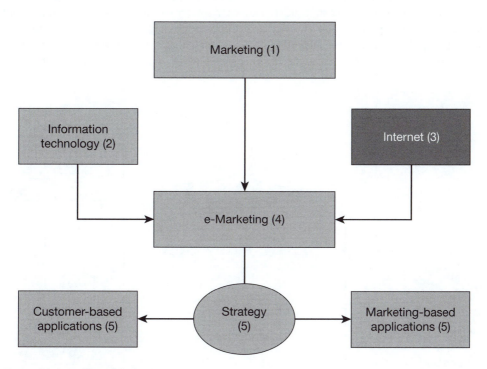

Figure P3.1 Outline of the book

There have been many changes within marketing as a direct consequence of the Internet. The Internet is a new medium that enables direct contact with customers. In the 1980s direct contacts became of interest to marketing after the breakthrough of direct marketing. Databases, laser printers and call centres made this direct contact a possibility, which in turn provided a direct knowledge of the customers and of the customers' response to marketing activities. Direct marketing was regarded as a form of direct communication; call centres became important for customer service and for direct sales. In the 1990s it became possible to use the Internet, which enabled all these functions to be carried out by the Internet as well. However, not only the focus (towards individual relationships) changed as a result of the Internet, but also the scope (reach) and methodology. The traditional media are called push media; here a message is sent to an undefined target group. On the Internet it is the visitor who takes the initiative, which enables an individual relationship to develop. The comparison of an angler who sits and waits for a fish to bite and a hunter who goes out looking for his prey is apt. With the traditional media the marketing department goes out to look for its prey and tries to reach and persuade it. On the Internet the visitor arrives at the site and weighs up whether this could potentially be a good relationship.

The Internet involves more than just selling: information provision, entertainment and communication are also important areas of application. Organizations will have to ask themselves whether the Internet supports the company strategy or whether it is actually an important guiding factor. In particular, companies that offer virtual products and services will use the Internet as part of their strategy and proposition. Games, music, information and software suppliers have had to adapt their business model due to the possibilities offered by the Internet. For other organizations the Internet is perhaps just an electronic brochure.

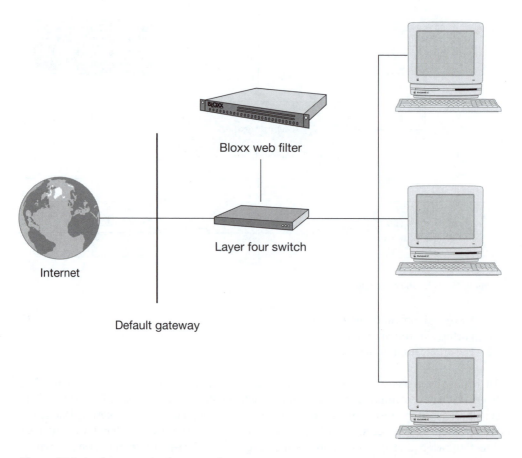

Figure P3.2 A telecommunication network

However, in all cases there has to be a good understanding of the application possibilities of the Internet, its specific functions and the wishes of the market.

The impact of the Internet within marketing has been multifaceted, but has also changed marketing from a market approach to purchasing support for individual customers. This part looks at the development of the Internet and its relationship with marketing. The functions of the Internet and the impact on marketing will also be examined. In conclusion, future developments will also be outlined.

Stand-alone computers, telephones, smartphones and other devices are linked to a server which in turn is linked to other servers. This produces a web of interconnected computers, the World Wide Web. Connections can be made using search words that are related to numbers. The basis is a telecommunication network, a physical and a virtual one.

10 The development of the Internet

At the start of the 1990s the first reports were heard of a new network for commercial applications; this was to be known as the Internet. At the time there were a number of developments going on in the United States that enabled contacts and commerce through this network. The first applications were aimed at online searches for information and advertising. Small-scale applications were developed whereby companies could offer their services, and customers – usually businesses – could establish contacts directly. There were also similar developments in other countries, such as Teletel/Minitel in France and Prestel and Ceefax in the UK.

In the Netherlands experiments were carried out with Viditel, Videotex and, for example, Memocom of the Dutch telecom provider KPN. This involved all sorts of new applications that were developed separately from one another and were responding to an increasing demand for direct contact. This was also a signal for the further application of telecommunication.

10.1 Development of telecommunication and interactive applications

The initial application of telecommunication focused on speech. The telephone is an example of this. The speech was based on a connection between locations, companies or private individuals. The development of this application could not be said to have been rapid, however. In 1960 only 40 per cent of households were connected to the telephone network, and there were still companies that only had one telephone; a telephone on each desk was by no means commonplace. Thanks to an increase in the capacity of the network in the second half of the twentieth century, however, all companies quickly got connected, each desk had its own telephone and every company its own switchboard, often with a telephone operator, but certainly with a central telephone number (you had to be put through to the appropriate extension). It seems strange to think about it now, but the direct external line was resisted for a long time for reasons of costs and to avoid private use; in the 1960s and 1970s the use of phones by staff for private calls while at work was frowned upon. The telephone was also regarded as an unwelcome interruption to the work. This view of telecommunication, the telephone, and its limited use in companies hindered its development.

For data traffic, to form a connection between computers a separate network was developed: the data network. Using this network, computers were able to pass on information, and the chances of mistakes and breakdowns were minimized. As a consequence, the risk of 'break-ins' could also be kept to a minimum. Companies signed contracts for a permanent connection, or a temporary data link through which access to this data network was shared with other companies. For technical reasons it was not yet desirable to use the normal telephone network for this.

10.1.1 *Special network for data traffic*

In the 1970s many countries built networks specially for data connections. Although the circuit-switched ordinary telephone network was used frequently for connections between computers, an increasing demand arose for a special/separate network for data communication. Many countries developed a special network for data traffic based on the standardized X.25 protocol. In the Netherlands the former state-owned postal company PTT built such a public network under the name Datanet 1. In everyday parlance the terms X.25 and Datanet 1 were used to refer to any network based on the X.25 protocol.

In addition to the telephone and data network there was also a telex network, which was separate from the telephone network. The advantage of the telex was that typed documents could be sent. These documents first had to be digitized. Initially, the message was recorded on paper tape and then on magnetic tape. The telex operator typed the document on a paper tape machine, after which the document could be sent. A speed of 300 baud was quite standard. The text was then printed out on the other telex machine at the receiver's end. Every company therefore had a telex number and a telephone number. The advantage was that a telex was a legal document equal to a letter. This was an important advantage, particularly for contacts and business agreements.

10.2 The road to the Internet

Interactivity and message traffic forms the basis for the Internet. In the most elementary form these are text messages that are sent (as with emails these days) or prepared in order to be consulted (as is done these days on websites, through blogs and on Twitter). The demand for speedy message traffic and interactivity grew in the 1980s due to a number of separate developments. A demand for more 'flexible' connections in every area arose, which led to the privatization of telecom companies and globalization.

At the end of the 1980s the demand for telecommunications and interactivity increased amongst both companies and consumers. In addition, there was a growing demand not only for a permanent connection but also for a temporary one (whenever convenient or required). This demand came from a technical and a social viewpoint. There was a change in social relationships and connections, and there was an increasing degree of individualization in the behaviour and demands of people. Technology facilitated this demand, through the personal computer (1981) and the new forms of computer services as described in Part 2. The integration of telecommunication within the information provision for companies and for consumers was in line with this development.

In early models a separate connection was made between a computer and a telephone. A modem was used to connect a telephone to a computer through a dial-up line. An acoustic coupler made data traffic possible through an ordinary telephone line; the speed, however, was very low at 300 or 1200 baud and text appeared on the screen character by character. It was, nevertheless, a direct connection between two computers, a 'peer-to-peer' connection.

Another important development was the privatization of the telecom companies. These companies were no longer state enterprises and had to compete in the market. As a result of this privatization money became available to develop new applications and at the same time most telecom companies aimed towards internationalization. As companies began to operate internationally increasingly often and more consumers travelled abroad, the demand for international telephone traffic grew. In the 1980s it was still quite normal for international networks to be connected together 'manually'. If you wanted to phone internationally you had to call an operator and give them the right number. Sometimes you had to wait for hours until the number was called and the call put through. The limited number of lines for international connections caused delays and the connection was sometimes of poor quality. The 1980s saw an increase in the number of satellites that took over the telephone traffic; the number of connections with the land lines also quickly increased and international telephone traffic gradually became automated. The linking of the networks gave rise to international collaboration.

In the mid 1990s telephone numbers became standardized on the basis of a ten-digit number. This led to a unique telephone number for each connection and each location, and later (after 1991) also for the mobile network. In addition, the investments in telecommunication increased considerably. As a result of the automation, digitization and the new possibilities offered by data traffic, new networks had to be developed. These networks were no longer just physical networks; virtual networks also became important. Bids had to be made for licences in order to acquire bandwidth and frequencies for telephone and data traffic.

A precursor to this international collaboration were the calling cards. These enabled a central number (often a freephone number) to be called, through which the call could be transferred. The payment then took place in the country of origin. The telecom provider purchased bundles at large discounts that were offered to the card users. As a result, advantage could be taken of the lower telephone rates. Because of the privatization of the telecom companies, extra investments could be made for takeovers and the development of new possibilities (infrastructure, technology and applications). This money no longer came from the government, but from other investments and through the issuing of shares.

As a result of increasing prosperity consumers travelled abroad more often, and because of the new possibilities offered by satellite television consumers were introduced to more international programmes. This was in line with the development of companies that increasingly started to focus on international markets. International networks of collaborating parties arose and there were many takeovers by or of foreign companies. The advertising world is a good example of this. As a result of the growth and takeovers, the advertising world became dominated by big, often American agencies that had offices in all the major countries (agencies such as Omnicom, Ogilvy & Mather, JWT and Saatchi & Saatchi). These agencies also worked for international companies that chose an agency for all their offices and for all the countries in which they were active. Advertising campaigns were often international campaigns, sometimes with just changes to the text and the language only.

As a result of this globalization a need arose to share information quickly, and there was a need, therefore, for telecommunication between the companies (offices). This demand was not only focused on speech but also on documents. Initially telex documents were used, but this had its limitations. Advertising agencies in particular wanted to share their drawings and campaigns. The fax provided the solution. A fax machine was installed alongside the telex. Within a few years, however, the fax, in turn, was replaced by the Internet. A fax machine is connected to a standard telephone line. A separate line is preferred, so that the fax has its own number, although private individuals often have their fax and telephone share the one telephone line, and therefore the same number. That is not a problem with an outgoing phone call or fax, but when receiving a phone call or fax it can be. Most fax machines, however, are able to recognize an incoming fax message, after which they process it; regular phone calls are transferred to the connected telephone.

The need for direct contact increased rapidly among companies in particular, as did the speed at which business had to be conducted. Due to these developments an integral use of documents increased quickly as well, and as a consequence also the complexity of conducting business, of the products and often also of the (business) relationships. A direct contact and a high response speed became increasingly important.

10.3 Development of interactivity

The demand for interactivity was a response not only to the wish for a direct answer to questions but also for customized services. The response to this came in various ways. Online it was through the connection of a medium with an infrastructure, for example, a telephone with a telephone network, or a computer connected to the telephone network or a data network and, of course, these days the computer connected to the telephone network or a mobile network. But there were also offline possibilities through customizing the computer software or making it interactive, thereby allowing a personal experience. There were developments on various fronts that would eventually lead to the acceptance of the Internet among a wide public.

10.3.1 Online interactivity

In various countries there were separate online developments, based on telecommunication and computers; for example, Minitel (France), Videotex (the Netherlands) and Prodigy (United States). The applications varied technically, but the basic ideas were the same: a computer-to-computer connection, use of the existing telephone network or a separate data network and the possibility of commercial applications.

Videotex

In 1971 the BBC carried out full-scale experiments by offering text information to consumers via the television under the name 'Ceefax'. In that same year the British Post Office demonstrated 'View data', the world's first videotex system. The layout principle was based on the Ceefax protocol, with 7 colours, 40 characters per line and 24 lines per page. Videotex was not transmitted through a television signal, but through a telephone line with a modem. This allowed it to be interactive. Pages were consulted by keying in menu numbers or by jumping directly to a page number (by using the famous 'star–page number–hash').

September 1979 saw the launch of the videotex service 'Prestel' in Great Britain. Over the years, Ceefax and videotex have met one another various times under the guise of 'interactive teletext'. By calling up a certain teletext page and then phoning a telephone number, the videotex pages could be viewed at home on the television.

In addition to videotex, in the 1980s and 1990s there were also many BBSs (bulletin board systems). These had a capacity of 80 characters per line but were limited to the ASCII character encoding scheme. It was only with the arrival of the personal computer that colours were added (the ANSI-BBSs).

These new developments were used by companies in order to appeal to consumers. The consumers, however, were still very reluctant. There was no infrastructure and there were still very few consumers who had computers. What's more, there were also the limitations of the telephone. Consumers often had only one telephone line, which was then occupied by the computer. There was still no integrated services digital network (ISDN) application nor were there any mobile telephones. This was an application that was based on data used by companies for communicating with one another and for business presentations.

In France this 'chicken and egg' problem was resolved by supplying both the infrastructure and the content. Every household in France received a special computer, free of charge, which was connected to the telephone. This computer had a direct link to a database, which allowed the user to search for telephone numbers as well as information about companies. Because this offered a database with telephone numbers, the telephone book was no longer required and the resulting cost savings helped to reduce the investments in this application. Although this French campaign led to each household having a telephone with a computer, this did not immediately lead to large-scale use. The information was considered too limited; and there was, of course, the barrier formed by innovation. It was technology, after all, which was a little frightening for the average householder.

At the same time as the Minitel development in France, in the United States other forms of interactivity were being developed. Prodigy was an interactive service intended for commercial applications that used a computer as the access medium, but in this case a separate data network was used. Consumers in particular made use of this, and could consult online services and buy products. In this application Prodigy was therefore one of the forerunners of the Internet.

Minitel

Minitel is a French network that uses the telephone line. It was introduced in 1982 and was another forerunner of the Internet. The system was used in France on a large scale because the hardware was supplied free of charge. In 2000 there were some 9 million terminals, allowing 25 million French people to make use of Minitel.

These days (2009) the system is still in use, although it is increasingly being superseded by the Internet. In France there is now even an ADSL version of Minitel.

In the Netherlands the introduction of Minitel (under the names Viditel and Videotex Nederland) failed to take off. In the Science Centre Delft there is a prototype of a PTT Telecom terminal.

Prodigy

The roots of Prodigy date to 1980 when broadcaster CBS and telecommunications firm AT&T formed a joint venture named *Venture One* in Fair Lawn, New Jersey. The company conducted a market test of 100 homes in Ridgewood, NJ to gauge consumer interest in a videotex-based TV set-top device that would allow consumers to shop at home and receive news, sports and weather. After concluding the market test, CBS and AT&T took the data and went their separate ways in pursuit of developing and profiting from this market demand.

Prodigy was founded on 13 February 1984 as Trintex, a joint venture between CBS, computer manufacturer IBM, and retailer Sears, Roebuck and Company. The company was headed by Theodore Papes, a career IBM executive, until his retirement in 1992. CBS left the venture in 1986 when CBS CEO Tom Wyman was divesting of properties outside of CBS's core broadcasting business. The company's service was launched regionally in 1988 in Atlanta, Hartford and San Francisco under the name Prodigy. The marketing roll-out plan closely followed IBM's SNA network backbone. A nationwide launch developed by ad agency J. Walter Thompson and sister company JWT Direct (New York) followed on 6 September 1990.

Thanks to an aggressive marketing campaign in the media, bundling with various consumer-oriented computers such as IBM's PS/1 and PS/2, as well as various clones and Hayes Modems, the Prodigy service soon had more than a million subscribers. To handle that traffic, Prodigy built a national network of POP (points-of-presence) sites that made local access numbers available for most homes in the US. This was a major factor in the expansion of the service since subscribers did not have to dial long distance to access the service. The subscriber only paid for the local call (usually free), while Prodigy paid for the long distance call to its national data centre in Yorktown, New York.

As is the case with the current Internet service providers (ISPs) the business model of Prodigy consisted of a subscriber's fee and revenues from advertising and online shopping. These last two were more important for Prodigy than the access fees. Use was made of a dial-up connection, as was also standard for the Internet in the 1990s (ADSL did not yet exist). At first online shopping was not successful. There were suppliers, but there was not much trust among consumers; trust about the items to be delivered and the possible guarantees. This was the same lack of trust that so characterized the early years of online shopping on the Internet (and still exists to a certain degree today).

It was due to the Internet that Prodigy, with its specific infrastructure and connections, got into difficulties. At the start Prodigy was still used as an ISP, but eventually this was not enough to survive. At present Prodigy is a dormant company.

VTN

At the end of the 1980s the world was at the dawn of the developments in the areas of data and telecommunication. Although no one could yet foresee the extent of the impact on the coming developments, it was clear that the monopoly of the Dutch state-owned PTT in the area of communication was a thing of the past. When the former PTT wanted to launch the successor to their information service Viditel, they set up the independent subsidiary Videotex Nederland BV (VTN). As successor to Viditel, it was VTN's task to run the new videotex service more commercially than the state-owned company would have been able to do itself. VTN was responsible for the administrative and commercial management of the new service; the purely technical management was brought under the new network administrators of Datanet 1 because of the technical similarities this had with the public packet-switched network. In contrast to the 'old' service Viditel, the new service was to be positioned in the market more widely and was expressly also aimed at private users. When the interest for videotex services decreased due to the emergence of the Internet, the organization continued to be used for a number of years as the parent company of Planet Internet and HetNet – two KPN Internet providers.

10.3.2 Text through television channels

Ceefax

Ceefax was one of the latest developments in interactivity – albeit based on the medium of television – when the BBC began to offer it in 1974. The name Ceefax was a play on the words 'see facts'. This illustrates that news could be shown on it in much the same way as is done today. Initially a special television was required for this, as a result of which in 1980 there were only 700 users. These days, however, televisions come with a Ceefax function as standard. The Ceefax function was and still is an information medium that does not offer the possibility of commercial messages. Since the 1990s it has been possible in various countries with similar Ceefax applications to place small advertisements on these as well. This application was and still is used a great deal by private individuals or to establish connections between individuals. Common applications are the telephone numbers for sex contacts (phonesex) and classified ads for sale and wanted services for houses and cars. In all cases, however, the commercial applications of teletext are very limited.

Teletext

The teletext signal is sent along with the regular television transmission in the picture lines that fall outside the normal picture. In the British system, Ceefax, the teletext signal is transmitted as part of the original analogue TV signal, but concealed from view in the vertical blanking interval (VBI) television lines, which do not carry picture. In poorly tuned televisions this is sometimes seen as ever-changing black and white dots above or below the image. This signal is filtered from the received signal using a built-in decoder, after which the user can search for the desired information using the remote control. This can also be used to access subtitles to certain television programmes (for example, for deaf people).

The developments in interactive possibilities were a response to user demand for customized services. The user also wanted direct information and to be able to use the service immediately. Teletext and Ceefax clearly show that there is a need for information. Even in 2010 there were millions of teletext and Ceefax requests per day. This is thanks to the convenience and user-friendliness of the medium.

10.3.3 Offline interactivity

In addition to the online services described above, for the most part based on a telephone connection, various initiatives arose that aimed at another form of interactivity. In the early days the computer memory and storage media for computers were still very limited, so efforts were made to look for other storage media. The video disc was an example of this. A video disc had large storage capacity, and could be played using special equipment. It was expensive, however.

In the early 1990s Philips launched a more compact solution, based on the compact disc, known as the CD-I. Information could be stored and then retrieved from this CD-I using a special player. CD-Is were initially made available with educational and encyclopaedic information as well as games. Then the CD-I player was connected to the television and later on portable CD-I players with their own screens were brought onto the market. The CD-I was never a great success. Fairly shortly after its launch the internal and external memory of the PC became much greater, which allowed more information to be stored on a floppy disk. In this way the computer acquired a multifunctional task. In addition, there was the introduction of the DVD, which also connects to the television but had a larger storage capacity.

SD and MMCD

In 1990 Toshiba and Time Warner developed a successor to the successful compact disc (CD), called the SuperDisk (SD). The developers of the compact disc, Philips and Sony, did not want their favourable market situation to be disrupted by a successor and waited for a long time to see which way the wind would blow. Meanwhile, experts at NatLab, Philips' research department, thought long and hard about a successor. In 1994 Philips and Sony presented the MultiMedia CD (MMCD). Although the capacity (playing time) of the SD was considerably greater than that of the MMCD, at 5 GB instead of the 3.6 GB of the MMCD, the MMCD had the advantage of being more compatible with the CD.

The demand for interactivity in the area of entertainment became clear with the CD, CD-I and the DVD. These days these media have also become highly personal due to the selection

Table 10.1 Development of interactivity and virtual application

Music/sound	Data	Films/video	Information	Pictures/animations
Magnetic tape, floppy disk, compact disk, DVD, MP3	USB stick, the Internet	Video tape, video disk, DVD, the Internet	Magnetic tape, floppy disk, USB stick, the Internet	Videotape, DVD, the Internet

possibilities offered by digital media such as the MP3 player. In fact, the CD as a data carrier is now no longer in favour and has been replaced by online storage possibilities, MP3 players and the USB stick. The demand for commercial services, such as seen with Viditel, Videotex and Minitel, was completely taken care of by the Internet, because of its ease of use and intensive infrastructure, as well as its international acceptance.

The development of interactivity can be seen schematically in Table 10.1.

Summary

- The demand for interactivity of companies and consumers led to the development of new applications such as the bulletin board.
- The basis of interactivity was initially the telephone, but later the Internet was used.
- The technological basis of the interactivity led to a slow acceptance among consumers. It was only after the use of the Internet began that this gained momentum.

11 The breakthrough of the Internet

Interactivity and messaging lie at the heart of the Internet. The online bulletin board was a clear forerunner, allowing messages to be both sent and posted. The messages posted could be read by many people. This functionality can now also be seen with the Internet, but in a more advanced form. A company that made this application popular was America Online (AOL). At the end of the 1980s this service was introduced onto the market, and by the early 1990s AOL was one of the first service providers to offer people outside the academic and military world access to the Internet.

The foundation for the popularity of the Internet had been laid. A number of developments were responsible for this:

- the arrival of the browser;
- the search engine;
- the user-friendliness of the medium;
- the simplicity of the network;
- the simple interface;
- international acceptance; and
- the commercial possibilities.

11.1 The browser

In the early 1990s the Internet began to increase in popularity. Academics and students used 'Gopher' in order to search the databases of other universities and libraries for scientific publications. There was also a (limited) bulletin functionality and the possibility to send messages to one another (if you had the correct address). The breakthrough of the Internet actually began in 1993 when a browser was launched with a graphical interface: the browser Mosaic. This allowed web pages to be viewed and made scrolling possible. As the web pages were still text-based this could be done quickly and easily. Later, other browsers came onto the scene that had greater functionality. Netscape was one of the first, and was followed (in 1995) by Microsoft's Internet Explorer. By 1999, particularly due to the automatic link with other Windows applications, Explorer became the market leader of browser software. These days this market leader role is under pressure, both because the European Union decided that the link was leading to an unlawful monopoly position for Microsoft and because Explorer is up against rival browsers, such as Firefox and Safari (Apple).

Browsers allowed users to view (navigate) web pages quickly and made looking for information online easy and user-friendly.

11.1.1 Gopher

When the World Wide Web was first introduced in 1991 Gopher was already popular. But when in February 1993 the University of Minnesota announced that it would charge licence fees for using Gopher, the popularity of the Gopher servers plummeted. Some people believe that this rapid decline was responsible for turning Gopher into a footnote in the history of the Internet.

Another opinion, however, is that the fall of Gopher was actually a result of its limited structure, which made it less flexible than the free-form HTML of the Web. With Gopher every document had to have a defined format and type, and the typical user had to navigate a single, server-defined menu to access a particular document. Many users found the artificial difference between menu and document in the Gopher system clumsy, and considered the open flexibility of the Web much more practical for free-form, related collections of documents and interactive applications.

11.2 Search engines

Another development that contributed to the popularity of the Internet was the search engine. Until the mid 1990s there were still registers of Internet users and websites, but it soon became clear that this was becoming impractical. A demand arose to be able to find websites and users (companies) on the Internet. One of the first search engines was AltaVista (1995). Advanced crawler technology enabled AltaVista to quickly search through web pages. This gave it a far greater reach than other search engines. At the end of the 1990s AltaVista was the most popular search engine, but this was about to change. The owner, Digital Corporation, was sold to Compaq, which considered the Internet to be of less importance; Compaq focused on selling computers. As a result AltaVista received no attention and no money was made available to invest in it. AltaVista was transformed into a portal function with a shift in focus towards shopping and free emails in order to generate more income. This was not a great success. Almost immediately new search engines were launched, which had better results and a greater reach on the Internet, such as Yahoo! and Google.

In some parts of the world Yahoo! is still dominant and the market leader (rather than Google). It began as a search engine but quickly developed into a new business proposition by promoting bonding among Internet users through free email as well as among companies by offering a portal function. This enabled Yahoo! to get an optimal return from the market, which it still does to this day. The considerable bonding created among users through free email and the search engine has led to a large number of visitors per day and a high frequent return behaviour, which in turn is interesting to companies offering products and services. The portal function provides the possibility of turning these visits into turnover. In 2002 Yahoo! already had some 97 million registrations for one of the Yahoo! services and 200 million visitors per year. In 2006 this number had already grown to 115 million visitors per month, compared with 95 million on Google.

11.2.1 Yahoo!

Yahoo! began as 'Jerry and David's Guide to the World Wide Web', but gradually acquired a new nickname. Yahoo! is an acronym of 'yet another hierarchical officious oracle', but David Filo and Jerry Yang insist that they chose this name from the word's general definition that originated from Jonathan Swift's *Gulliver's Travels*: rude, unsophisticated and uncouth.

For this reason the word Yahoo! should be spoken with an emphasis on the first syllable. Yahoo! was initially only hosted from a workstation (*Akebono*), while the software remained on Filo's computer (*Konishiki*). The 'yet another' goes back to the UNIX program yacc, which stands for 'yet another compiler compiler'.

On 12 April 1996 Yahoo! went public on the stock exchange with an initial US$33.8 million (by selling 2.6 million shares at US$13 each).

The popularity of Yahoo! increased quickly, and it soon became a one-stop shop for all popular activities on the Internet. It now encompasses Yahoo! Mail, a webmail service, Yahoo! Messenger, a popular instant messaging service, Yahoo! Games, Yahoo! Entertainment and various other news and information portals as well as an auction.

11.2.2 Google

Google is another popular search engine. The business model is clearly different from that of Yahoo!, and Google also has a different reach. What is striking about Google is the calm look for users: there are no loud advertisements or distracting messages. The Google business model was based on 'AdWords', which involves the buying of search terms rather than advertisements. In doing so, it formed the basis for the Internet of today.

The strength of Google lies in the ranking methodology based on search words. The search word ranking is calculated on the basis of the search words that appear the most on a page, the qualification of the sites that are linked to the most and the words with which this search is carried out. The ranking on Google is commercially very important, because most users who look at the search results for a particular search term do not look beyond the first page (70 per cent); 20 per cent will have a look at the second page, but only the few diehard searchers look further. Being at the top of the Google search results is therefore very valuable for a business. The algorithm that Google uses for this, however, is a secret. Other techniques have to be used in order to positively influence the ranking. Many hyperlinks to the site from other sites can have a positive influence on the ranking. Also the mention of a certain search term on the site can lead to positive results.

The numbers of unique visitors on the ten most popular websites in 2008 are listed in Table 11.1.

Table 11.1 Number of unique visitors on the Internet in 2008

1 Facebook.com: 590 million visitors per day
2 YouTube.com: 490 million visitors per day
3 Yahoo.com: 400 million visitors per day
4 Live.com: 330 million visitors per day
5 Wikipedia.org: 260 million visitors per day
6 MSN.com: 250 million visitors per day
7 Baidu.com: 230 million visitors per day
8 Blogspot.com: 210 million visitors per day
9 Microsoft.com: 190 million visitors per day
10 Qq.com: 190 million vivitors per day

Source: Google.com

11.3 User-friendliness, networks and interfaces

The subjects that are discussed in this section address the rising popularity of the Internet. User-friendliness and simplicity are keywords in the following subsections.

11.3.1 User-friendliness

In addition to the introduction of the browser and the search engine, it was also the development of websites that helped the Internet to acquire the position it enjoys today. The websites were no longer text-based, like the databases of the early 1990s. Thanks to the graphical interface it was possible to make visually attractive graphical web pages. This increased their ease of use and user-friendliness, but it also made the Internet more fun to use. This development became clear at the end of the 1990s. The infrastructure, however, was not yet ready. As a result the transmission speeds were not sufficient for the heavier websites which then led to the system slowing down. Users became frustrated with all these graphics-heavy websites that took an eternity to load. The abbreviation of the World Wide Web, www, also began to be known as the 'World Wide Waiting'.

Thanks to increases in transmission speeds to 1 Mbps – and nowadays to 10 Mbps or more – these delays are a thing of the past. However, web designers still have to take speed into account; delays lead to irritation among users who may not want to wait and will surf elsewhere.

In general, however, the Internet has become highly accessible to everyone. The combination of the browser with information, the possibility of being able to quickly click on links to the relevant website, being able to find information and websites by using a search engine and the fact that it is possible to use normal texts has made it easy and fast to use. Current developments such as 'smartphones', the Blackberry and netbooks have removed virtually every barrier to accessing the Internet.

Once the user is on the Internet, it is important that a website can be found quickly. As mentioned above, in the early years there was a register that could be consulted. In addition, there were books one could buy which listed websites, similar to the telephone books or Yellow Pages. In order to increase the findability, it was decided to use names that were linked to a number. The number (IP number) in turn was linked to a website. A numerical identification can be tricky: people find it harder to remember numbers rather than names so it is not an ideal system. For this reason the Internet also has a name that refers to a certain number. This number is the Internet user or the web page. The numbers are classified into groups and countries by adding suffixes to a domain name (the highest level), such as *net* and *com*. In the early days only businesses were allowed to register a domain name, which was a clear indication of the commercial possibilities of the Internet. These days private individuals are also allowed to do this.

Table 11.2 lists the number of domains in some top level domains as at 1 December 2009.

IP addresses

An IP address, in which IP stands for 'Internet protocol', is an address with which the NIC (network interface card or controller) of a host in a network can be addressed unambiguously within the TCP/IP model (the standard of the Internet).

Every computer that is connected to the Internet or a network has a number which makes it visible to all other computers on the Internet. This is similar to telephone numbers. In

Table 11.2 Number of domains in some top level domains as per 1 December 2009

Top level domain	Number of domains	Top level domain	Number of domains
.com	83 592 799	.at	902 725
.de	13 295 902	.fr	1 604 981
.net	12 593 517	.se	931 611
.uk	8 082 887	.pl	1 103 270
.org	7 934 179	.es	1 200 000
.info	5 444 925	.no	456 479
.eu	3 142 632	.cz	627 472
.biz	2 016 198	.fi	200 000
.it	1 787 840	.pt	294 233
.us	1 640 529	.ie	135 397
.ch	1 343 000	.is	27 000
.li	57 375	.tk	[untraceable]
.dk	950 067	.lu	47 289
.be	975 013	.nl	3 677 351
.ru	1 130 000	.tr	137 861
.sk	201 864	.jp	1 133 081
.au	1 100 000	.mx	381 052
.cn	13 680 729		

Source: www.zooknic.com

order to make it possible for computers to find and identify one another, they need their own number. This number is the IP address. An IP address on the Internet is usually linked to a company. This makes it possible to trace who is responsible for actions carried out under a particular IP address. For people who work from home, the IP address identifies their Internet provider. As a result, contributions on the Internet are hardly ever anonymous. The person behind an IP address can usually be found, sometimes directly but sometimes only with the collaboration of the judiciary.

11.3.2 Simplicity of the network

No technical knowledge is required to use the Internet. What's more, very little investment in access facilities is necessary: a computer or telephone is sufficient. Users usually already have a mobile telephone network, a cable connection or a telephone connection. There are no specific commands, and no jargon is needed. Simple language, often one's own mother tongue, is sufficient. This has all helped in the popularity of the Internet. What's more, the costs involved in Internet use are low. With ADSL these days you pay a fixed amount per month.

It is also possible for companies to get a presence on the Internet very quickly. The design and construction of a fully interactive website with all the 'bells and whistles' requires the work of specialized companies, but a simple website can be built quickly by anyone. Special software, which is very cheap to buy these days or which comes with the computer itself (such as with Apple), enables users to build websites very easily without any knowledge of programming. Standard templates are usually used; only the text and navigation model need to be prepared before the website can go live. It is, in fact, child's play, and practically every company, large and small, now has their own information website on the Internet.

11.3.3 Simple interface

Anyone who wants to can access the Internet. Most computers that are bought already have browser software preinstalled, or browser software, such as Firefox, can be downloaded for free from the Internet. Only a few individual details need to be entered: name, service provider and a number of personal particulars. These days this can be done in a matter of minutes. For businesses, too, this can be arranged easily. A domain name and one's own website are sufficient. Due to the standardizations in protocols, as already outlined, interfacing has become very simple. This simplicity, the acceptance by suppliers of computer software (such as Microsoft), the many service providers and the many facilities that the Internet can offer the user, make Internet access and use easy. As a result, the users and suppliers of content can concentrate fully on using it for whatever they want.

11.4 International acceptance

The Internet is a worldwide platform, hence the 'www'. Since the early 1990s international agreements have been made regarding the provision and connection of all sorts of documents and computer applications. For the findability of web pages and documents a URL (uniform resource locator) was developed as a uniform addressing method. In order to format documents HTML (HyperText Markup Language) was used, which supports not only formatted text, images, videos and other multimedia, but also hyperlinks (clickable references) and forms. And lastly, HTTP (HyperText Transfer Protocol) was used for retrieving documents. Through monitoring these agreements closely a universal platform arose that has become very easy to use. The disadvantage of other platforms (such as Minitel, Prestel and Prodigy) was the choice of technology and facilities. These were often specifically tailored to these applications and therefore lacked a universal foundation, which was not the case with the Internet. What's more, it was anticipated that businesses would make use of the Internet. As a result there was a supply of content, which was important and directly accessible for the consumer, as was described in the development of interactivity. As it was also possible to gain access to the Internet from various domain areas (the extensions of the countries), there arose a feeling of familiarity and solidarity. In the technical area, local (telecom) facilities were used, meaning that the local telecom providers gave local access. This local access was later replaced by other another methodology, ADSL, so the telecom costs were no longer visible.

The local image and perception is still very important for the acceptance and use of the Internet. Eighty per cent of Internet use takes place with local (country-related) parties. It is not visible to the Internet user where the application is hosted, whether in one's own country or abroad.

The structure of the Internet is based on a connection of local host computers (ISPs) linked to a central Internet backbone (Figure 11.1). This is a series of computers that are connected to one another worldwide. The service provider takes care of the connection to the Internet and the URL ensures that the correct website is approached. The unique IP addresses ensure that each user (computer) is identified and consequently addressable (in order to send emails or to register the user's behaviour).

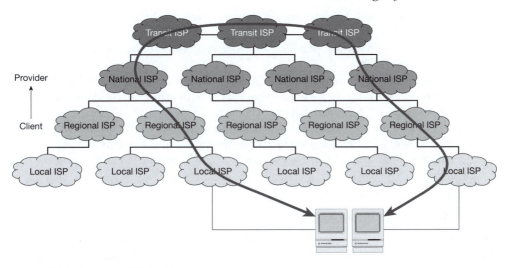

Figure 11.1 Structure of the Internet

Source: http://www.isoc.org/inet99/proceedings/1e/1e_1.htm

11.5 Commercial possibilities

The commercial possibilities of the Internet seem to be almost limitless. Chapter 14 will demonstrate that the Internet greatly affects an organization's commercial strategy and processes. There are various reasons for this, such as:

- a worldwide coverage;
- a high penetration of users in each country;
- a complete acceptance of this sort of information provision; and
- the possibility of direct, interactive communication.

There are, however, clear rules that have to be observed. The Internet, a medium for virtual applications, is different from a physical medium. Users can always make use of it, whenever they want and wherever they are. The information can remain available permanently, and the data has been registered and is accessible at all times. Once it is on the Internet, your history will always follow you. The Internet never forgets and the more capable user will always be able to find old information. The communication is also direct, and based on interactivity. This aspect requires a change in perception and a different execution from what businesses were used to. And it is here that the strength, as well as the weakness, of the commercial applications lie. A different interplay between businesses and customers, between businesses themselves and between customers themselves is the result.

11.5.1 Internet terms

- *Web page*: a page on the www; pages can have both a fixed or a changing content.
- *Website*: a coherent collection of pages, usually on the same computer.
- *Web application*: a collection of pages that together form an application.
- *Hyperlink*: a link to a page within a page; this provides navigation between web pages.

- *Search engine*: a web application with which pages can be searched (for example, AltaVista and Google).
- *Web server*: a computer that provides web pages via HTTP, or a program that provides web pages via HTTP.
- *Web browser*: the program with which the user accesses the World Wide Web; it has to be able to use a URL to retrieve a web page via HTTP or another network protocol, such as FTP, Gopher or NNTP; and display the retrieved page, if the page is in HTML, plain text or if it contains an image. Other sorts of documents can be displayed with plug-ins or separate applications. Many HTML pages use JavaScript, which allows pages to be dynamically modified; the web browser therefore has to be able to interpret and execute JavaScript.

11.6 Acceptance of the Internet

The Internet was very quickly accepted by businesses that saw the commercial possibilities. Private individuals were initially still reticent. There first had to be sufficient content in order to make the application interesting. The use of bulletin boards and fairly soon afterwards email ensured a quick acceptance amongst users. The Internet has had a worldwide impact, but users still prefer to use local sites. This preference, however, does not apply to facilities: hotmail, Gmail and Yahoo! Mail are used by everyone without them realizing that the server and service providers are located abroad. This results in a stratification in the use of the Internet into:

- access;
- general services/infrastructure/facilities;
- specific services via websites; and
- commercial services.

Summary

- The breakthrough of the Internet was prompted by the browser.
- The Internet is user-friendly.
- Companies accepted the Internet because of its commercial possibilities.
- Users accepted the Internet because of the bulletin boards (information function) and email (communication function).
- The Internet is accepted worldwide but its use is still very much determined locally.

12　The application of the Internet

The application of the Internet is related to the functions of the Internet. The functions determine the specific applications by suppliers and other users. Four primary functions can be distinguished:

- communication;
- information;
- transactions; and
- facilitating/infrastructural.

Both the user and the supplier determine the use of the Internet. The Internet is in fact a menu of possibilities from which the supplier and the user can choose. If a business does not want to sell through the Internet, then the transaction function is not used. The same applies if the user does not want to buy through the Internet. And yet in these cases the Internet would still have an influence on the (buying) behaviour of customers, as will become clear in this chapter.

12.1　Communication function: direct personal communication

With the communication function, use is made of the possibility of the Internet to connect suppliers and buyers to one another. This can be direct and interactive; for example, using software applications such as Skype and a webcam communications can include instant messaging and visuals. There can be a delay in the communication, such as with email, weblogs and Twitter. These media provide a direct form of communication. For marketing it is important that there is a direct contact with (potential) buyers and customers. Through the Internet a communication takes place towards a defined personal recipient, such as the email address. The basis of direct communication is direct marketing; with marketing it is mass communication. Direct marketing is often personal but it can also be impersonal. For example, when distributing flyers the communication takes place on the basis of a postcode and house number (a location). This is also the case with all sorts of unaddressed printed matter. In direct marketing we can distinguish between interactive and semi-interactive communication as well as personal and impersonal communication:

- addressed communication, such as direct mail;
- unaddressed communication, such as door to door leaflets;
- non-interactive communication such as direct mail; and
- interactive communication, such as telemarketing.

These types of communication also form the basis for commercial communication using the Internet; the medium may have changed, but the objective of the businesses (selling or maintaining a relationship) has not. Internet-based communications may be personal and semi-interactive (email, blogs), personal and interactive (chats, Twitter, webcams) or undefined (FAQ, guestbook, spam).

With direct personal communication the communication can be spontaneous; the user (customer) determines when it is most convenient. For businesses this is an unpredictable form of communication, and therefore also difficult to organize.

A number of forms of communication using the Internet are described in the text below.

12.1.1 Webcam and chat

Webcams, separate or built into a laptop, allow for direct interactive communication with images. Direct, spontaneous communication includes communication with a webcam or through chatting. The user determines when this takes place, as it is at that particular time that he or she would like to have contact. This is often the case with a complaint or during a buying process. The customer may suddenly want support and send a chat request or cam request. An organization must be geared towards this, as the customer wants to buy precisely at this moment. If the customer receives no response, he or she may consider buying elsewhere. The communication has to be to the point and based clearly on the user's question. This can be difficult for the person at the receiving end of the communication request, as it may not be known in advance what is going to be asked. The recipient must therefore have sufficient knowledge or the necessary facilities to be able to answer the question or have the necessary knowledge/information systems. We will first look at answering the questions. Afterwards we will deal with chatting.

Answering questions

The person who answers the customer queries must be sufficiently knowledgeable about the products and trained, but because the deployment of this employee is very difficult to schedule, increasingly more use is made of supporting facilities. This often results in a division between front-line support and back-office support. The back-office support comprises the specialists, while the front office houses the generalists. This structure is often chosen for technical support. The front office can answer many of the questions but if a problem or question is too specific it can be handled by the back office. In this case the customer would be transferred to a technical specialist. It is also possible for a customer to be phoned back or to receive an email with an answer to the question. Figure 12.1 illustrates this system structure.

As the user may require support at any given time of the day or night and the permanent deployment of personnel is very expensive, possibilities were sought for providing customers with answers as efficiently as possible without requiring any direct contact. A semi-interactive contact was the solution: users seek the answer to questions through the use of the system themselves. A simple form of this is 'frequently asked questions' or 'FAQs', which comprises a database of the most frequently asked questions linked to standard answers. In many cases this is sufficient. In some cases, however, the answer to an FAQ will not be enough. In order to avoid personal assistance being required, there is a subsequent step which connects the customer to a knowledge base. Here other search criteria can be used. It is often also possible to do a semantic search, whereby the question is interpreted by the system and an answer is given. The question 'What is my bank balance?' may be answered with the

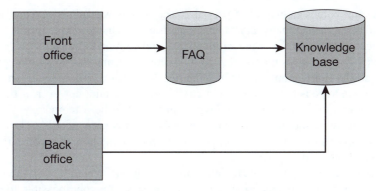

Figure 12.1 System structure for handling questions with the Internet

question: 'The balance of your savings account or loan?' The question 'What is the balance of my loan?' can be answered with the question: 'The balance at this moment or as of 1 March?' Such a dialogue is based on interpreting the question, further questioning by the system and then providing the correct answer. A well set-up system can ensure that the need for personal support via chat, email or webcam is greatly reduced.

Chat

Another form of direct personal communication is chat. Here you can exchange messages with other people who can respond directly to them. Through public chat boxes you can chat about anything; through specific theme-oriented chat boxes you can meet like-minded people. For businesses, this form of communication is effective for product support. In particular, problems with computers and software can often be solved efficiently using chat. By explaining a problem in a chat room, other people with similar problems can give advice. Other subjects can, of course, also be discussed in these chat rooms, which may prove negative for an organization. What used to happen at dinner parties, now takes place in chat rooms. However, the barrier to being negative is much lower on the Internet, and messages can also stay there for a long time. Organizations need to develop a policy for registering data on the Internet and for an (active) role in chat rooms. In this way they can gain insight into the experiences of users and customers. Negative messages should not be refuted, as this can be counterproductive. Rather, lessons should be learned from them. Chat rooms obviously can, in fact, be used in this way as a form of market research. The research may not be representative, but certainly provides an indication. For this reason it is a good idea for organizations to allow their marketing staff to actively participate in fora.

12.1.2 Twitter

Another recent form of direct communication is Twitter, which allows an immediate and personal response to messages. People can also use Twitter passively, which means they just follow other Twitterers and read their messages, their 'tweets'. It is up to the organization or person whether to respond and in what manner. Via direct messaging ('DM') a personal response is given, via @ a public response is given and via retweet you can forward a message publicly. By adding tags to certain names, you are constantly kept up to date if that name or word is being used. For example, businesses can add a tag to their own name. As soon as the name comes up in a tweet, they also receive that tweet. This way they know what is being said about the company and can respond directly. Thus a unique form of interaction arises between people that the organization knows and complete strangers.

In this way it is also possible to create a 'buzz' or to ensure that your company is being mentioned all the time: simply Twitter. Whether this form of communication has lasting power or is mere hype is not yet certain in 2010. What is certain, however, is that there is a demand for direct communication. If Twitter turns out to be a temporary phenomenon, it will undoubtedly be succeeded by other forms of direct communication. The smartphone will play an important role in this; it is, after all, a personal medium that you carry with you all the time and can be used anywhere.

Twitter may be replaced by 'near field communication', which allows the user to see exactly which of their contacts are currently in the area. It is then possible to send these 'friends' a message. Online weblogs, location-based services and interactive chat rooms will also maintain the communication between people in the future. This will result in communities that bond like-minded people both on the Internet and in the physical world. Businesses will be able to communicate directly with these like-minded people, but will also know when they are in the shop or in the area. These forms of direct communication, which are facilitated by the Internet, are still in the early phases of their development.

Box 12.1 Spam

Article 13(1) of the Privacy and Electronic Communications Directive requires Member States to prohibit the sending of unsolicited commercial communications by fax or e-mail or other electronic messaging systems such as short messaging services (SMS) and multimedia messaging services (MMS) unless the prior consent of the addressee has been obtained (opt-in system).

The only exception to this rule is in cases where contact details for sending e-mail or SMS messages (but not faxes) have been obtained in the context of a sale. Within such an existing customer relationship the company who obtained the data may use them for the marketing of similar products or services as those it has already sold to the customer. Nevertheless, even then the company has to make clear from the first time of collecting the data, that they may be used for direct marketing and should offer the right to object. Moreover, each subsequent marketing message should include an easy way for the customer to stop further messages (opt-out).

The opt-in system is mandatory for any e-mail, SMS or fax addressed to natural persons for direct marketing. It is optional with regard to legal persons. For the latter category Member States may choose between an opt-in or an opt-out system.

For all categories of addressees, legal and natural persons, Article 13(4) of the Directive prohibits direct marketing messages by e-mail or SMS which conceal or disguise the identity of the sender and which do not include a valid address to which recipients can send a request to cease such messages.

For voice telephony marketing calls, other than by automated machines, Member States may also choose between an opt-in or an opt-out approach.

Source: http://ec.europa.eu/information_society/policy/
ecomm/todays_framework/privacy_protection/spam/index_en.htm

12.1.3 Email and newsletters

Other direct forms of personal communication are email and newsletters.

Email

With the email there is a direct contact between the sender and the receiver. There is, however, a delay in the response (if a response is given at all). Email is often used for commercial messages to customers and other registered parties, but also to inform customers of any personal developments. The more personal the email, the better the response.

Impersonal, unsolicited emails lead to irritation. Often these are spam messages. In the Netherlands there has been a ban on sending unsolicited commercial emails since 2009. It is only permitted to send messages to people you know or who have requested an email. This can be done through an 'opt-in', whereby the customer indicates that he or she wishes to receive newsletters. The difference between 'opt-in' and 'opt-out' lies in the activity that is asked of the customer. With opt-out the box has already been ticked: 'Yes, please keep me up to date on any new information'. If the customer does not wish to receive this, he or she has to remove the tick. In the case of the opt-in the customer has to actively tick the box requesting further information.

Opt-in system

Opt-in is the system that is used for the bulk distribution of (often periodic) emails or text messages. Here every receiver has to give their prior permission for the email or text message to be sent to them. This is usually done by someone filling in their email address or mobile number in a registration form on a website, or by sending a 'subscribe' mail to a registration address.

The opt-in system is used for all sorts of applications, such as closed or public discussion lists, announcements, newsletters, e-zines and the marketing communication of businesses. Experienced Internet users follow the rule that the permission first has to be confirmed. This is called a confirmed opt-in, or double opt-in. The verification usually consists of a neutral email (that is to say without any content to which the permission relates), which is sent to the registered address which the receiver has to confirm by responding by email or by clicking a link.

Newsletters

The newsletter is another form of direct communication used by organizations, through which customers and other subscribers are regularly kept up to date on relevant developments. This is an electronic form of the old paper newsletter. Most businesses do not take into account the specific requirements that an electronic newsletter has to meet. The newsletter arrives at the receiver's mailbox unsolicited and often at unexpected times. The messages are often standard messages that a business wishes to send, usually information about the company. There are a number of rules that should be followed for a newsletter to be successful:

- no unnecessary pictures, video, animation or Flash;
- only relevant information that is of interest to the receiver;
- genuine pieces of news that would please the receiver;
- short messages (maximum of five lines) and a link that can be clicked on for further information;

- an interaction possibility (response), but also a possibility to prevent the receipt of further messages;
- no more than five messages at a time (there can't be that much news!);
- and finally: consider when the customer would be reading this newsletter and gear your mailing to this.

The newsletter is still regarded as a medium for showing a product range. The opening percentages are therefore very low, on average 15 per cent. It is a good idea to analyse the opening percentage, the clicks of the messages and the duration that the newsletter is read. These will all provide lessons that should be taken into account when sending the subsequent newsletter.

12.2 Information function

In addition to communication, the Internet is also often used for acquiring and disseminating information. Businesses in particular use their own website for the dissemination of information. This can vary from generic information about the organization, such as the vision, the mission, the management board, the personnel and contact details, to specific information. Specific information includes information about the products, operating instructions, FAQs or newsletters. This specific information can be located by a visitor on the website of the supplier.

Ranking and good websites are important conditions in the commercial information function of the Internet.

12.2.1 Ranking

Often commercial information is provided so it is important that the website attracts many visitors. This can be realized through:

- a high ranking on the search engines;
- a high ranking on selling sites/marketplaces;
- affiliate marketing;
- specific services such as comparison services; and
- a good domain name.

It is not easy to get a high ranking on search engines. The first page of hits on a search engine is very important. Seventy per cent of people who search using a particular search word do not look beyond the first page. Approximately 20 per cent or so look at the second page, and only 10 per cent are willing to look any further. For this reason businesses need to be on the first page. This can be achieved by buying a place on this page through an advertisement or an advertisement linked to a search word (for example, through AdWords). It is also possible to influence the search ranking by creating greater traffic on the site (for example, many quality referrals). The ranking is determined by, for example, the popularity of the link, so the more the site is linked to from good-quality sites, the higher the ranking.

A few steps to get to the top:

- Make sure that you have a good, specific domain name.
- Ensure that your website is mentioned on various other sites.
- Ensure that the correct key words are present in the document; repeat the key words in the text a number of times.

- Enter the specification of the website fully and well; also use as many unique key words and descriptions as possible.
- Avoid Flash as much as possible when showing the content of the website. This can of course be used for specific components of the sites, such as animations or clips.

Google itself is an information site. Visitors go on Google because they are looking for information. This is an important fact as this determines the phase in the buying process of a customer. Google is only the first step in this buying process. We will look more closely at this in the next chapter.

Other information-oriented sites include portals. A portal is a general site that usually provides information but also refers to other websites. It is this information function that makes the portal interesting for the visitor. The information is perceived as objective. What's more, the visitor can go straight to a webshop. Portals usually receive a great deal of traffic as well as many referrals due to the strong information function. The better and more objective the information, the more often it is referred to, and hence its higher ranking on Google.

12.2.2 Information sites

In case of the information function there is a user who is looking for information and a supplier providing that information. This match has to be good and efficient in order to 'bind' visitors. In some cases the information can be difficult to find on the site, resulting in visitors giving up and going elsewhere. The effect is then counterproductive. A good website is an important source of information, whether something is bought or not. For information sites, speed, clarity and a good key word on the site are important. Webshops have to win the trust of their visitors. Good information on the webshop, the terms of delivery and the payment possibilities are important. There has to be good product information on the products available, so that customers know precisely what they are buying, who they are buying from and what they can expect. It is particularly important on the Internet that trust is gained and customers have to be helped in making their purchases.

There are various types of information site, including:

- orientation sites;
- general information sites; and
- search sites.

Orientation sites

On orientation sites general information is provided about a particular theme. Tourist sites are an example of this. They do not give specific information, but provide general information about a country or region, or for example about theme parks. Visitors go to these sites to find out more about what there is to do. Fashion sites are another example: what is the latest fashion or what shall I wear today? Student information sites are also an example of orientation sites where you can find general information about, for example, studies, educational institutions and preliminary training.

General information sites

General information sites are more specific than orientation sites. Information can be provided about products, people and companies. This involves, for example, specific information about the use of products, product composition, where products are available, dealer information, FAQs and application information. It is on the basis of the products that the information is collected, either as a step in a buying process, or as general orientation or if there are any problems. These sites do not have any specific sales (transaction) function. Sometimes it is not even possible to buy, but what you often see is an advertisement placed on the site. In this way some of the costs can be recouped.

There are also sites with personal information. An example of this is the police register with the most wanted criminals, as well as sites with 'babes', celebrities or sports and pop stars. In the business world LinkedIn.com is an example of an information medium that has the potential of a social medium (see Chapter 14).

Many businesses have a website that does not have a buying function. The website contains general information about the company: what it is, its objectives, financial details, information about the management board, contact details and perhaps information about the opening hours. This is clearly an example of an electronic brochure. The site is intended only as an information medium for contacts who may wish to do business or who wish to get in touch with the company. The commercial impact is, of course, extremely limited and the website only contains relevant information that has been determined by the supplier.

Search sites

Visitors go to search sites only to find something; it is not possible to buy anything directly and visitors are referred elsewhere. Google is an example of such a search site. The Dutch site Marktplaats.nl is another example. Here it is not possible to buy directly either, but people are referred to others from whom they can buy. Generally speaking 'portals' are search sites. A portal is a sort of shop window, from which you are referred to relevant sites. Portals lead to a clustering of information. Good portals attract many visitors, which makes them interesting for advertisers. Google, Yahoo! and many sports sites are examples of this. Marktplaats.nl, for example, receives almost 7 000 000 unique visitors per month. For marketing this is a good opportunity to realize exposure.

12.3   Transaction (sales) function

With the transaction or sales function a commercial transaction takes place. Customers can buy on the Internet. Internet use is very much focused on this transaction function, but not deservedly so. Only 10 per cent of all activities are aimed at buying on the Internet; the other activities are mainly focused on communication and searching for information. The facilitating function of the Internet is only now being applied, particularly through mobile Internet networks and the Internet as a medium for identification, authorization and mobility.

With the transaction function a subdivision can be made into physical products and virtual products. This section will look at the difference between the two. It will also examine the generation applications of the Internet.

12.3.1 *Physical versus virtual*

The difference between physical products and virtual products lies primarily in the way in which they are sent: virtual products are downloaded whereas physical products have to be sent through the mail or by courier. The Internet is ideally suited for virtual products. There is no waiting time, and the products can be loaded and used immediately after purchase. It is therefore not surprising that increasingly more virtual products are being offered on the Internet, but also that physical products are being given a virtual component.

Music is an ideal virtual product and was therefore one of the first virtual products to be sold on the Internet. The music could be loaded immediately onto the computer or an MP3 player and listened to by the purchaser. A physical component was no longer required.

The ongoing debate about books also looks at this virtual element. If a book is also made as a virtual product, an e-book, then a physical component is no longer necessary. This implies that bookshops will disappear from the high street and customers will simply load books onto their e-reader. Efforts are now being made to encourage the need to continue making physical books: because customers want them, because the colour illustrations are so much more attractive or because physical books have a longer life.

It will be clear that the first phase of transactions on the Internet allowed a breakthrough for virtual products, for which little interaction is needed. This was followed by the advent of products that were physical but did not need any specific sales support (such as books), followed by products with little interaction. These days we also see products which require a great deal of interaction being sold on the Internet. The new possibilities offered by social media, webcams and, of course, mobile Internet have contributed to the possibility of removing all limitations. The various relationships between product form and the potential for interaction are examined in Table 12.1.

The movement of selling on the Internet is shown in the arrows in Table 12.2. It started with virtual products that did not require any support. However, thanks to the support that the Internet can provide, particularly through Web 2.0 and soon also 3.0, the transaction possibilities with the Internet will become practically boundless. This will help to make the

Table 12.1 Relationship between product form and interaction possibility

Form/interaction	Physical	Physical and virtual	Virtual
Much	Cars, houses	Meetings, communication	Private banking, investments
Little	Fashion, wines	Diet products, teleworking	Information, games
None	Food	Books	Music, banking services

Table 12.2 The development of the Internet as a commercial medium

Form/interaction	Physical	Physical and virtual	Virtual
Much	Cars, houses	Meetings, communication	Private banking, investments
Little	Fashion, wines	Diet products, teleworking	Information, games
None	Food	Books	Music, banking services

Internet a fully fledged commercial medium that is capable of competing in all areas with the current media and the current sales possibilities (trade shows, retail and personal sales).

In addition to the dimension of interaction and virtuality, the product itself also determines the selling possibilities on the Internet. Physical products are harder to sell than virtual products. In particular, the logistic handling (picking, packing and sending) is expensive. On top of this, the buyer always has to wait for the product to be delivered, despite a guarantee of delivery within 24 hours. A product also consists of various components: a core and the actual product. This can be physical, such as with foodstuffs, or virtual such as music. The manifestation can also be physical, such as is the case with the packaging or the information carrier. With virtual products such as music and software it is possible to make them physical by placing them on a physical component such as a CD. With the Internet the physical component (CD or MP3) is separated from the virtual product (music). Transport through the Internet is possible when the buyer has the physical component needed, such as computer, iPad or iPhone. Services can also be a virtual component belonging to a physical product, such as a manual. These services consist of providing information, support or communication, and this can, of course, be done very successfully via the Internet, the telephone or a webcam. The imaginary value is the perceived idea a buyer has about the product. The association that is made is, of course, always virtual. Brand perception, perception in general and use association are examples of this. These are virtual components of a product. Advertising in particular contributes to this imaginary value of a product and the Internet plays an increasingly important role in this. In the future, once the Internet has matured, this role will become even more important (Figure 12.2).

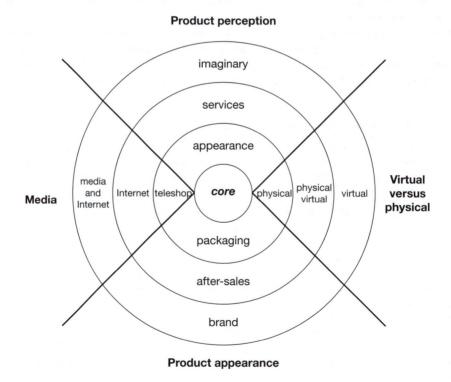

Figure 12.2 Product perception and media

12.3.2 Generation applications

These days the application of the Internet is also indicated in generations. With the basic generation the Internet was used as an information medium, based on a large amount of information distributed over sites and feature sections. The Internet user was a passive consumer in search of this information. Little involvement was expected, but then it was not possible either. It was a bit like walking through a library, now and again taking a book off the shelves, having a look at it and then returning it, until the preferred book was found. In the generation approach this application was called 1.0. In addition to the websites – the electronic brochures – it was also possible to communicate by email, but the commercial applications were very limited. Web 1.0 is mostly associated with the 1990s, the first phase of the Internet (and therefore an advanced form of a bulletin board) (Figure 12.3).

Since 2004 there has been a new generation, both in terms of the users (younger people use the Internet much more than older generations) and the technology: larger bandwidths, faster Internet connections and new interactive possibilities with the software. This was Web 2.0. The emphasis of Web 2.0 lay more on communication and participation: social networks, sharing your opinion, collaborating, combining websites, referring to other websites, communicating and videos. Interactivity, in fact, lies at the heart of Web 2.0. Some aspects of this generation of the Internet are:

- discussion forums;
- chat;
- weblogs;
- web video (e.g. YouTube);
- sharing photos (e.g. Flickr);

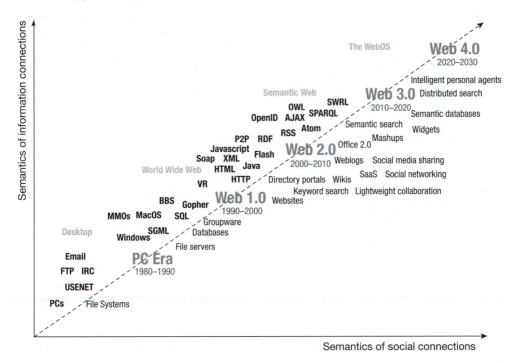

Figure 12.3 Development of the Internet

- network websites (e.g. LinkedIn, MySpace, Facebook, Twitter);
- online office tools (e.g. Google Docs);
- RSS feeds; and
- virtual worlds (e.g. Second Life).

The Internet user has now become an active consumer and producer. With Web 1.0 the user was passive, always searching for relevant information. With Web 2.0 the user has become part of the information provision and the use possibilities. Users create their own world with sites they want to be involved in or associated with. This has become a personal world (and a successor to Second Life). This world began for children with Habbo Hotel and for adults with Hyves and Facebook, but these personal worlds could also be found on other social media networks and interest sites.

The new generation application is called Web 3.0. It is not yet clear exactly what this will entail. It is probably a combination of physical and virtual, applications of mobile Internet, location-based services and near field communication. The development will ensure that users become the centre and the Internet facilitates what they do, regardless of where they are. Users are tangible, available and traceable and the possibilities and facilities are grouped around them. This is seen in the strategy of Microsoft, whose Phone 7 groups services around hubs. These hubs are activity oriented and group all the services that the user needs.

Box 12.2 Designed for life in motion

With Windows Phone 7 Series, Microsoft takes a fundamentally different approach to phone software. Smart design begins with a new, holistic design system that informs every aspect of the phone, from its visually appealing layout and motion to its function and hardware integration. On the Start screen, dynamically updated 'live tiles' show users real-time content directly, breaking the mould of static icons that serve as an intermediate step on the way to an application. Create a tile of a friend, and the user gains a readable, up-to-date view of a friend's latest pictures and posts, just by glancing at Start.

Every Windows Phone 7 Series phone will come with a dedicated hardware button for Bing, providing one-click access to search from anywhere on the phone, while a special implementation of Bing search provides intent-specific results, delivering the most relevant Web or local results, depending on the type of query.

Windows Phone 7 Series creates an unrivalled set of integrated experiences on a phone through Windows Phone hubs. Hubs bring together related content from the Web, applications and services into a single view to simplify common tasks. Windows Phone 7 Series includes six hubs built on specific themes reflecting activities that matter most to people:

- *People:* This hub delivers an engaging social experience by bringing together relevant content based on the person, including his or her live feeds from social networks and photos. It also provides a central place from which to post updates to Facebook and Windows Live in one step.
- *Pictures:* This hub makes it easy to share pictures and videos to a social network in one step. Windows Phone 7 Series also brings together a user's photos by inte-

grating with the Web and PC, making the phone the ideal place to view a person's entire picture and video collection.

- *Games:* This hub delivers the first and only official Xbox LIVE experience on a phone, including Xbox LIVE games, Spotlight feed and the ability to see a gamer's avatar, Achievements and gamer profile. With more than 23 million active members around the world, Xbox LIVE unlocks a world of friends, games and entertainment on Xbox 360, and now also on Windows Phone 7 Series.
- *Music + Video:* This hub creates an incredible media experience that brings the best of Zune, including content from a user's PC, online music services and even a built-in FM radio into one simple place that is all about music and video. Users can turn their media experience into a social one with Zune Social on a PC and share their media recommendations with like-minded music lovers. The playback experience is rich and easy to navigate, and immerses the listener in the content.
- *Marketplace:* This hub allows the user to easily discover and load the phone with certified applications and games.
- *Office:* This hub brings the familiar experience of the world's leading productivity software to the Windows Phone. With access to Office, OneNote and SharePoint Workspace all in one place, users can easily read, edit and share documents. With the additional power of Outlook Mobile, users stay productive and up to date while on the go.

Source: http://www.microsoft.com/presspass/
press/2010/feb10/02-15mwc10pr.mspx

12.4 Facilitating function

The development of the Internet involves the development from information medium to participation and then to the centralization of the user. The future will be clearly geared towards the facilitative possibilities of the Internet, such as described previously. The Internet is the same as air, radio or television. The Internet is everywhere and available whenever you want to make use of it. But in contrast to radio and television, you yourself have also become part of the Internet. Because of the smartphone, mobile devices and perhaps also because of identification possibilities based on chips, you, the user, have become the centre and can have services offered to you that you need at any particular moment. Cars have access to hotspots and can be monitored on the Internet, and navigation systems are programmed to avoid traffic jams and to be guided by the Internet. And the driver can always hear (and see) what emails come in and immediately change his or her route. Everyone is able to gain access to this type of facility (via the telephone) and everyone can choose to have their own personal world. The evolutionary developments lead towards individualization, connectivity and agility in a dynamic world that constantly requires modifications, but in this case it is the user who determines what happens and not (just) the provider.

12.5 Influence on marketing

Over the years the Internet has gained more and more influence on businesses, consumers and consequently also on marketing. From the very beginning the possibilities of direct communication were recognized. The Internet influences:

Table 12.3 Evolution model for the application of the Internet

Classical marketing	Customer-oriented marketing	Network-oriented marketing, participation and interaction
Supply oriented	Interaction oriented	Time, need and location oriented
The supply is central. Many websites with information. Electronic brochures. Low speed when connecting. The computer is central.	Social networks, users are part of the information supply. Users choose sites for interaction and communication. Combination of computer and mobile device.	Users are central, and can be tracked and traced. Information and services are geared towards needs. Mobile device plays the leading role.
Web 1.0 as of 1992	Web 2.0 as of 2004	Web 3.0 as of 2010

1. communication;
2. information;
3. supply;
4. location of the shop; and
5. power.

The way the application of the Internet has evolved is illustrated in Table 12.3.

12.5.1 Influence on communication

It was the direct marketing industry that was the first to recognize the possible applications. We saw this in the form of direct communication by email, but also through newsletters and mailings. Spam is actually a continuation of the mass mailings of the 1980s, when address databases were first bought in order to be able to send unsolicited mail. In the 1990s these mailings were increasingly being carried out via electronic mailings. Eventually this was restricted by legislation about unsolicited mail (spam) in most countries.

The communication possibilities allowed by the Internet have had a great influence on marketing; customers can be approached directly, and a direct contact is also possible for customers. This interaction has led not only to a closer bonding with customers but also to different customer expectations. Customers expect to receive information, to be kept up to date on relevant developments and to receive speedy answers to their questions. A direct consequence of this is that the 'window of opportunity' becomes increasingly shorter. The moment a customer asks a question, he or she expects a quick answer. If none is given, then he or she will look and buy elsewhere. Organizations therefore have to employ a more inter-active communication at times that are convenient to the customer, often in the evenings.

12.5.2 Influence on information

In addition to the influence on communication, the Internet also influences the information that customers can find about products, services and the total package. From the Internet they now know straight away what to buy, where to buy it and at what price. Transparency leads to suppliers having a better understanding that the price has to be realistic in the eyes of the buyer. The competition is also on the Internet, in the form of unknown suppliers, sometimes even based abroad. There is transparency on the basis of price, terms of delivery and product properties. As a consequence customers speak their mind and in the shop will quite happily negotiate the price, as they know the price on the Internet.

12.5.3 Influence on supply

Supply is also influenced by the Internet. Until recently the local retailer would select the product range from which a customer could choose. These days customers increasingly determine what they want to buy first and then decide where to buy it. The local shop's product range and therefore the retailer's choice of products are no longer the decisive factors. The customer decides what is bought and where, and subsequently implicitly also what the retailer has to buy in. The choice of the customer determines the composition of the product range. If a shop does not sell that preferred product, the customer will not settle for a substitute product but will simply look elsewhere (often on the Internet). A retailer has to adapt to the change in this buying behaviour. An example of this is the bookshop. When buying a book or a CD, in order to make a well considered purchase customers increasingly choose an Internet supplier, for example Bol.com, Amazon.com or Managementboek.nl. Local retailers lose some of their turnover as a result. But by making timely changes to their product range, into high-emotion products, bestsellers, impulse purchases and magazines, they can keep afloat. Other books (the more well-thought-out purchases) are bought on the Internet. Customers don't often order books at the bookshop anymore. If one has to order a book it is often easier to do this at home, and it is usually cheaper as well. The same development has occurred in the music world, which has also seen the emergence of downloadable products. The music shops can only really compete by offering impulse purchases or very selective choices.

12.5.4 Influence on the location of the shop

In addition to the influence of the Internet on the communication function and the information possibilities for customers, webshopping has also had a huge impact. Location is increasingly often multi-channel, where different values and rules apply, as we will see in Chapters 14 and 17. The choice of a physical shop, a webshop or both is very much determined by the wishes of the customer.

12.5.5 Influence on power

The greatest influence that the Internet has had on marketing is on the balance of power; this is no longer determined by supply but by demand. It is no longer the supplier who determines what is supplied, at what price and who can sell it: the customer now determines what is bought when and at what price. This shift in power from the supplier to the customer has had a decisive impact on the application of marketing activities and the customer's choice regarding where to buy. Marketing is no longer about just waiting passively for someone to turn up. Marketing no longer uses passive media such as the newspaper or television in order to persuade customers to buy. Marketing has to be a dialogue; it involves an interaction with customers, as well as binding and motivating customers. This development is the result of the customers' use of the Internet.

Summary

- The Internet has been completely accepted as a communication, information and sales channel by consumers, telecom companies and suppliers.
- The Internet is, in fact, a standard infrastructure and you can decide yourself how you wish to use it: as a supplier using websites, as a communication medium through blogs, chats or video or as a sales channel. The Internet can, however, also be an infrastructure for accessing people by telephone (such as Skype). Furthermore, it provides navigation and location services (through location recognition) and the recognition of products and people through, for example, an RFID chip.
- The Internet has had a huge impact on companies and consumers. Physical boundaries have disappeared and the virtual boundaries are unknown. Boundaries now only exist in people's minds; the possible applications have had an effect on the behaviour of people and on business functions. This will cause marketing to change; after all, not only is customer behaviour (buying behaviour) changing, so too is the potential to make and maintain contacts with customers.
- The Internet leads to a large degree of transparency, new structures and different expectations. The marketing discipline should recognize this change and use the application possibilities of the Internet in order to intensify the relationship with customers, to find new markets and to remain competitive on the market with various unknown suppliers. This determines the future of the organization and its ability to remain attractive to customers.
- Because of the Internet boundaries have become blurred; everyone can have access to information and a 24/7 economy has arisen without limits. Users make use of the Internet in different ways, depending on culture, age and experience, and, in the case of businesses, depending on the marketing orientation and the business model.
- The application of the Internet has considerable consequences for the relationship between an organization and its market, customers and suppliers.

Part 4

Internet strategy

The customer in power

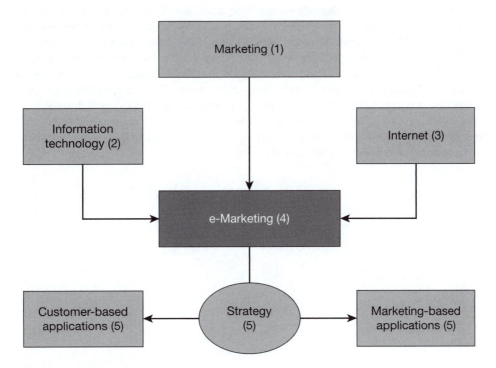

Figure P4.1 Outline of the book

The Internet is used in many applications. For an organization, however, it is important to determine which application is best suited for its strategy. An organization cannot determine this independently. Both external and internal factors have to be taken into account, including the competition, suppliers and international developments, as well as the wishes of the customer. Internally there has to be a commitment from the management board as well as the IT and marketing departments. Marketing in particular is very important in this selection process. Marketing has to bear the final responsibility for the use of the Internet; after all, contacts with external parties are arranged through the Internet. In the event of an open application of the Internet this would mainly be customers and visitors who would like to be involved in the organization. What's more, the manner in which the information is provided, its content and form, is a responsibility of the marketing department. The IT department is important because the Internet has many IT aspects and should also be a part of the IT infrastructure. A good collaboration between marketing and IT is essential if the Internet strategy is to succeed.

Another important aspect is the choice of suppliers. This can be the hosting supplier, the software supplier but also the design company and the web builder. An organization should not want to do everything itself, as greater efficiency is gained through a collaboration with external parties. What's more, the experiences of other customers can be used. Another important point is the release strategy. The Internet is currently just at the beginning of a development. Changes in technology and its use are following one another in rapid succession. And there are also style aspects such as design and use of colour. The Internet strategy has to be regularly tested against these developments. We have seen the breakthrough of smartphones, mobile Internet, the use of tablets with specific user possibilities and automatic identification with RFID chips. On top of this, sales via the Internet are also increasing considerably. An organization has to constantly ask itself whether the chosen strategy is still the right one. Modifying the website every two years is not at all unusual, neither is reviewing the strategy every year or the results every month. With the Internet external developments, in particular, have to be followed closely in order to determine the necessary response from the organization. This requires sound analyses, as well as a clear understanding of visitors and customers and a good insight into the results.

13 Developing the Internet strategy

The Internet is a specific channel through which customers search for information about products, people and companies. The Internet is, in fact, a pull medium: customers search for information, while the reverse is true for media companies, which look for customers. This different approach makes it necessary to develop a good strategy for using the Internet, based on the expected wishes of customers. This strategy cannot be regarded in isolation from the company strategy (vision, image and objectives), from the marketing and sales strategy and from the IT strategy. In all cases the application of the Internet must be a part of these strategies.

13.1 Determining the strategy

The general objectives of an Internet strategy are aimed at the market and very specifically at the relationship with the market. This can vary from business to business, as we will see in Part 5 of this book. Examples of business objectives for an Internet strategy are to:

- come closer to customers in order to be able to communicate directly with customers and market players;
- save costs, both in the communication and in the sales;
- make the market more transparent, by providing information to investors, but also for building the brand and after-sales services;
- be able to maintain direct contact with registered parties; and
- optimize processes.

Table 13.1 shows the intended advantages of these objectives and their effectiveness.

13.2 Objectives of websites

The website reflects the objectives of the business. It may, for example, inform visitors about the organization, communicate with customers, inform visitors about products, encourage people to buy and provide an after-sales service.

13.2.1 Informing about the organization

Websites that only give information wish to inform visitors about the organization, the structure of the organization, the staffing, contact and location details and often also the financial situation. The Internet is, in effect, used as a facility to show an electronic brochure in order to enable people to quickly gain a good picture of the organization. These sorts of websites

Table 13.1 Advantages and effectiveness of Internet strategy objectives

Objective	Advantage	Measurement of effectiveness
To come closer to customers and enable direct communication	This is important for the control function in the communication, for responding to market developments and for assessing a direct response from the market (market research)	The effectiveness is measured on the basis of the number of visitors, the length of time that visitors remain on the site and the number of page views
Cost savings	This form of communication is faster than the traditional media and can also impart more information. Any use of the traditional media can be short and to the point: simply refer to the website. Also when handling questions from customers, such as with after-sales, FAQs and emails are more efficient than for example a call centre	The effectiveness is measured on the basis of the number of visitors to a specific page, the time that the visitor stays on the page, the number of emails, the number of telephone calls
Visibility in the market	Through an active communication policy by using Web 2.0 media, including YouTube and other video services. Through an active policy with search engines, online marketplaces and comparison sites. Through attractive web design and visual styling and services	The effectiveness is determined by the number of clicks at other sites (click through ratio), number of returning visitors, time on the site, total number of site visitors
Direct contact	By linking log-in services to profiles and companies, specific services can be offered. These may include: questions on the use of products, special price offers (business-to-business) and stock levels, terms and conditions of delivery as well as framework contracts. The access is the log-in code that gives a certain view of the information that leads to targeted, specific communication	The effectiveness is measured by the number of users of the service, the intensity of the use and the return ratio
Process optimization	By linking the website to the internal processes a larger process optimization can be realized. This is the case for example with banks where payments are automatically processed within the process, but also with orders and logistics services. The link between orders and stock levels allows the purchasing to be optimized	The effectiveness is measured by the number of users and the number of transactions, total cost savings per department and process handling

are used by organizations that do not have immediate sales objectives. Their sales usually take place through other channels, such as retailers, shops or resellers. These websites are intended to support the sales by creating trust in the organization that imports or manufactures the products. Often financial details are shown on the websites as well, such as investor information in order to inform potential investors and to encourage them to become interested.

13.2.2 Communication with customers and visitors

Communication is used to build a direct relationship with the visitor. The communication can be direct communication with the website, by providing information or by giving an answer to expected questions (FAQs). It is also possible to give direct support through the customer service using a chat function, email and webcams. Particularly when a customer needs support during the buying process, or after the purchase, this can be a very useful function. This will help to create a direct relationship, and contact details, such as purchase details and email address, are saved directly. The primary objective is support; the sale usually takes place through other channels. Examples of websites designed with this is mind are those of electronic suppliers such as Philips and Sony. The sale takes place through retailers, but the product support can be given through the website (for example, after registering). Other forms of direct communication are the use of Web 2.0 possibilities, such as social media and Twitter.

13.2.3 Product and purchasing information

Product and purchasing information is information given on the products as well as the terms and conditions of delivery, including payment possibilities. The product information is often linked to the visitor's search criteria. A visitor may be searching for a specific product (direct search), a group of products (indication of the range) or an experience (going out, leisure). A good search possibility on the site ensures that the site can respond to the visitor's questions efficiently. If this does not happen, it will quickly lead to irritation. Various blogs, guestbooks and FAQs also contribute to providing support to the purchasing process on a site.

13.2.4 Motivating visitors to buy

The visitor is a potential buyer. Not only is information given about the webshop and the products, but trust is also created in order to encourage buying. This trust is generated through:

* a clear design;
* a good look and feel;
* simple navigation;
* a quick buying process;
* various payment possibilities, including payment in arrears;
* carrying the home shopping quality mark;
* clear terms and conditions of delivery; and
* transparency in the delivery (possibility of viewing the logistics process).

A direct communication will also be part of attracting visitors to the site and enticing them to buy.

13.2.5 After-sales service

Another objective of the Internet strategy can be the after-sales service. In this way the buyers of certain products receive, for example, user's information, information regarding faults, new releases and addresses of service centres.

This after-sales service is important for expensive consumer products. Registration of the purchase leads to guarantee rights, but for the business it provides an insight into who bought

Table 13.2 Site types and corresponding business types with examples

Type of site/Internet function	Type of business	Examples
Information site/information	Large businesses, no sales directly to consumers, often B2B. Often also listed on the stock exchange	Unilever, Philips, Océ
Communication site/ communication	Large businesses, work with distribution channel, no direct sales to private individuals, strong brands, support in the buying process, specific product information. Sometimes also active on Web 2.0 sites	Sony, Douwe Egberts, Asus, Acer
Selling site/selling	Webshops and physical shops; the aim is to sell. Much product information. Often also identification of 'return' behaviour. Registration of visitor details. Also increasingly more active on Web 2.0 sites	Webshops
After-sales site/aftercare	Often no direct selling, but through distribution channel. Very much consumer oriented	Sony, Apple

what and where. This can then form the basis for further communication. This allows businesses that sell through a distribution channel to still gain information on who has bought their products, and enables these businesses to approach those buyers directly with product information, new products or upgrades. It is also possible to activate certain products after they have been purchased (for example, Microsoft applications on the computer) whereby a further product support is possible. In actual fact, in doing so the manufacturer provides supporting services for the sales channel, which helps to create more trust among the buyers as well as more efficiency for the retailer. In addition, it provides the manufacturer with more insight into the buying process and the customers. Table 13.2 gives examples of types of function of the Internet specific for certain businesses.

13.3 The Internet strategy

The Internet strategy is part of the company strategy, as well as the marketing strategy, and depends upon external and internal conditions. Figure 13.1 shows this schematically.

For the development of an Internet strategy a number of phases can be identified: a conceptual phase, an implementation phase and an operational phase. Each phase comprises a number of subareas.

13.3.1 Conceptual phase

In the conceptual phase the Internet concept is developed. This will always have to be done in line with the company's objectives and has to be part of the marketing and sales strategy. The Internet will therefore have to form an integral part of the marketing and sales plan.

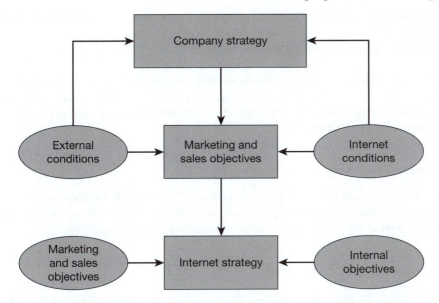

Figure 13.1 Relationship between business strategy and the Internet

Table 13.3 provides a model which shows the focus of each part of the conceptual phase. Each phase is then examined separately, with extra attention given to the final phase: request for proposal (RFP).

During the conceptual phase the management will also have to focus on the possibilities of the organization and their strategic consequences. This requires a large involvement by the management board. The area of application cannot be isolated. Tasks for the management board include:

•   determination of the strategy and budget;
•   the realization of the IT application;

Table 13.3 Phases and focus in the conceptual phase

Phases	*Focus*
1. Review the preconditions	An internal focus based on the company strategy, marketing strategy and organizational possibilities (also the budget)
2. Review the external possibilities	Market developments, strategy of competitors and the wishes of customers. Determine the possibilities based on the ORCA model, an outside-in approach
3. Define the objectives of the Internet strategy	Determine the objectives of the Internet concept
4. External review with potential clients, advisors and market consultants	Make a long list of suppliers and examine the possibilities
5. Crystallize the RFP as a basis for the internal reviewing and acceptance and as a basis for the choice of suppliers	On the basis of the shortlist an RFP is sent to potential suppliers. The RFP is a detailed plan of the concept

- the possibilities of acceptance of customers and the consequences in the market and for marketing; and
- the business model, costs and payback time.

Within the conceptual phase attention to these strategic aspects also has to be set out in a management document in which the plan is summarized. This should include a summary of the plan, the business model (costs/overview of yield and payback time) as well as an investment proposal as total overview.

Review the preconditions for an Internet strategy

Based on the model in Table 13.2 the preconditions of the Internet strategy can be determined. These preconditions consist of the company objectives, the marketing strategy and objectives as well as the determination of the internal and external conditions.

Review the external possibilities

When determining the external possibilities the market is investigated, including an analysis of the buying process of customers, the Internet strategy of the competition and the external possibilities of suppliers (approximate). It is important here to employ an outside-in focus. This involves finding out the market developments and possibilities as well as the buying process, and where the Internet can play a role (based on the ORCA model, see Table 13.4). For a further explanation of the ORCA model see Chapter 14.

Define the objectives of the Internet strategy

Determining the objectives on the basis of the external developments and the internal possibilities is, in fact, the concept that indicates the Internet strategy, the intended objectives and how these are to be realized. Part of this phase is a mock-up of the intended website and a navigation model. A rough description of the functions is also given.

Table 13.4 Application of the Internet within the buying process based on the ORCA model

Orientation	Research/information	Communication	Action
Information regarding the organization, Twitter, social media	Information regarding products, shop location, delivery information, user's information, product comparison	FAQs	Shop location
		Chat function	Supporting the buying process
Information regarding products		Social media	
		Email	Online shopping basket
Videos	Operation instructions	Blogs	Purchase confirmation
Animations	Guestbook	Webcams	Tracking and tracing
Links/AdWords	Blogs	Newsletters	Delivery confirmation
		Telephone	
Anonymous	Usually anonymous	Usually identified	Always identified

External review with possible clients

External review means that a general evaluation of the concept is carried out with possible suppliers, and a selection is made of possible partners for the development of the Internet proposition. These could include fulfilment partners, software suppliers, hosting and design suppliers and information suppliers.

RFP – a request for proposal

The RFP describes the concept as completely as possible on the basis of the intended objectives, the functions and the observed preconditions. An important part of the RFP is a scoping, whereby the dimensions are determined, such as the number of visitors, the maximum number of visitors at any one time, the number of orders per time period as well as the maximum number of orders per day, backup procedures, service levels (SLA), the update procedure, and payment and delivery procedures (time). This concludes the conceptual phase. The plan is written in detail, the dimensions determined and the objectives, processes and actions defined. A rough cost–benefit analysis is made as well; a specification can only be made once all the cost components are known and the suppliers have all submitted a quote. The end of this phase is an extensive request for proposal (RFP) as part of the conceptual plan.

An RFP is used in order to be able to compare various possible suppliers with one another. When comparing offers the pricing and the product or service supplied are often determining factors, but an RFP compares more than this. An RFP process provides a structure to the comparison process as it also looks at, for example, references, experience, offer conditions, working methods and guarantees for both quality and delivery dates. It is also possible to make a standard comparison between the various possible suppliers, as the response to the RFP is given in the same structure. An effective RFP gives information on what the business objectives are for the project, the principles and criteria, the growth path and the timing. Suppliers are also able to give specific detailed responses to the proposal by making suggestions and recommendations. An RFP is often a single step in the choice of suppliers. Sometimes the RFP is preceded by an RFI (request for information), whereby only information is asked for, and followed by an RFQ (request for quotation) whereby a specific quotation is requested.

Sometimes a longlist of potential suppliers is made to whom an RFI is sent. On the basis of the first selection, potential suppliers are requested to participate in the RFP (the shortlist), and in the final phase a comparison is made on the basis of an RFQ with a very small number of potential suppliers.

The advantage of an RFP is that it allows potential suppliers to be compared on objective grounds. Because of the RFP's structured approach the information is grouped in the same manner, which of course simplifies the comparison. What's more, the suppliers know that a choice will be made and that there are various potential suppliers, which will often lead to more competitive quotes being given. It is also clear that comparisons will be made on the basis of facts. There is no point in supplying vague or exaggerated information and irrelevant details.

The content of the RFP provides the potential supplier with an immediate source of information. In addition to the project details, information will also be given regarding the business, the history, the issues and the objectives of the project (as well as the financial objectives). A confidentiality clause is usually part of the RFP, the 'non disclosure agreement'. There is also a timetable for the RFP indicating by what date the response to the RFP has to be returned. This concerns the date on which a decision and firm agreements are made concerning the delivery dates.

13.3.2 Implementation phase

The implementation phase starts with the assessment of the RFP. The suppliers have given their feedback concerning the draft and on the questions that have been asked. A selection is made on the basis of the answers given. This selection also means: a choice for a central control role for the Internet department (the envisaged Internet manager), a choice between internal or external realization, and a choice between an external software package or in-house development. In addition, the necessary interface is determined, a detailed cost–benefit report made and the project plan drawn up. This forms the basis for the decision-making. If a positive decision is taken regarding the draft, the partners and the project plan, the implementation phase can start.

Table 13.5 provides a model which shows the focus of each phase during the implementation phase, then each phase is discussed separately.

Table 13.5 Phases and focus during the implementation phase

Phases	Focus
1. Drawing up project plan and appointing project team	Clearly defining responsibilities, activities, dependencies and decision points
2. Putting together technical team and technical realization	Building the system and interfaces, both back office and website
3. Forming department, hiring personnel and describing job profiles and responsibilities	Setting up operational user's environment, marketing communication and web management
4. Testing system, procedures, interfaces and concept	Testing all processes and functions and checking them against the objectives and the original concept and principles
5. Final review, possibly trying out test site	Last test of beta version before the system goes live. Often tested with a small group of users, but in a real-life situation
Management	*Involvement*
There is a steering group in which the manager with the final responsibility is chairman (and also responsible for the budget). The project manager and proposed e-commerce manager are members of the steering group. Sometimes there is also a sounding board group with users and other officials	Management (budget and realization) Project manager (progress and quality) e-Commerce (operational environment)
Management document	Management summary of the progress report including financial report
Final report	Completion document

Drawing up the project plan and appointing the project team

Phase 1 involves not only drawing up the project plan and appointing the project team, but also determining responsibilities, the timing of reports and a decision-making procedure. What's more, the members of the steering group are appointed which include at least the project manager and the person in charge of the budget.

In this first phase the contours of the project are determined, the roles and functions indicated and a timetable established. The interaction moments are also determined, that is to say the delivery dates at which the progress of the project is critical.

Putting together the technical team and technical realization

The technical realization takes place under the supervision of the project manager. Processes are described, including those that are related to other business functions. Reporting is defined, the dashboard determined and the analyses set down. This phase sees the actual building of the concept, the website, the underlying systems and the interfaces with functions, departments and supplier.

Forming the department, hiring personnel and describing job profiles and responsibilities

In phase 3 the department is formed, the personnel hired and trained, the communication determined, the triggers decided upon and the system loaded with text, pictures, videos and product information. In addition, photos of the products are added, links are made with suppliers and information sources added (such as RSS, really simple syndication).

Testing the system, procedures, interfaces and concept

In phase 4 the system is tested on the basis of functionality, performance, dialogue and interfaces. Trial orders are placed, mailings sent, analyses run and the dashboard tested. In addition, the system is presented to those involved in the Internet.

Final review, if necessary trying out the test site

A final review of the draft is carried out on the basis of the principles, the scoping and the dimensions; the plans, therefore, as set out in the conceptual phase. After this the site goes live, although this will perhaps be low profile, without too much publicity so that any teething problems can be remedied before the definite site goes live.

Box 13.1 Example contents of the RFP

- Introduction and objectives.
- RFP process.
- Objectives of the Internet strategy.
- Functional requirements front-end.
- Functional requirements back-end.

- Web architecture and design.
- Fulfilment requirements.
- Back office specification.
- Project implementation and timing.
- Service level agreements.
- Non-disclosure agreement.

13.3.3 Operational phase

In the operational phase everything has to run well. There will be regular consultations concerning the results. The basis for this is formed by the dashboard, the comprehensive analyses and the developed scorecard. A regular technical performance check will also be carried out. Each year the concept has to be evaluated on the basis of (visitor) experiences, market developments and technical developments.

The structure of a typical standard Internet department is shown in Figure 13.2. It includes the following functions and departments:

- *the e-commerce manager*: a manager with a great deal of marketing knowledge and experience in (direct) communication as well as experience of and an affinity with new media;
- *a communication manager*: initiates the communication, manages (triggers) and reports, and is responsible for the sales results; and
- *a webmaster*: is responsible for the website, for the content (the content management system, the CMS) and design as well as the layout of the information, and for keeping it up to date.

The department may be complemented by a support department, which provides customer support and support to suppliers of products and services, and by an analysis and reporting department that constantly analyses the website, generates real-time actions and provides an overview of the results.

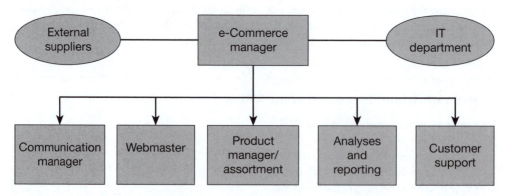

Figure 13.2 Possible Internet department

Table 13.6 Phases and focus during the operational phase

Phases	Focus
1. Organization	The organization has to think from the perspective of the customer. The focus is on direct, regular and targeted communication with the customer
2. Marketing	A cross-channel approach whereby the Internet is focused on the customer and the shop aims to support the Internet or the Internet supports the shop. There has to be some sort of recognition and the direct customer approach can also take place in the shop or together with the shop. Part of marketing must also be: increasing customer satisfaction, stimulating return behaviour, and being distinctive in relation to the competition and continuing to be so
3. Reporting/analysis	Continuous analyses on customer-based key performance indicator. Reporting must be action-oriented. There is a distinction between operational analyses, which are always immediately accessible, and complex analyses, which are made regularly. For the direct decision-making the operational analyses are important in order to be able to modify direct actions and campaigns. For the regular reports the analyses are tested against the scorecard and the indicated key performance indicator and strategy

Technical responsibility will usually not be part of this Internet department's remit but will be under the IT department or an external hosting partner. Logistics, finance and payment services also fall outside the scope of this department.

The model in Table 13.6 shows the emphasis for each phase of the operational phase.

13.4 The place of the Internet strategy within marketing

The Internet strategy is closely related to the marketing and sales strategy. The Internet strategy is part of the marketing strategy for the market positioning and marketing activities and of the sales strategy for direct communication and online sales. The communications and the marketing activities have to be univocal. The information on the site regarding the organization has to be in line with the information that the marketing department disseminates among other media. The Internet strategy has to be part of the marketing plan (as a submodule).

The sales plan also has to describe the Internet as a submodule. Customers use the Internet for orientation, information and sometimes also to buy. The sales department has to describe the application of the Internet from the perspective of sales. These two submodules – marketing and sales – are integrated within the Internet strategy, which includes various aspects such as design, updating, fulfilment and management.

In order to make an objective choice of partners, an RFP has to be set up. Here one should look not only at the costs (price) but also at all aspects that are important within the Internet. Based on the choice of suppliers an implementation plan is formulated and the strategy realized.

Summary

- The application of the Internet within an organization cannot be isolated within a particular department or function.
- Because of the large impact that the Internet has on external relationships, the Internet must be part of the marketing strategy.

- The management board and management must be directly involved in the decision-making concerning Internet applications. The website is an organization's calling card for external parties as well as other business functions, and the organization must adapt itself to the changes.

14 Applications of the Internet

As we have seen in Part 3, the Internet offers various functions; communication, information and commerce are the most important, but there is also the supporting, facilitative function. These functions are based on the users of the Internet and therefore also on the relationship between the information provision and the user. When developing a strategy for the application of the Internet one must always take into consideration the aim of the Internet use, what a user uses the Internet for and how this relationship can be optimized. This means that there has to be some insight not only into the user of or the visitor to the website but also into how the Internet fits within the organization and its commercial strategies. This chapter will take a closer look at these aspects; the purpose of the Internet user will be analysed first, followed by the application potentials for businesses.

14.1 Why does someone visit a website?

The reason why someone visits a website depends on the aim. This may be:

- a commercial aim (to buy something);
- an information aim (to find something out); or
- a communication aim.

14.1.1 The commercial aim

Businesses want to sell something while customers wish to buy. This may seem the same thing, but in practice they each require a totally different approach; after all, they are two sides of the same process. If a business wishes to sell something it investigates the application possibilities of the marketing instruments and activities. The business is then highly focused on bringing about a transaction: how can customers be motivated to buy? Price is an important marketing instrument for realizing this, certainly when it is linked to a product. Through advertising, the price and the product perception are communicated and customers are stimulated to buy. In retail the location and product range play an important role in attracting customers. But are these also the reasons why customers buy on the Internet?

In the physical world customers usually buy from a local shop, often routinely, such as with convenience goods, or in the town centre such as with shopping goods. In all these cases the action radius of the customer is important (based on mobility). What's more, products are sometimes bought on impulse (for example, because of a discount); these may be spontaneous purchases or even semi-conscious purchases, where the customer is actually planning to buy, but a motivation is still required. The questions that the potential buyer asks the seller are part of a motivation process. The customer is persuaded to buy this particular product. The physical process of the sale is a contact between the seller and buyer, and between the product and the buyer. Elements that play a prominent role in this are therefore the environment (location and product range), the seller (trust and expertise) and the presence of the product (seeing, feeling, smelling).

Selling versus buying

On the Internet the buying process is different. The customer does not come across the product by accident, the seller is not physically there and the environment is different (at home or at the office). As a result, the buying experience for a customer is totally different; but the possibilities for a seller are different, too. The seller does not see the customer, cannot respond to questions or body language and the product cannot be shown physically. Another important factor, which can be disruptive, is that the customer has to wait for the product when buying on the Internet: it has to be sent to the buyer's (home) address. Often the products still have to be made or finished off before they can be sent. There is therefore a time interval between buying and use.

Because of the various functions of the Internet as well as the differences in the use of the Internet, there will be an interaction between the use of the Internet and the purchasing of products. This interaction may be that the Internet does everything, from the very first (buying) intention up to the purchase itself; that the Internet only has a supporting role in the purchase in the shop, through information and perhaps also through communication; and in some cases (for example, with convenience goods) the Internet may not play any role whatsoever. With the Internet one has to think about the buying process, and for each phase it has to be determined what function the Internet has for a customer.

This buying process can be represented in an ORCA model:

- *Orientation*: This is the first phase in which a customer becomes aware of a potential need and begins to explore the possibility of buying something. This orientation can be conscious but also subconscious by just asking questions during a conversation.
- *Research*: This is the information phase in which a customer searches for information by going from shop to shop, looking at products and acquiring information. But the Internet is also used for consciously looking for information, by surfing, googling or by visiting websites and comparison sites.
- *Communication*: In this phase the purchase is seriously considered and very specific purchase information is asked regarding the product, the price, the services or the delivery times.
- *Action*: In this phase the product is bought, on the Internet at the webshop or in the physical (local) shop.

All these steps can be taken on the Internet – where the customer takes the leading role – but also without the Internet, where a customer is led by what is on offer in the shops and the information given by the sellers. A combination is also possible, where a customer decides what the Internet is used for (often information, but also buying) and what is done in the physical shop (often communication and the purchase). It will be clear that this multichannel approach for the customer plays an important role in the buying process. These days the Internet is integrated within this buying process. Because of the accessibility of the Internet and its simplicity of use, approximately 80 per cent of buyers of shopping goods go first onto the Internet to find out information and people's experiences with a product before deciding to buy. The purchase itself usually still takes place in the shop (out of habit). It is expected that in the next few years the Internet will mature to such a degree that the distinction between physical shops and virtual shops fades away. It is expected that in a few years' time between 35 per cent and 40 per cent of the purchases of shopping goods will take place on the Internet.

The impact of the Internet, however, is much greater during the buying process because already now 80 per cent of people, but soon almost everyone, use the Internet as a medium for information and communication. On the basis of the buying behaviour a model can be designed for this (Figure 14.1).

The classification in Figure 14.1 is based on the Myers-Briggs Type Indicator (see for example www.myersbriggs.org and www.raymondklompsma.nl) which makes a distinction between people's behaviour and their buying behaviour. This buying behaviour can in turn be projected onto the behaviour on the Internet, and a distinction made between four types of visitors: competitive, spontaneous, humanistic (based on feeling) and methodical.

- *Competitive visitors*: These prefer to make a decision quickly based on facts. They ask themselves as they visit a website why they should be there, they wonder whether the site is credible and how it can help them realize their goals. Amazon.com serves these visitors by providing on its website a short summary of the author, book, price and delivery time. For the competitive visitor this is sufficient information on which to base a decision.
- *Spontaneous visitors*: These tend to decide on the basis of emotion. They are not easily distracted by facts, but rely upon their feelings. They consider it important that a product can be tailored to their own wishes. Good service is important. They respond well to special offers and promotions. Amazon.com serves these visitors by offering books at interesting discounts. The spontaneous visitor will be keen to take advantage of this.
- *Humanistic visitors*: Although humanistic visitors base their decisions on emotion, their decisions are well thought-out. They like to know the company behind the website. The

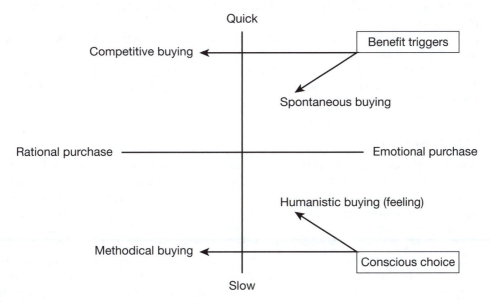

Figure 14.1 Buying model

experiences of others are very important. Why should I trust you and who actually uses your products? These are typical questions for the humanistic visitor. Amazon.com serves these people by providing book reviews on its website, but also by showing what other people bought within the same category.

- *Methodical visitors*: These take their time in making their decisions that are based on facts. These visitors are curious about the entire process and the background to the product. They do not rush into making a decision. They make deliberate choices and like to see testimonials and guarantees. Amazon.com offers these visitors the possibility of reading a number of pages of a certain book before the actual purchase. The methodical visitor will then sleep on it after which they will decide whether or not to buy the book.

Source: www.raymondklompsma.nl

The rest of this subsection will look at the decision-making process, the guided choice and the buying process.

The decision-making process

Buying depends on the type of product and the type of customer. Based on the buying process of a customer, a distinction can be made between an emotional purchase and a rational purchase (a conscious purchase) and between a quick decision maker and a slow decision maker. These types are shown in Figure 14.1. Customers who buy slowly are also conscious customers who clearly first want to consider what they want, and need to be motivated to buy this product. These customers will have to be informed well. Often they will also want to acquire as much information as possible, go from shop to shop in their search for information, look at products and talk with the sales staff before making a decision. Expertise and trust is very important for these customers. The role of the Internet during this buying process will mainly be aimed at the information function. Armed with the information that they have gained through the Internet they will go to the shop to check whether the information that they have found themselves is correct. They have a strong preference for buying from shops that they trust.

With this knowledge, based on information from the Internet, they will make a rational purchase; but with the knowledge and the persuasion skills of the salesperson, the right atmosphere and the right motivation there will also be an element of an emotional purchase. The salesperson will have to add to this and use the right arguments. Figure 14.2 shows this schematically.

Guided choice, triggers

Not all purchases are conscious purchases by any means. Convenience purchases, for example, are often routine purchases; in these cases there is therefore not a conscious buying process. Other purchases may, however, involve quick decisions or an emotional wish to buy a particular product *now* (impulse buying). Selling triggers can have a good stimulating effect on this type of purchase. For the rational motives incentives such as price as well as 'buy now', or 'only in combination with this product' or 'buy before 10 o'clock in the morning' help. For emotional purchases the triggers are often aimed at a special design, a special product, the presence of a celebrity, a good salesperson, pleasant music or other emotional triggers. The buyers make a quick decision regarding the purchase and tend not to go to another shop to see whether the product is cheaper there. For the buyers the time is *now* (and

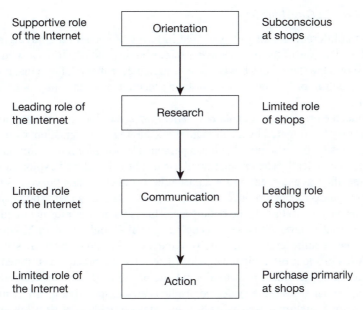

Figure 14.2 Relationship between the Internet and a shop within the buying process

therefore also for the salesperson). The role of the Internet will therefore be essentially different and will depend very much on the extent to which the customer is Internet-oriented. Figure 14.3 illustrates the distinction between high and low Internet orientation.

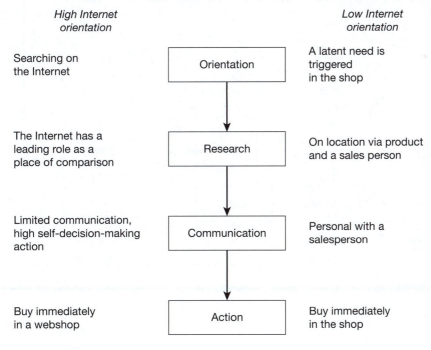

Figure 14.3 The buying process

Buying process: the ORCA model

The role of the Internet can also be analysed in terms of steps in the buying process (the ORCA model). The role of the Internet in conscious buying can be shown in a buying model. This model shows the steps that a buyer goes through before making the actual purchase. The last step – the action or buying step – can take place either in the shop or on the Internet (Figure 14.4).

In this model the orientation is explained in the first phase. This can be conscious, because the customer may be triggered by a comment while having a conversation, by a chat session or through a website. It is also possible that a person is looking for more information without going into too much depth. The orientation phase is a little bit like an exploration phase, but there is no specific buying intention for a particular product. A latent need is stimulated. In the orientation phase it is determined whether or not this need is real. The latent need may then disappear once more or become opportune. This is when the information phase begins.

This phase usually starts with a search engine such as Google, Bing or Yahoo!. The need is shown in a few specific terms. The search engine gives links to relevant sites and the search can begin. A brand site is often visited quickly. The selection process has started and a number of products are selected. A visit to a brand site has to lead to a motivation to buy these products. On comparison sites the selected products are compared rationally with one other. Chat features are sometimes used as well. These days quickly writing a few messages on Twitter is enough to get quite a few tips. Webshops are visited to look at the product range, the price and the alternatives. The preferred webshop is often determined on the basis of the

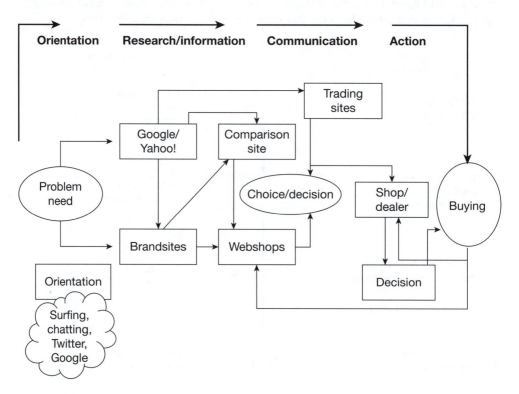

Figure 14.4 ORCA model

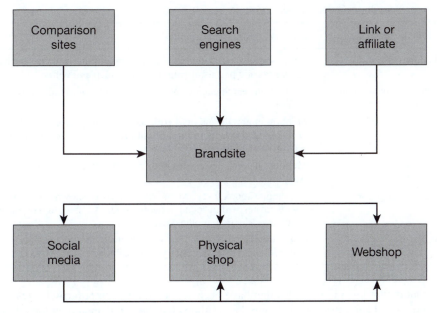

Figure 14.5 Traffic flow in the buying process

links given by the search engine, but even more so by the links at trading places, affiliate sites and on comparison sites. A business therefore has to ensure that it has a ranking on these three in order to get hits for its own website; this often has to be paid for through an adlink, adword or a price per click. Figure 14.5 shows this in diagram form.

No purchase without comparison

The Internet is increasingly being used as a source of information when buying products. More than 90 per cent of consumers go online to get advice on certain articles before making their purchase on- or offline.

The order of shops that offer a particular product on price comparison sites is based on price, with the cheapest supplier at the top of the list. The webshops are therefore unable to influence their position on a comparison site except with their sale price.

Reputation is a very important and valuable factor for webshops and manufacturers. Consumers are able to share their experiences with reviews concerning a particular product or webshop. These reviews are often accompanied by scores or ratings. They make the service of the shops more tangible and the choice whether or not to buy a particular product easier. A team of content specialists check all the reviews on their reliability and content before they are published on the website.

A number of criteria are important for a comparison site:

* The shop must be easily accessible.
* The shop needs to have been registered with the Chamber of Commerce for at least one year.
* The website has to have been active for at least six months.
* Consumers (before buying a product) have to be able to find contact details, payment methods and shipping costs on the site.

Table 14.1 Phases in the buying process (ORCA model)

Phases in the buying process	Contact possibility of supplier
Orientation phase	Chat rooms, social networks, mention on popular websites such as news sites and portals, mention in chats such as Twitter
Research/information phase	Mention in search engines but also high in the ranking and with AdWords
	Mention in portals and marketplace(s) both in AdWords and with the affiliates section with referral possibilities or mention in search sections on the site
	Mention in comparison sites both with the ranking and with AdWords, banners
Communication phase	Action guestbook, user groups, social networks, own user groups, own websites within social networks such as LinkedIn, Hyves and Facebook. Mention at other user groups
Action phase	Quick buying processes, 'buy now' buttons on relevant sites, link with affiliates (offer direct buying possibility)

Shops that do not keep to the rules that have been set down may temporarily be suspended or even removed from these sites. Not only webshops see the value, manufacturers, too, see the benefits of comparison sites. In the past manufacturers were not very keen to have their name linked to a comparison site. Many comparison sites focused primarily on price comparisons.

An important point for the sales moment is *clarity*. Be clear in the method of delivery and payment. Ensure that the indicated delivery time and stock information is accurate and that consumers receive their products within the time they expect. Being able to view the status of the order gives customers the sense that they have some control over their orders. This applies to the payment methods as well. Be clear about the costs involved for a particular payment method as these sometimes vary quite a bit. Ensure that the customers know in advance where they stand.

Table 14.1 shows the phases in the buying process based on the ORCA model.

Based on the products offered by the webshop and the acquired information a customer can decide whether to buy the product directly online or to first go to a shop to have a look at the product. The urgency of having the product, the available time, and the trust in the web-shop and the product play an important role in whether a person buys on the Internet or in a shop. Based on these considerations a company with a webshop can determine its own strategy for removing these barriers. The buying criteria of the customers are:

- *The degree of necessity*: necessary immediately (shop), necessary quickly (shop or the Internet), no rush (the Internet is preferred).
- *The time available*: little (the Internet), limited (the Internet or shop), plenty (the shop is preferred).
- *Trust*: plenty (the Internet is preferred), limited (the Internet or shop), little (the shop is preferred).

A webshop has to respond to these buying criteria with information, trust and convenience. This can be done in various ways, as shown in Table 14.2.

Physical shops also have to respond to these buying criteria in order to attract customers and not lose them to webshops (Table 14.3).

Table 14.2 Internet response to the various buying criteria

Buying criteria	Internet response
No local presence	Home delivery or delivery at fixed service points. Can also open up a physical location
Necessity for customer	Quick ordering procedures, speedy delivery, collection service. Order today, delivered tomorrow
Little time	Simple ordering process, customer recognition
Little trust	Home-shopping guarantee hallmark, various payment methods, including payment upon delivery such as COD and giro slip, good navigation, guestbook and a physical collection point
No physical contact	Intensive communication and customer recognition, both by email and on site. Keeping a record of customer data and buying history

Table 14.3 Response of physical shops to the various buying criteria

Buying criteria	Response of physical shops
Physical presence	Open more smaller shops in small town centres and neighbourhoods. Offer a limited product range (bestsellers); the other products can be ordered online (also in the shop) and collected the next day
Necessity for customer	Quick delivery of Internet orders, which can also be collected in the shop. The customer would therefore not have to wait for the logistics service provider (click and collect facility)
Little time	The same solutions linked to the Internet. The combination of the Internet and physical shops (many smaller shops) is a strong concept
Little trust	The customer can see and touch the products, and the salesperson can provide good support. As with the Internet, here, too, a 'no questions asked money back guarantee' within 14 days
Feeling/emotion	Emotion in the shop, Internet access in the shop with specific terminals for customers and sales staff. Later also 'near field communication' facilities, 'augmented reality' and very specific 'narrowcasting'. Integrate physical with virtual and add emotion. Shopping has to be fun too!

14.1.2 Research/information

The buying process and the need for information often go hand in hand. This is why so many businesses provide information on their website not only on the product itself but also on its use. In some cases a separate website is made in response to this need for information. Physiotherapists, for example, set up a special information site about physical ailments, complaints related to old age or sports injuries. As a result not only does this position them high on the Google hit list (due to the number of hits and the number of referrals), but their authority is enhanced, too. By including a hyperlink to the site of the practice, this directly also leads to more customers (patients). Another example is the Dutch site www. onrustigebaby.nl which provides information on restless babies, such as babies that cry constantly, which is a common problem for young parents. This target group would tend to go and search on the Internet first when looking for information about this problem. The target group is people between the ages of 25 and 40, a group characterized by their intensive Internet use. In addition to the information on the site there is also a link to a site that provides specific products for babies that cry excessively (as well as other products). Here, too, we see a combination of information and products in separate sites that are linked to one another.

We will now examine information sites in more detail and take a closer look at user-generated content.

Information sites

The combination of information sites with commercial sites offers many possibilities. The information sites can, for example, have more links, which results not only in the ranking going up but also possibly more income being generated. The information sites can develop into a portal, through which suppliers (not competitors) can offer their services regarding this particular theme. The party that starts this process can keep control of it and ensure that the information is in line with the product or the service that is primarily being offered, and that the competition are not included on the site. It is important for the visitor that everything comes across as authentic and honest.

It is the separation of information from commercial services that leads to an objective perception among customers, and consequently also to a higher return visit percentage. Visitors will remember the site or add it to their bookmarks or favourites, and carry on returning if there is a specific need for information, such as regarding injuries or products. Brand manufacturers as well as large retailers benefit from developing such sites alongside their own site or by joining other market leaders that have a similar site. This helps to generate traffic to their own website – a 'spider in the web' concept. This is also the idea behind being mentioned on a comparison site. Visitors are looking for information and product comparisons, and are then also given links for the next step in the buying process: communication and purchasing.

In addition to commercial information sites, both direct and indirect, there are also general information sites, which only provide information and possibly also mention sources. This information can be found in libraries, news sites and news sections and in online encyclopaedias. The encyclopaedia Wikipedia, which is generated by the users themselves, is particularly popular for general information and has taken over the role of the traditional encyclopaedia, but with the limitation of having user-generated content.

Wikipedia

Wikipedia is a project of the non-profit organization Wikimedia Foundation, based in Florida, USA. The aim of Wikipedia is to create a free Internet encyclopaedia in every language. Under the umbrella of the Wikimedia Foundation there are various multi-language projects, of which Wikipedia is the oldest, most well known and most successful. The name Wikipedia is a linguistic blend (portmanteau) of the Hawaiian word *wiki* and the Greek *encyclopaedia*.

The articles included in this encyclopaedia, which is actually written on the Internet, are considered to take a neutral standpoint. In theory, Wikipedia can be edited by anyone in good faith. And this is also why Wikipedia cannot give any guarantees regarding the correctness and balanced quality of the information provided. What's more, due to the open nature of the project vandalism can be a problem to a greater or lesser degree.

The Dutch version can be found at nl.wikipedia.org and contains more than 580000 articles. The English version is the largest, with 3100000 articles. On 15 January 2010 more than 14 million articles in 271 different languages can be found on the entire Wikipedia.

In general usage, a wiki (such as in Wikipedia) is a web application that allows web documents to be edited jointly. The term originates from the Hawaiian term *wiki wiki*, which means quick, speedy or agile. WikiWikiWeb (also known as Ward's Wiki) was the first wiki application ever written. It was developed in 1994 by Ward Cunningham in order to simplify the exchange of ideas between software programmers. It was based on ideas developed in HyperCard stacks that he developed in the late 1980s. He was also the first to link the wiki application Ward's Wiki to a server.

Encyclopaedia sites have the same goal, but can be of a better quality as the information on these sites is verified by experts. Wikipedia does have a team of experts who try to ensure that the information submitted is of value to Wikipedia and its visitors. Commercial information, for example, is not permitted in any form whatsoever.

User-generated content

Keeping information up to date is very time-consuming. We often see websites being launched with relevant information, but then afterwards nothing more is done to them. But information can become obsolete all too easily. It takes a great deal of effort to keep the information current and companies very often do not see the point of this. There are then a number of possibilities open to them: linking with other sites, RSS feeds or user-generated content.

With a link to another site use can be made of news services that offer the information as a subscription. These suppliers then supply specific sections or categories on the site and maintain the information sites for third parties. Another possibility is to do this automatically by linking certain subjects to another site, which automatically uploads the information. These are RSS feeds. Information sites, such as news reports, sports sites and technology sites ensure that subscribers are kept informed of the latest developments. This information – the RSS feed – can then be sent to a smartphone or computer. On the site the RSS feed is a separate section so that any new information can be constantly available on the information site without any kind of involvement. The visitor to the site is often informed that this information is an RSS feed from a third party, but this is not essential. In this way visitors can continuously be attracted with up-to-date information from third parties.

The information – the news – is made for a particular party, but with the aim of making it in syndication, and therefore suitable for various websites. This can be done by modifying the format accordingly – RSS (really simple syndication) or simple simultaneous publication. An RSS feed on a site can often be recognized by the orange XML block, or the blue RDF block. Sometimes the abbreviation is mentioned in the text – XML, RSS or RDF.

But there is also the option of allowing the visitors themselves to publish information on the site. This is often done on technical support sites where users try to resolve problems in discussion through publishing standard solutions on the site or through a blog. With blogs visitors can leave behind information that other visitors can then consult. The site administrator needs to provide the section and a good search functionality. This saves the technical helpdesk a great deal of time. Some information sites about books (Amazon.com, Barnes and Noble) provide the possibility of reviews. This allows readers to publish their opinions of a book (or a film). Such reviews help a potential buyer in making a decision. Also sites where emotion plays a role, such as sports sites, often have blogs where the fans can share information or thoughts with one another. Sometimes separate sites are made as well, such as fan sites or even hate sites. Like-minded people can then tell one another about their feelings and load photos, videos or cartoons onto the site. This is a form of social media and did indeed lead to the establishment of special social media sites such as Facebook, YouTube and LinkedIn. The implications of social media sites as part of a marketing strategy are discussed in Chapter 18.

Today photos, videos and cartoons are also loaded onto public sites, such as YouTube, and the video clips themselves become a source of search possibilities and information. As a result, YouTube, for example, is often also used as an alternative for the text-based site Google. This also demonstrates the shift that is taking place towards user-generated content in the search for information. The text-based sites on which the Internet was founded are increasingly being replaced by sites that offer audio, video and moving images. These can be on the websites themselves, but also through special sites. The website www. hetnieuwewinkelen.com, for example, is entirely based on videos. Brief summaries of the books are given, whilst interviews provide more information on the subject. Dynamism is guaranteed by the interviews. By regularly posting new interviews the site stays up to date and provides a reason for visitors to come back. This is a new development for websites: images and sound instead of text.

14.1.3 Communication

Information is often presented in the form of text. This comes from the time-honoured art of printing, in which text was the method for sharing information with others. Later, images (in addition to drawings) were added. Again at a later stage photos were added. This was the situation in standard advertising through the printed media.

Online media, such as radio and television, gave us another other way of transmitting information, namely words and sound as well as moving pictures, although we were constrained to specific, medium-determined circumstances. You needed to have a radio for the sound and then a television for the moving pictures.

Because of the limited capacity of the early computers (until the mid 1990s) and the limitations of data transport (until the early twenty-first century) our ability to communicate and provide information via computers was constrained. The companies that specialized in developing websites in the 1990s were often directly or indirectly affiliated to advertising agencies (communication agencies). In view of the limitations of the technology and experience of these companies the websites were strongly text-based. Even these days this is still the case. Text as a form of communication originates from the printed media, but the Internet is different from the printed media in many ways:

- Reading text on a computer screen is not always easy.
- The dialogue with the reader is different on a computer screen (short sentences).
- Scrolling can lead to irritation as the text cannot be displayed in one go.
- The visitor is searching for highly specific information that has to be offered as concisely as possible.

Texts and text-based sites on the Internet do have certain advantages:

- The sites load quickly and are easy to navigate.
- It is possible to have links to pictures and video.

- It is possible to insert hypertexts, which allows for highly specific searching based on associations.

It is important that websites are geared towards the 'restless visitor'. The information that is presented in text form must be brief and clear. The essentials must be clear within a few sentences, and if the visitor wants more information he or she should be able to click on a link in order to access a larger document. The use of hyperlinks makes the document multifunctional. The user is then able to personalize the information. The use of hyperlinks in the text is to be encouraged – they give the opportunity to support the text with images and videos, giving visitors the ability to choose their preferred medium.

Online chat, videoconferences and free phone calls

Since 2008 we have seen a breakthrough the functionality of video contact. This can now take place through Skype for direct contact or teleconferencing software for direct online communication, but also (delayed) via videos on websites and specific sites (of which YouTube.com is the most well known). In particular the ability of the new generation of video cameras to enable a direct link with a computer provided a breakthrough. It is now possible for everyone to quickly make a video and upload it to their preferred website. Within two years on YouTube more than 1 billion videos have been viewed. These videos can be searched and selected according to subject and tags. These tags in turn are grouped (and associated) so that the videos are easy to find. In addition to the direct search possibilities, related videos that meet the same conditions are constantly being offered. This responds to the thinking of the visitor, who is increasingly focused on associations.

The manner in which the communication takes place is also responded to. Communication via written text is not necessarily the best form of communication. Reading text is a skill that is learnt (usually at school) and the interpretation of text is also a skill in itself. People are, however, familiar with auditory and visual communication, which is a typically human form of communication. Through the Internet it is possible to disseminate information in this manner to a large public. The technology facilitates the possibility and the visitor interprets the sound and images. The younger generation in particular has a strong preference for this form of communication; after all, this is the world in which they live. The older generation have been trained in communicating through the written word and although they may prefer sound and images, text is the form of communication with which they are familiar.

In the future it is likely we will see considerable developments in video communication, and YouTube.com and similar sites will be important channels. For commercial suppliers it has become increasingly important to have a presence on YouTube and to provide information via video. It is easy to incorporate this commercial application by making a link on the company's website to its video on YouTube.com.

Communication is often very specifically aimed at a personal contact with a company, sometimes to ask a question but also to share a comment. Guestbooks allow customers to do this, giving them the chance to indicate whether or not they are satisfied. Guestbooks can be consulted by others, who can then contribute to a positive image of the organization.

Within the need for communication we also see certain specific needs, such as on the user group sites and social media. Both applications are based on communication, but they also serve a common purpose. This common purpose may be highly specific, but it may also be latent or not present at all. Examples of this are the user groups where users inform one another about applications, make known their complaints or give tips. Sometimes all they want to do is talk about a specific subject. Examples of this are the chat features concerning football clubs, car makes or other brands. Customers talk, discuss and inform one another because they share, for example, a hobby, a product or a passion for a particular club.

Another specific purpose can be to maintain contact with one another. Social media are good examples of this. Within a social medium, groups are formed around themes or people. With Facebook, friends networks are formed around people, which can also overlap one another. The idea of this is to keep in contact with one another as efficiently as possible, but also to see what others within the network are doing. Another purpose is to be able to follow one another; in the real world you can lose contact with people, but with Facebook you can always be found.

14.2 Social media

Using social media Internet users can look for one another very deliberately. This can be done interactively in chat rooms or via chat sites such as Twitter. But it can also be done passively via registration sites such as www.linkedin.com, www.hyves.nl, www.facebook.com and many other varieties of these. Like-minded people who have similar goals and have something in common search for one another via sites where other like-minded people come and where there is no special control function by third parties.

Web 2.0 and social media are often used interchangeably because the functionalities of Web 2.0 are often incorporated within social media. There are, however, clear differences between Web 2.0 and social media. Web 2.0 implies that not only is there a special focus for the practicability of interaction and user-generated content, but also that the technology used by the Web services support interaction. Social media have been around far longer than Web 2.0; they just started to use the Web 2.0 technology when it first became available. Bulletin boards such as those that were used in the 1980s were already examples of social media. In the early years of the Internet (the 1990s) these bulletin boards were an important element of the Internet. Because of the technology social media merely became more advanced and were applied more widely.

The following distinctions can be made between the various forms of social media:

- private versus business;
- information versus interaction; and
- personal-oriented versus theme-oriented.

The entirety of social media can be illustrated in diagram form as shown in Figure 14.6.

14.2.1 Private versus business

There has to be a reason to take part in a social network. With respect to the private individual possible reasons would include the interests of the person or the wish to keep in contact with people. Examples of private social networks are Hyves and Facebook, which are used to stay in contact with others. In addition, there are many sites where information is shared or where interaction takes place around hobbies, interests or other common factors (such as politics, sex or parenting). These sites are also suitable for commercial purposes, providing the product or the service fits in with the expectations of the participant. Themed sites may incorporate additional services that fit in with that particular theme, perhaps commercial services as well. This is more difficult with sites that are aimed at maintaining contact with

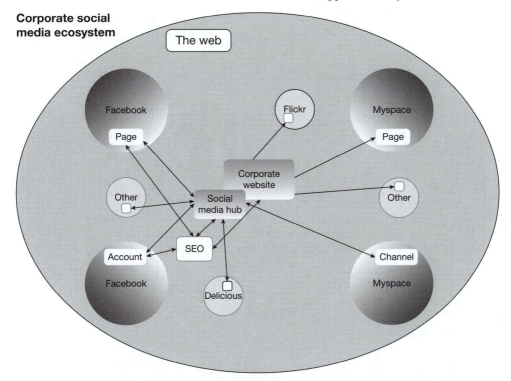

Figure 14.6 The social media marketing ecosystem

Source: http://davefleet.com/2010/01/2010-social-media-marketing-ecosystem/

others. Visitors come for the contact (communication with others) and not for information or links to commercial sites. Care therefore has to be observed when placing commercial messages or links to a site that is intended for social contact. This can cause so much irritation among the visitors that it can have an adverse effect.

It is also possible to form personal groups within these sites. The perception of a brand (product or shop) can be so great that a person may want to be in contact with that brand or other fans of the brand. A fan site within a private social network gives a company a good opportunity to get to know their customers and to maintain contact with loyal customers. Areas of interest based on profession, position or company can also be successful with commercial social media such as www.linkedin.com or www.plaxo.com. On the basis of these groups specific information or commercial messages can be displayed. The members will also appreciate regular messages.

The formation of social media is illustrated in Figure 14.7.

14.2.2 Information versus interaction

A social network enables interaction as well as the sharing and provision of information. For sites that are aimed at users of a certain (technical) product, support and information often already creates a sense of belonging, as does keeping the users informed of updates of certain products. Technical support, help in the event of viruses and user information are all aspects of such a site. The GPS technology company Garmin, for example, allows all its users to read

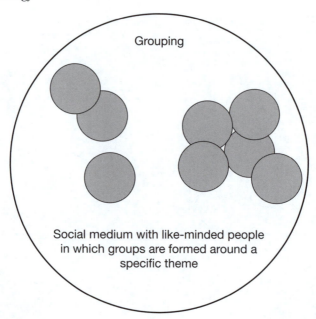

Figure 14.7 The formation of social media

out the data from its equipment and keep it available for later reference. Users of the Garmin sports watch 'Forerunner' can automatically save the information that the watch saved during a training session (heart rate, intensity of the exercise and the course covered) on their own page on the company's website. This allows a training session to be analysed and compared with other training sessions. If desired, the user also can share the information on a certain route with others.

This facility is also a strong component of the site www.myasics.com. Various runners can keep records on a particular route, supplemented with specific data, and share the information with other runners.

The commercial possibilities of these types of social networks are based on the products and services of the supplier. In both cases there is no capacity to interact, although this would be possible technically.

14.2.3 Personal versus themed

At personal sites people wish to see others and keep in contact. Examples of this are Facebook and Hyves, as well as LinkedIn and Plaxo. After registering on such a platform you can include your personal information on the site and publish photos on your profile. The various relationship sites are also examples of social networks that have the purpose of allowing people to meet and follow one another if they so wish. Through the built-in communication and chat function it is possible for participants to keep one another informed of what they are doing and stay in contact. You may of course be looking for a relationship, but these sites can also be regarded as friends sites. They provide the possibility of becoming friends with like-minded people and maintaining these friendships.

LinkedIn is more to do with business contacts. This allows you to keep track of business colleagues even when they change jobs or alter their contact details. In fact, LinkedIn can be seen as a replacement of the old card index box, but in a modern form with new function-alities. It fulfils the wish to be visible and traceable; this can be necessary if you are looking for a new job or another assignment. Headhunters frequently use these sites. It is relatively easy to find candidates that meet a certain profile. Also people who would like to find another job or who are self-employed or small businesses looking for new assignments actively keep their profile up to date and ensure that they remain visible. These types of sites have limited commercial applications for third parties.

Eight tips for approaching people on LinkedIn:

1. Your subject line must be gripping and personal.
2. Introduce yourself properly, just as in real life.
3. Write a personal message, possibly alluding to something you have in common.
4. Explain why you are approaching the person.
5. Do not tell everything, but refer to one or two interesting aspects. Your purpose is not to inform 100 per cent, but to stimulate a response.
6. Do not place the ball in the other person's court, but ask when and where you can contact him or her. After all, you want something from them.
7. You can quickly find personal information on Google or websites such as www.wieowie. nl. (Make sure you have the right person; there are, for example, seven Cor Molenaars in the Netherlands. If you are looking for a general or popular name then refine your search question in Google.)
8. Check if the person has a Twitter account. Here the average Internet user tells more about what he or she is interested in or doing. Twitter is also useful for sending brief messages (but bear in mind that this is a public channel).

Source: www.sprout.nl, 8 March 2010

With themed sites it is a theme that is the binding factor. In this case suppliers can place commercial messages that are directly related to the theme without this causing irritation to the members. At football sites you therefore see information on football travel, football clinics and football gear. In addition, products and services that fit in with the user's profile can also be appropriate. For example, if many young men visit the sites, you can offer cloth-ing and videos, products that are in line with the interests of this group and that grab their attention.

14.3 Keeping in contact

The key to a successful Internet strategy is to encourage visitors to continually come back to the website of the supplier. With information sites this is possible as there is always some-thing new being added to them; commercial sites have to have a similar dynamism. This dynamism can be created by varying the product range or by having special offers. Within the fashion sector collections often change every month, so the collection on the site will also have to be changed. This, of course, has to be clearly shown on the site, and customers natu-rally have to be informed about it. One component of a successful Internet strategy is therefore also an active communication policy. This active policy may consist of:

- regular mailings, with a selection according to the type of customer;
- regular news reports; and
- on-site triggers.

The regular mailings to customers lead to customers visiting the site directly. The mailings do, however, have to be personal, both in the form of address and in the message. The best thing to do is to use the variable purchase data, that is to say what was bought in the past. This will make it more likely that this person will be stimulated to visit the site. Impersonal mailings that do not make use of this purchase history have a much lower response rate. A good example are the mailings of Amazon.com which refer to previous purchases.

The mailings can be created specifically without a follow-up action being planned. These single-shot mailings are often theme-oriented: a Christmas mailing, a spring mailing or a summer mailing. The content of the mailing has to refer to this particular theme.

A multi-shot campaign can, of course, also be developed, whereby follow-up actions are planned immediately. These follow-up actions consist of reminder mailings if there has been no response or if it has not led to a visit to the site (or if the person has visited the site but has not bought anything). A CHAID analysis is made of the response and non-response, and a reminder can be prepared that is sent at set times in the event of non-response (Figure 14.8).

The main mailing and the sub-mailings are generated on the basis of the buyer profile, using purchasing history or past communication behaviour. As a result, the main mailing can consist of many variants. The variation therefore entails the specific customer variables.

In addition to direct communication, a multimedia campaign may also be opted for. The themed communication in that case takes place through traditional media such as newspapers and television, but is also simultaneously followed up by direct communication such as described above.

An advanced form of direct communication is campaign management. Campaign management consists of a number of components:

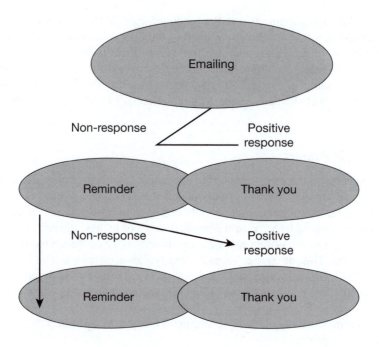

Figure 14.8 Response analysis and communication

- the campaigns;
- the triggers; and
- the analyses.

The campaign is based on a main campaign and is supported by sub-campaigns, based on the trigger response and non-response. Typical here is the trigger non-response and the follow-up in communication. This is actually a simple form of triggered communication. The analyses that result from this are mainly response analyses and yield analyses.

Another form of campaign management is based around triggers on the basis of behaviour – behavioural targeting campaigns. The behaviour can consist of not only historical buying behaviour, based on past purchases, but also 'buying moments', where the time interval between the buying moment and now is the trigger. If, for example, the customer has not bought anything in the last two months, a mailing is sent; if there is no response to this then a special offer can be sent, for example, after a month. This also involves standard communication, but now the trigger is a time interval. Such triggers could also be the date at which a contract is extended or terminated. Other triggers based on time include birthdays, wedding anniversaries, births and other important life moments. Based on personal customer data, selections are made every day that are then linked to a standard mailing. When this campaign management system is fully applied, hundreds of standard communications can be prepared which can be experienced as personal.

Another sophisticated trigger is based on analyses, such as the most recent buying moment, the last purchase amount, how long someone has been a customer and also possibly products associated with the most recent purchase. A formula that describes the customer value is the RFM (recency, frequency and monetary) value. RFM values indicate how often a customer buys (the basis is therefore the time interval), how many items from the product range are bought (the breadth of the purchases is the trigger, so it therefore concerns associations) and finally the value of the purchases themselves. The total determines the customer value, assuming that the best customer is one who returns regularly, buys many different items and spends a great deal of money. Suppliers will try to use individual triggers to increase the value per element (RFM value). Sophisticated campaign management triggers and good customer-based analyses form the basis of this.

14.4 Action

Then finally comes the action: after the orientation, research/information and communication the purchase is made. A buyer makes a choice between buying physically or on the Internet. Various considerations determine this choice, such as the experience with buying on the Internet, the age of the person, the available time or the necessity of the purchase. Also playing a role in this choice are whether or not the purchaser is mobile, whether shops are in the neighbourhood or whether the shop meets the specific needs of the buyer. We can also consider the role of the retailer and the salesperson, the product range, the layout and design of the business and the service provided. Physical shops have to motivate customers to buy in the shop for emotional reasons; on the Internet people usually have rational reasons for buying.

For webshops it is important that they can be easily found, through AdWords, links and top-of-mind position, but also through intensive communication. Through mailings and newsletters the shop is continually brought to the attention of the potential buyer; however, by adding links it becomes easy to go directly to the supplier's site.

14.5 Internet use

The use of the Internet very much depends on experience, age and gender. What's more, the environment in which you grew up and where you find yourself now are also important factors. As a result, there is a large degree of diversity in the use of the Internet. Suppliers really have to take this into account when designing their websites and when defining the processes, including navigation models.

Based on experience and the moment that someone comes into contact with the Internet and gains experience with this medium, *and* integrates this medium within his or her own behaviour, two groups of Internet users can be distinguished. The difference in behaviour results from the moment a person comes into contact with the Internet. People's behaviour is strongly influenced by their youth – their teenage years. This behaviour is determined by the environmental conditions in which the person grew up, such as family, social class and material possessions. Friends, school and study also influence later behaviour. What's more, in the teenage years a person consciously comes into contact with all sorts of possibilities that will determines their later life: the sports chosen, favourite sports team and musical preferences. An important factor is a person's contact with technology and the possibilities it offers. And it is this that determines how he or she will deal with technology later.

In the previous chapter we looked at people who came into contact with computers in the 1980s. This generation is not nervous about using computers and is quite skilled in using the equipment and software. But there was no Internet at that time. That came later, in the 1990s at the earliest. A generation that had already matured into adults looked on with amazement at all the possible applications. Their behaviour, after all, had largely already been formed before all these possibilities were offered by the Internet. For these adults use of the Internet came later, while they wondered about the actual advantages of the Internet. In the early years of the Internet it did not really offer many advantages; only the bulletin board function and email. Later you could also surf and buy. It is because the Internet was developed later that the generation born before 1975 use the Internet differently to the generation born after 1975.

We will now discuss the differences between those people who have grown up with the Internet and those who came into contact with it much later in their lives. We will also look at the difference in the use of the Internet between men and women.

14.5.1 Natives and immigrants

We can refer to people who have grown up with the medium of the Internet as 'natives', and those who came into contact with it later in life (during adulthood) as 'immigrants'. This same distinction is visible in the physical world, something which gives colour to society. There are also differences in the use of the Internet. Young people use the Internet intuitively; they have a better feel for what has to be done, what is possible, what is logical and what value can be attached to transparency and communication. Young people are also much more active on social networks; they have a greater need for communication, as well as for attachment and recognition. Older people use the Internet more consciously; they make comparisons more with the physical world, the world that they know so well. This generation consciously decides whether or not to use the Internet, and imposes the same moral values on the Internet as in the physical world. They have little interest in actively using social networks: surely they can do much better in the physical world? They have a different need for communication, which is less interactive (via media) and more direct in the physical world, with more of an interest in using the Internet for information (email, blogs, guest-books).

This is why there is such a difference in the use of the Internet: intuitive versus conscious/rational and the difference between feeling and conscious suspicion. This difference is certainly not a value judgement, but it is important for those providing information on the Internet. Young people tend to compare more; they tend to base their decisions on colour, layout, navigation and pictures, while the generation pre-1975 tend to look at explanations (rationality versus intuition). Young people like to give their opinions on social networks, while the older generation tend to look for information only. This dichotomy, which is important for commercial processes, also leads to a different buying behaviour which in turn is affected by the behaviour-forming elements as well as current circumstances, such as the availability of local shops and how much time one has. In addition, it is the natives who have a strong need for physical control; in order to see whether expectations are realized and to have the correctness of their choice confirmed. The native relies more upon a personal feel.

In addition to this generic dichotomy, age is also an important factor in Internet use. Other factors, such as time, playfulness, responsibility and existing behaviour, also play a role. Young people play computer games more than older people, while older people tend to look more for information than the younger generation. Older people tend to go on Google for information more often, while young people visit social networks.

14.5.2 Women versus men

Another distinguishing factor in Internet use is gender. Women use the medium differently to men. Women are more conscious in their use, more rational, whereas men are actually more emotional. In the buying process this leads to a conscious choice of the site (webshop) among women. But in addition to this conscious choice, women are more loyal. Once they know that the site sells the items or provides the information they need, they will return more. If the item is not found, then women will continue looking. Because of their trust, women tend to buy different types of articles at their preferred webshop (providing this fits in with their expectations). It is therefore a good idea for women's fashion webshops to also sell children's clothes and even casual clothes for men. After all, women buy not only children's clothes but very often also the casual clothes for their partner. Men, in contrast, display a completely different style of behaviour here; they are more straightforward as well as more specific. Men's fashion websites do not offer any children's or ladies' clothes.

Other associations also apply clearly for men and have to be very logical. For example, on football sites we see football products as well as football travel. There would be no general sports items or general holidays, as the connecting association is football, not sports in general. Analysis of Internet traffic clearly shows that men visit more sites when using the Internet and surf more than women. Although women tend to visit fewer sites per session, they do have more page views as they search for other items. When designing a website all these aspects of the buying behaviour have to be taken into account: a short route for men and quick decision makers, and the correct associations for female decision makers. Associations for men should have a strong relationship with the product that is to be bought: shirts with ties and cufflinks are very logical, but socks are regarded as less so.

Table 14.4 provides an overview of Internet use according to age and communities (social media).

Table 14.4 Behaviour according to age and communities used

Age (years)	Focus of Internet use
0–10	Games and educational programs
	Videos and clips
10–15	Communication via chat rooms, msn, Googletalk
	Communities, such as Facebook
15–20	Information regarding education (school)
	Communities, such as Facebook and hobby/music sites, chatting, downloads (music)
	Gaming, information for education (school) and information for specific purposes (sports, holiday, hobby)
20–30	Communities, such as Facebook
	Chat via chat rooms
	Information for many purposes (school, hobby, news)
	Online shopping, particularly clothing
	Online banking
30–45	Integrated in normal life for communication (chat, email, Twitter, blogs), information (subject- and problem-oriented). Professional sites like Plaxo and LinkedIn
	Buying (few restrictions)
	Integral within behaviour
	Communities often themed or commercial
45–60	Commercial use
	Email
	Conscious search for information
	Rational purchasing, such as music, books, holidays and wine
	Particularly information oriented
	Functional use
	Little community use, chiefly LinkedIn
Above 60	Rational purchase of virtual products such as airplane tickets, holidays, books and music
	Functional use
	Community themed

14.6 Analyses

More than any other medium, the Internet offers vast possibilities for measuring various factors. When someone visits a website, how they arrived at the website, which pages they viewed and for how long and at what point they left the site can all be registered. This information is recorded in web statistics packages. Examples of these are Google Analytics,

WebTrends, Omniture, Yahoo! and Web Analytics. Analyses of the web statistics can be used to improve online campaigns or the website itself. Easy-to-read reports and dashboards can also be made using them (Figure 14.9).

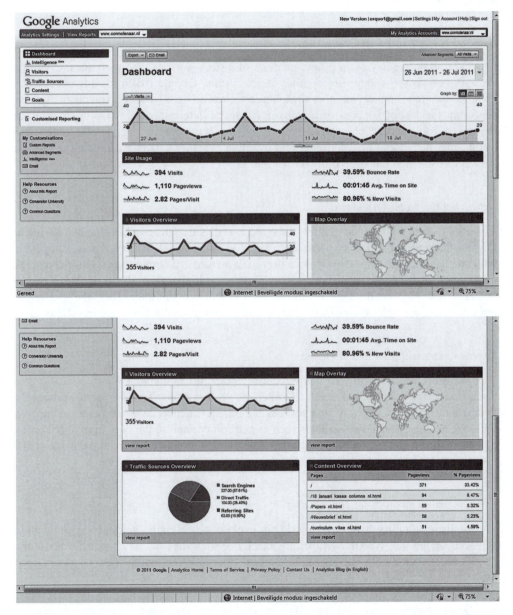

Figure 14.9 Examples of reports made using the web statistics of Google Analytics

14.6.1 Web statistics

Web statistics can produce interesting information regarding where the visitors come from and how long they stay on certain pages of a site. Other research methods for the Internet are also looked at below.

Where do the visitors come from?

It is interesting to carry out a proper analysis of a site's various visitor sources. Common examples of visitor sources are organic search results, Google AdWords advertisements, email newsletters, banners on other sites, blog articles and links (referrers) on other sites. By analysing the visitor sources of a website it can be determined which sources produce the most visitors and which sources the most buyers. If the costs of the various sources can also be clarified, it can be determined, for example, whether a banner campaign or Google AdWords campaign has been profitable or not.

Improving the pages on the site

It is also good to analyse the quality of the pages on a site. This can be done by looking at the time that a visitor stays on a particular page. You can also look at the percentage of people who do not look further on the site once they have arrived at a certain page. This percentage is called the bounce rate. If this percentage per page is higher than 80 per cent, this means that more than 80 per cent of visitors did not look further than this page. The page is therefore not interesting enough to click further and could probably benefit from improvements.

Yet even more web statistics analyses

Web statistics packages provide many reporting possibilities that allow further analyses to be carried out, such as 'funnel analyses' (where do visitors drop off in the ordering process?). Furthermore, periods, pages, visitor sources and other elements can also be easily compared with one another. Specialist agencies such as netprofiler analyse the data from a marketing perspective and provide advice regarding the returns produced by campaigns and the effectiveness of a website.

Other research methods for the Internet

Web statistics produce hard data, but do not explain why certain visitors carry out certain activities on the site, who the visitors are exactly or what they like or do not like about the site. In order to find out more about these areas, other research methods are necessary such as:

- *Online questionnaires*: At the end of the visit to the site a questionnaire can be initiated which asks about the reason for visiting, the visitor's satisfaction regarding the site and any areas for improvement.
- *Usability research*: A number of consumers (usually 5–15) are invited to carry out a number of tasks on the site. These examine what they did and why, and what they believe can be improved on the site.

- *Eyetracking-usability research*: This is the same as standard usability research, but now the eye movements of the consumer are also followed. This identifies the areas of the site that receive the most attention and those areas that are viewed little or not at all.

It is difficult to predict the behaviour of visitors in advance. However, when designing sites and processes, the expected visitors and their related behaviour can be taken into account. This is often difficult. It is easier to simply respond to the visit by registering what a visitor does, where the visitor comes from and when the visitor leaves the site. This is done using products such as Google Analytics, whereby the Internet use preceding the visit is recorded. It can also indicate where the visitors log in, how long they stay on the site and where they go on from there. This produces a more general picture of the visitors. Specific analyses of the website can determine what a visitor has been looking at, the mouse behaviour, the click behaviour and of course how and when they move on elsewhere. By using this analysis as a basis it is possible to create general profiles, which can be used to optimize the design of the website.

Google analyses regarding the number of visitors, the visit time, the use of the browsers and the log-in location

More knowledge of customers can also be gained, so that whatever is being offered can be modified accordingly. Based on the IP number it can be determined what a visitor has done on the site. This information can be saved until the visitor returns (within a certain time interval). This information can then be used for a specific special offer. If a visitor had looked, for example, at a flatscreen TV but did not buy it, the next time he or she visits the website a special offer can be made for this television. The (unique) IP number forms the basis for this registration. If a visitor logs in using an access code it is even easier to make this connection. If the access code consists of an email address and password it is then also very simple to send an email. This data is therefore part of the core process.

Special offers that are based on the click behaviour are also called behavioural targeting (BT). The behaviour is taken as the basis for the interaction and dialogue. In the future, once the use of smartphones becomes more commonplace, this will allow the Internet and the physical world to be connected. The search behaviour on the Internet is registered on the basis of the mobile number or the number of the smart chip. As soon as this number is recognized during a visit to a shop, messages can be sent to the smartphone, the narrowcasting system or to the salesperson!

14.6.2 Measuring success

The success of any campaign can be measured by using the analyses that are carried out and checking the results against the starting points. This can be done in a structured way using a scorecard. Based on the scorecard the components can be determined and the results set down in a structured manner. The components of this scorecard consist of the financial perspective, the customer perspective, the website perspective and the organization perspective. For each component the success factors and KPIs (key performance indicators) are determined. This produces the overview given in Table 14.5.

In addition to this analysis based on the scorecard methodology one can also look very specifically at the measurement elements and results. Here certain predetermined variables are important. These variables are displayed in a dashboard for management purposes (reporting), but also in order to be able to take direct action. The comparison with a dashboard

Table 14.5 Overview of success factors and key performance indicators per component of the scorecard

Success factor	Key performance indicator
Financial perspective	
Turnover realized via the Internet	Total turnover
	Turnover per campaign
	Turnover per customer
Costs	Total costs
Profitability	Campaign costs
	Costs per order
Customer perspective	
Total reach	Target group to be reached
Visit	Number of visitors
	Number of page views
Conversion	Conversion ratio visit–customers
	Conversion ratio use shopping basket–real buyers
Retention	Number of returning visitors (frequency)
Website perspective	
Content	Quality content
	Currency of content
Ease of use	User-friendliness
	Navigation
Technical performance	Loading speed of site
	Loading speed of pages
	Purchase handling
Organizational perspective	
Organization	Structure
	Responsibility
	Response times
Systems	Link with ERP and delivery
	Link between e-marketing modules
	Link with analysis systems
Processes	Reports

is significant here, because when driving a car KPIs are also visible for the driver, so that measures can be taken immediately in response to deviations. Important key factors include:

- CpC – cost per click;
- CpO – cost per order;
- AOV – average order value;
- CTR – click through rate;
- return rate; and
- basket value.

Based on the above factors the success of the Internet strategy can be measured. It eventually comes down to determining how many visitors arrive at the website, how many orders are placed (the conversion), the costs per order and the yield per customer. In these cases it involves measuring the effectiveness of the Internet application. It is of course also important, as we have already seen, to measure the effects per customer. How many customers visit, and how many new visitors, what is the RFM per customer and what is the response to the promotions per customer? From the perspective of e-marketing the effects on the customers and how these effects can be optimized (customer-oriented approach) are examined. What's more, the effectiveness of the tools (the Internet) are analysed in order to optimize the Internet strategy on the website.

14.7 Impact of the Internet on marketing communication

The Internet is an important medium for making and maintaining contact with customers. The Internet makes interactivity possible, but the behaviour on the Internet can also easily be measured. This allows a great deal of knowledge to be gained about visitor numbers, the visit time and visitor profiles. As a result of this knowledge, it is also possible to maintain more direct and personal contact with customers. Sound analyses, however, are necessary for this, as well as communication strategy based on behaviour and 'triggered' communication and knowledge of the buying behaviour. As a result, customers will perceive this as customization and great loyalty will be stimulated through the direct communication. The Internet should not be regarded as an electronic brochure but as an interactive means of communication which provides information, allows for communication and enables purchases to be made. In the near future the medium will become even more personal due to the use of smartphones and tablets, and through the integration of location-based services.

Summary

- Internet use is not generic but is in part dependent on the age and gender of the user.
- The Internet enables the behaviour of the visitors to be measured. This must form the basis of the marketing communication.
- Through the application of the Internet, marketing communication will become more personal and direct.
- The behaviour of customers can be both at an individual and at a group level, as can be seen from social media.
- Groups of customers are no longer predefined but are determined on the basis of behaviour.

Part 5

Marketing strategy in a dynamic world

Company orientation

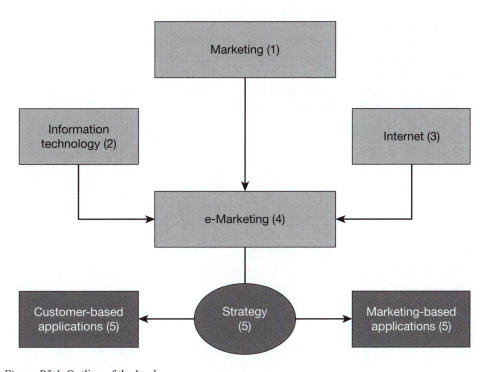

Figure P5.1 Outline of the book

We have seen in the previous sections how marketing has evolved over the past 40 years from a focus on products and the relationship with the market (generic), to a target group focus. Since the 1990s the marketing focus has shifted to customers and customer relations. This shift has been brought about by the rapid changes in markets, the shift in consumer (and company) demand and the application of information technology (IT) and the Internet. This has created a greater dynamism in the markets, among customers and thus also in marketing. For an organization it is important to make the right choice of marketing instruments, activities and sales channels. It is also important to make the right choice for support from IT and the Internet. This choice depends on the market circumstances, but also on an organization's focus.

The choice can only be made by marketing if it is clear where the management's focus lies, what the market circumstances are and which marketing orientation is possible based on these starting points. The organizational focus and the management objectives derive from the organization's mission and the objectives of the owners (stakeholders). With a financially driven objective it will be mainly profit and shareholder value which are important, while with a cooperative concept it is the interests of the members (often customers) that matter most. With the current rise in companies driven from a financial perspective, given the interests of investors, the organization will aim for profits. This profitability can be focused on the short term, because investors want to cash in or wish to sell their shares within the not too distant future. In such cases an interest is often acquired in an organization which is not focused on operational excellence, where costs may be lower and the profits are thus higher. These are all aspects that are significant for marketing and the choice of marketing orientation. In fact the choices for marketing orientation and the value disciplines are also determined by the origanizational focus and the stakeholders' interests. The consequences of this will be expressed in the competitive position.

15 Marketing orientation as a competitive model

The degree of customer focus of an organization is a determining factor for the marketing strategy and its execution. The customer focus may comprise a product focus aimed at an optimum alignment between the customer and the use of a product. The product must meet the customer's expectations. The customer focus may also comprise a relationship with a more or less uniform target group. In that case, the determining factor will be the position of the product within the target group, coupled with the customer satisfaction. In both cases, however, there is a low degree of customer focus because a product-based relationship with an unknown customer is involved. By definition, customer focus is based on personal interactions with a known (identifiable) relation. The individual customers are known and direct contact is maintained with them. In some cases, products will be tailored to customers and there may also be scenarios in which products are developed in collaboration with the customer (with a sharing of risks). The latter scenario involves a very close collaboration between the customer and the supplier.

15.1 Value disciplines

The use of marketing as well as the application of IT will differ with each scenario. In each case a different method of organization and management focus will be required. IT in particular will be a distinguishing factor. The degree of customer focus will determine the structure of the organization as well as the use of IT and marketing. However, it is important that the choice the organization makes is integrally applied to all business activities and relations. If this is not the case, there will be friction, compromising the customer relation and the organization's competitive edge.

A sequential selection process involving strategic choices and the choice of marketing focus is shown in Figure 15.1.

An example of a strategic approach focused on customers, the organization or the product is given by Tracy and Wiersema in their book *The Discipline of Market Leaders*. Based on these starting points, they define three value disciplines:

- customer intimacy;
- product leadership; and
- operational excellence.

Their conclusion is that organizations should focus on one of these value disciplines in order to be successful (Figure 15.2).

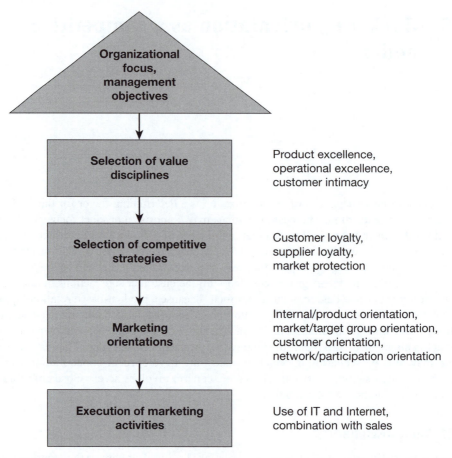

Figure 15.1 Sequential selection process involving strategic choices and the choice of marketing focus

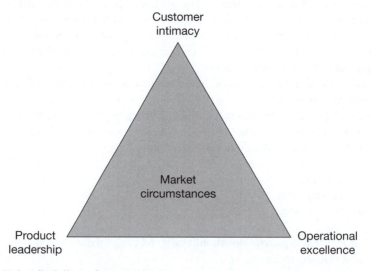

Figure 15.2 Value disciplines of an organization

15.1.1 Customer intimacy

The relationship with the customer is regarded as the most important proposition. It is important to cater for the wishes and requirements of customers. This requires insight into customers as well as a proper response from customers to messages. The aim is to create a close, sustainable relationship and a high level of customer satisfaction. This can be achieved not only by adapting the various marketing instruments to the wishes and requirements of individual customers, but also by modifying the marketing activities accordingly through direct communication and building a tailored brand and product image. The vision underpinning customer intimacy is that it is best to provide customers with an 'end-to-end solution'. In this context, the customer lifetime is more important than the profit per transaction.

15.1.2 Product leadership

The products should be 'best-of-breed', and should create a clear distinction from the competition. This distinction may be objective or relative (in the eyes of customers). An example is Apple, which always characterizes itself by a distinctive product proposition, innovation and a different design. This is why Apple is regarded as a product leader. In such cases, customers attribute an added value to the products and are willing to pay a premium. Is the iPod really better than other MP3 players? Is a MacBook better than other laptops? The vision underpinning product leadership is that an organization should always offer state-of-the-art products.

15.1.3 Operational excellence

Operational excellence is especially important in competitive markets. Lower costs will result in higher profit margins or the possibility of offering products at lower prices. It is precisely through lower operational costs that competitive advantage can be achieved. This is possible through lower costs per unit (lower wages), the use of technology (for example, the Internet) or process optimization. Another possibility is to achieve economies of scale (for example, by expanding the sales area or through increased market penetration), so that the costs of production can be reduced or more favourable purchasing conditions can be agreed to. The vision underpinning this value discipline is that an organization should always offer reliable products at competitive prices with the most favourable delivery conditions.

Thus, a significant customer segment will remain.

Whether consciously or subconsciously, organizations will select one of the three strategies above as their principal focus. If no choice is made, a 'stuck in the middle' situation may arise in which the organization will lose ground to specialists in each of the three fields.

The following consequences are possible with regard to the various relevant aspects of the products and services to be provided.

The consequences of operational excellence may include:

- lowest price;
- highest reliability of delivery;
- outstanding logistics management;
- limited assortment; or
- an optimum use of automation and the Internet for process optimization.

The consequences of product leadership may include:

- technological innovation;
- product or service innovation;
- a quick time-to-market;
- knowledge exchange and gathering for product or service development; or
- use of automation for product innovation and market relationships (suppliers, supply chain).

The consequences of customer intimacy may include:

- mass customization;
- one-to-one marketing;
- partnerships;
- client relationship management (CRM); or
- an optimum use of IT for customer insight and of the Internet for communication, information provision and transactions.

These value disciplines are important for determining the organizational focus as well as the use of IT and the Internet. This focus will make it possible to achieve a distinctive edge in terms of the value discipline, which in turn will result in competitive advantage.

15.2 Competitive strategies

It is also possible to determine the use of IT and the Internet on the basis of Porter's five forces model (see Chapter 6). This mainly involves increasing the market entry thresholds, which makes it difficult for new parties to enter the market and the competitive struggle. This focus will also implicitly determine the market conditions. Whereas with Tracy and Wiersema the distinction between market suppliers involved a significant focus on a value discipline, in Porter's model the focus is rather on the relationship with and between market parties as well as shielding the market from new suppliers and (substitute) products. This is represented schematically in Figure 15.3.

The use of IT and the Internet not only requires a greater investment for newcomers, but also for existing market parties. According to a 1994 study by the MIT (Multi-year Infrastructure and Transport) programme, investments in IT do not result in an improved competitive edge, but rather in equality of competition. IT investments result in higher market entry thresholds, greater efficiency, improved information provision and closer market relations. Each market party will have to participate in order to survive. This is what creates this equality of competition. A company that does not participate in this process will no longer play a role in the market. The use of the Internet, direct contacts with suppliers and customers and the alignment of business processes will make it increasingly difficult for new parties to enter the market.

If newcomers nevertheless want to gain market share, they will have to come up with a distinctive portfolio, concept or sales methodology. Initially, the Internet offered this opportunity. The Internet can still serve as a sales channel to countries in which Internet penetration and adoption still lags behind the country in which the supplier is based. For example, Amazon.com initially had a market share for English books in the Dutch market. However, as a result of the current market position of Bol.com, Amazon.com's market position has become marginalized.

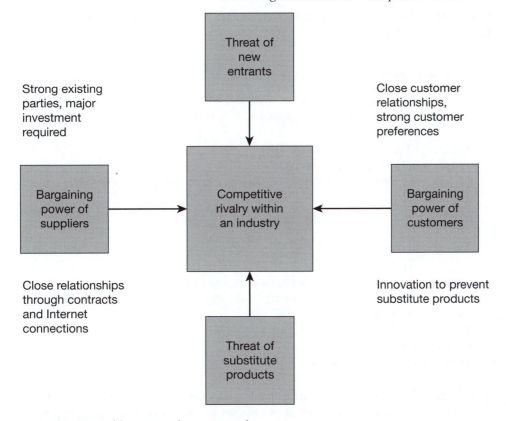

Figure 15.3 Competitive strategy in present markets

To create competitive advantage, organizations must distinguish themselves in the market in respect of other suppliers as well as ensure that their products and services are distinctive in the eyes of consumers. According to Porter, there are a number of methods to achieve this:

- a low-cost strategy;
- a differentiation strategy; or
- a focus strategy.

The low-cost strategy involves selecting ways in which the costs can be reduced (for example, through outsourcing, the use of technology or efficiency). Porter focuses on a broad, externally oriented approach to this strategy, while Tracy and Wiersema focus rather on an internal approach.

The differentiation strategy is similar to the value discipline of product excellence. Differentiation involves looking at all aspects of the product and service portfolio, such as the combination of product and service (after-sales service), customer support, the product composition and the product design.

The focus strategy comprises the clear selection of a strategy aimed at cost reductions, differentiation, market share or customers.

That a proper execution of the selected strategy can result in competitive advantage is something that Porter and Tracy and Wiersema agree on. If no clear selection is made, a stuck-in-the-middle situation is created. Marketing will execute the chosen strategy by selecting the best marketing orientation.

15.3 Market dynamics

As we have seen in Chapter 2, the market dynamics have increased in recent decades. There are general as well as demand-specific reasons for this. General reasons include:

- increased affluence (disposable income);
- a larger supply of high-quality products;
- the adoption of new technologies by businesses and consumers (for example, IT and the Internet); and
- globalization.

Demand-specific reasons include:

- a faster succession of product innovations (changes and renovations);
- changes in buying behaviour (for example, the advent of fun shopping as a pastime and later web shopping);
- the impact of advertising;
- newcomers on the market; and
- a strong fashion-consciousness.

Another factor is the adaptation of the technology discussed in Part 2, such as automation, IT and later the Internet. This resulted in changes in customers' knowledge and buying opportunities as well as the relations between suppliers and their buyers. Not all markets have changed with equal force. Some market conditions have essentially remained the same. This particularly concerns markets in which a great many investments have been made or have to be made to enter the market (see Porter's five forces model). Examples are oil extraction, the petrol sector, the raw materials market and the chemical product sector. The market for medical products is a similarly difficult market to enter; the market keeps growing while the number of market players remains limited. The change lies in the product offering, which is the result of highly capital-intensive product innovations.

Market dynamics strongly determine the structure of organizations, their decision-making process and their marketing focus. Fast market changes require a quicker decision-making process, a more flexible structure and a more intimate relationship between marketing and the customer. In some cases, structural relationships between suppliers and their customers will even be required.

Table 15.1 provides a schematic representation of the changes involved as well as their consequences.

15.4 The impact of CRM

Precisely as a result of the evolution of the marketing concept from products to customers, an evaluation has taken place with the marketing vision as well: the focus has shifted from transactions to relationships. Initially, this evolution and change in vision was triggered and supported by the use of automation in the 1970s and 1980s (see Part 2) and later by the use

Table 15.1 Cause and effect of market changes

Market changes	Change	Consequence
Consumer demand	Increased affluence, greater disposable income, greater fashion-consciousness, adoption of new technologies, changes in behaviour as a result of geographic, demographic and psychographic differences	An increased focus on individual customers and target groups. Intensive advertising to ensure a top-of-mind position as well as a direct approach. Need for insight into customers
Product offering	Products of a higher quality, elimination of bad products. A large number of innovations. Technology is integral to products. Fewer local and more international brands	Distinction from the competitors through brands, intensive distribution. Increasing power of distribution (points). Fight for the shop shelves. Eroding margins
Manufacturers	Focus on international level, powerful distinction between market leaders and followers. Intensive investments in technology	International collaboration and acquisitions. A focus on greater efficiency, market broadening as well as market shielding
Technology	IT used to create efficiencies, use of ERP platforms, later CRM for customer intelligence. The Internet as a sales and information channel. Changes in the supply chain as a result of extranet, RFID, tracking and tracing, VMI	Strong need for process control, insight into processes, results and efficiency (cost control)

of the Internet (Parts 3 and 4). As a result, marketing has not only changed as a discipline; the role of marketing within the organization has changed. In fact, a divide between operational marketing and strategic marketing was created. Operational marketing predominantly focused on the performance of marketing activities, while strategic marketing focused on the development of a customer-oriented marketing concept. This development was promoted, among other things, by the use of CRM software, which was strongly advocated by automation providers such as Siebel Systems (now Oracle) and SAP.

According to the vision of these automation providers, a CRM application was required for an organization-wide adoption of customer relationship management and customer-oriented thinking. In this framework, automation would lead the way and marketing would follow. The decision-making process chiefly involved an automation investment as well as involvement of the IT organization. The impact of a CRM strategy was supported by the CRM solution across the organization, but not yet by the marketing vision. Some of the reasons for this were that:

- automation traditionally had no affinity with marketing;
- marketing traditionally had no affinity with automation;
- the CRM budget involved an automation budget;
- the marketing function did not form part of the management and was not involved in the decision-making process; and
- marketing was (and often is) strongly associated with marketing communication, which is an operational activity.

With the implementation of a CRM system, organizations were forced to record customer relations and to use this information. As a result of the discrepancy in the involvement of marketing and IT as well as the differences in focus, more often than not the implementation of the CRM vision would result in disillusionment: although the CRM system operated well, it was left unused by marketing and sales!

Another problem was associated with the organizational focus. CRM uses leading customer relations (in fact customer intimacy) as its starting point, while many organizations wanted to focus on operational excellence because of a strong focus on price. Within boards of directors there was also a strong focus on profitability, return and shareholder value (in the 1990s). Shareholder value was strongly associated with profits and share prices. This resulted in a strong focus on cost control and operational excellence. The financial function was strongly represented within the board of directors, which meant the decision-making process was often based on short-term profitability and expected profits. Marketing was not represented in the decision-making process or had no real vigour if it was. CRM was implemented as the result of the strong hype created by automation providers as well as the 1990s hype of adopting a customer focus as an important new competitive weapon.

15.5 Marketing as value discipline

As a result of the developments discussed above, marketing found itself in a difficult position. In some organizations, marketing was marginalized into marketing communication in support of sales. However, this situation changed in reaction to the advent of the Internet. Particularly in the last few years, the impact of the Internet has become so big that the organizational position of marketing is gaining ground again. The use of the Internet has resulted in direct relationships with customers, insight into market relations and direct interactions with customers and suppliers alike. Added to which, the Internet is no longer just a communication medium but also a sales medium, and its use can result in greater efficiency. An integration of operational excellence and customer intimacy is taking place as a result of this development. This means the marketing profession will change and an organization's marketing activities will vary according to the marketing vision and market circumstances. There will no longer be a clear-cut use of marketing that is the same for all companies. Rather, the use of marketing will strongly depend on the dynamics of the market circumstances, the selected value discipline and the use of IT and the Internet.

15.5.1 Marketing orientations

The marketing orientation comprises an orientation on external market parties and circumstances that other organizational units and functions are aligned with. The marketing orientation is synonymous with the way in which marketing is applied; it is associated with the product, customer loyalty and market dynamics. Other organizational aspects, such as the management style, organizational size, information provision and decision-making processes are also partly determined by the marketing orientation. The marketing orientation of an organization will also determine the use of marketing instruments, the marketing activities and the use of e-marketing. A stable market will be characterized by transparency between the suppliers and a homogeneous demand. There will be limited product differentiation. Since in these market circumstances the market determines the price, a strong focus on cost control is only logical. Consequently, the management will strongly focus on products, costs and market share.

The associated value discipline is operational excellence. There is a strong internal focus and a push approach is adopted with regard to the market. This is typical of the internal orientation or product orientation of marketing. There will also be a focus on the market if it is susceptible to changes as a result of product innovations, newcomers to the market or the advent of new technology. It is precisely in such circumstances that competitive strategies and a target group approach are significant; the organization will give priority to market developments over product development and the product concept. This is a market orientation or a target group orientation. Both approaches in fact comprise the classical marketing approach as described in Part 1, namely bringing products and services to the market.

However, the markets have become less stable, particularly in recent years. The use of the Internet in particular has resulted in greater transparency and internationalization (newcomers to the market), while consumers are showing a different buying behaviour. Especially in the case of highly dynamic markets a more intimate relationship with customers is required to acknowledge these changes and to ensure their loyalty. For this reason there will be a greater management focus on customers and customer relationships, so that insight into individual customers, buying processes (ORCA model) and direct communication become important; this involves the customer orientation.

However, this can also result in a strong management focus on collaboration with customers, users, buyers, suppliers and possibly other market parties. This collaboration may involve a limited degree of contract-based collaboration or intensive cooperation, for example in the case of VMI (vendor-managed inventory), relationships with a select group of suppliers or other types of collaboration. This involves a network orientation or a participation orientation.

Figure 15.4 provides a schematic overview of marketing orientations. A divide has occurred between the market/target group orientation and customer-focused orientation. Among other things, this indicates the difference between the classic marketing concept and the new marketing approach, which does not focus on the product or market, but rather on individual customers and interactive customer relations.

The line indicates an increase in market dynamics. The bigger and faster the market changes (dynamism), the more organizations will have to focus on customers and ensure their loyalty.

15.6 Strategic consequences for organizations

It is important for organizations to have a competitive advantage. This can be achieved by shielding the market from newcomers or competitors, or through a strong focus on a value discipline. This value discipline can be product-based (product excellence), cost-based (operational excellence) or based on close customer relationships (customer intimacy). Organizations must consciously select one of these value disciplines to distinguish themselves within the market. There is also an interplay between organizations and the market circumstances. This interplay is determined by the typical characteristics of the organization, the marketing focus and the market circumstances. In the case of stable markets, organizations will place a greater focus on distinguishing themselves through their product proposition. If market segments can be identified, the market position and the ability to cater for the wishes of this segment will play a significant role. In the case of increasingly dynamic markets, the individual relationships with customers will become especially important; loyalty leads to customer retention. Particularly in the case of capital-intensive products, organizations will strive towards a collaboration with the customer, joint product development and risk sharing.

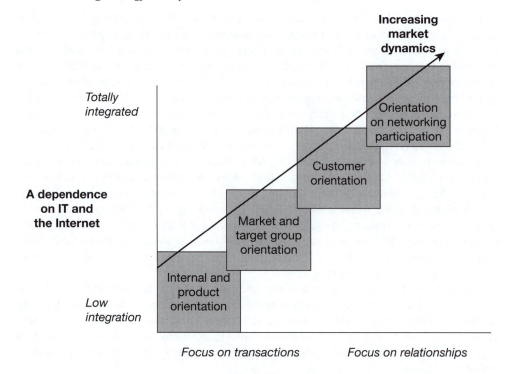

Figure 15.4 Marketing orientations of an organization

This is the ultimate form of customer focus, customer participation and interaction or network orientation.

Summary

- The marketing circumstances determine the marketing orientation of an organization.
- Competitive advantage can be achieved by focusing on a single value discipline.
- As a result of the market dynamics and quick changes in customer demand, a high level of customer focus must be present across the organization.
- CRM applications and the use of the Internet form a key success factor in dynamic markets.

16 Applying market orientation

As we saw in Chapter 15, a marketing orientation is an orientation towards the external market parties and market conditions to which other organizational components and functions are adapted. The marketing orientation is synonymous with the way in which marketing is applied, and goes together with the product and the dynamic in markets. Four orientations can be distinguished here:

- internal or product orientation;
- target group or market orientation;
- client orientation; and
- network or participation orientation.

For each orientation there are determining market circumstances, an application of the value discipline, a different culture and management style and naturally a different application of marketing instruments and activities. All these differences mean that the application of e-marketing will also differ – both the application of IT and application of the Internet.

16.1 Internal orientation: product focus

With an internal orientation the management focus is primarily on the quality of the products or service provision and the efficiency in the production and distribution process (Figure 16.1). There will be little distinction between other products and services in the market. The marketing conception is equivalent to the sales conception. Marketing's main focus will also be marketing communication.

Ansoff was a particular proponent of this orientation. The Ansoff model is based on product distinctions in markets. It must be noted that Ansoff developed the model in 1965, when there was little dynamism in markets and the focus of marketing was strongly orientated towards sales, and marketing was applied mainly by 'fast movers' who communicated with a mass market. These were therefore also typical market conditions for this internal or product orientation.

To achieve efficiency an organization also wants to standardize the products as much as possible. Automation, particularly in the production process, obviously helps here. Product development is a development where the aspiration is modifications to enhance or improve the quality of production and distribution. Packaging is modified (such as plastic bottles to avoid returns, or squared packaging to increase the effective shelf space). Product development is an activity of research and development, a department which is separate from the marketing department. Marketing is an activity which is focused strongly on distribution and marketing communication (Figure 16.2).

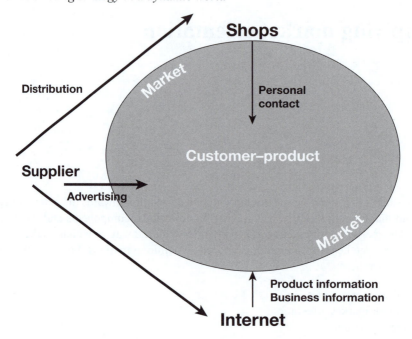

Figure 16.1 Classical marketing, selling via a market distribution channel and mass communication

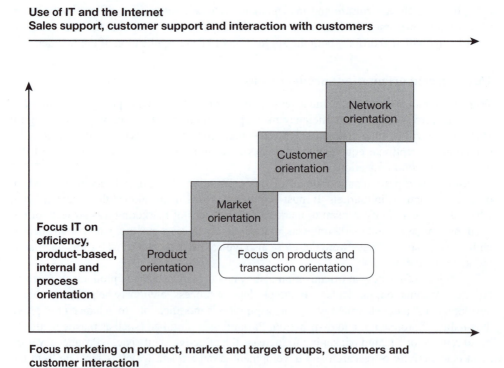

Figure 16.2 Product orientation

16.1.1 Customer relations

Customer relations in an internal orientation will occur mainly at the product level. Habit and continuous availability ('never out of stock') play an important role here. For distribution points such as supermarkets, customer relations will consist mainly of location, local availability, range and transaction reward. It is unsurprising that it was in fact supermarkets which applied loyalty programmes in the 1990s. Before that time there were already many savings programmes which rewarded customer transactions. Technology made it possible to link customer details to purchasing details, as occurs with the bonus card. A modification to the checkout system and a card with a magnetic strip is sufficient. This yields a great deal of information about purchasing, and an insight into the shopping trolley. Some supermarkets have introduced changes to their shelf arrangements on the basis of combined purchases in the shopping trolley. Wal-Mart claims to have achieved a significant turnover increase in this way. Often items are offered by department, such as fruit and vegetables, meat and chemist items. Analysis of shopping trolleys puts cocktail nuts alongside the beer, and soup alongside the dessert. The creates simpler shopping and a logical shopping route. This is the basis for customer relations based on analysing purchases.

16.1.2 Distribution

A large degree of efficiency is aspired to within distribution. Applying automation leads to lower costs. Examples of this are the application of RFID (radio-frequency identity) tags on pallets. With an RFID tag, data can be stored on the chip; the chip can also be read remotely. This enables a different, more efficient storage methodology. Products no longer have to be looked for, and the oldest products are identified in such a way that they can be delivered first.

The application of active RFID chips has also made the distribution process more transparent. This is the basis for tracking and tracing, which enables customers (and suppliers) to follow the goods via the Internet. There is no longer any lack of clarity on when goods will arrive, even if they are supplied from China.

In the shop, RFID tags can be read during warehouse controls and also, if agreed, by the suppliers, giving rise to different collaborative forms. The best-known collaborative form in this field is VMI (vendor-managed inventory). With VMI responsibility for stock at the distribution point resides with the manufacturer, the supplier. The responsibility only changes at the moment of 'entering the shop', or in some cases after the sale. Suppliers would like to have an ongoing insight into stock levels, to be able to manage the risk. They aspire towards greater efficiency in supply by supplying automatically once stocks have passed a critical level. The shopkeeper no longer has to order; it occurs automatically. This application is also possible without RFID tags, by interlinking computer systems. The shop's stock system is then linked to the supplier's sales system. Deliveries are expedited on the basis of framework contracts.

This application is, in fact, a hybrid form of marketing orientation. Nothing actually changes for marketing, hence the internally focused orientation. Nor does anything change for the value proposition (operational excellence). But a great deal does indeed change for the supplier, because they supply in accordance with the participation model, the network orientation. The supplier's objective is a sound relationship with clients, while for the client it is a high degree of efficiency.

16.1.3 Price

The price is based on the cost price – a cost-price-plus methodology. The focus on efficiency (operational excellence) is important here. The cost price calculations and the profit calculations are based on transaction-based costing. The profit is determined per transaction and must be positive. Prices are used for communication with clients: a high price is associated with high quality, a low price is used to persuade customers to buy. The prices are based on the product's cost price; the focus of marketing is to bring about a transaction.

A price different from that in the shop is sometimes used on the Internet (dual-pricing methodology). The difference cannot be justified by lower costs, but by building customer knowledge so that focused direct communication is possible. Greater turnover can also lead to more discount from manufacturers, so that the total margin rises. For a dual-channel strategy and a dual-pricing strategy, consideration of the marketing orientation is essential. Alongside the product orientation, for the Internet a target group or customer orientation will be necessary to be able to stimulate repeated buying behaviour.

16.1.4 Communication

Marketing communication for an internally focused marketing orientation is strongly focused on mass communication. This is communication to a mass market – customers and buyers are unknown – and it is about inducing a transaction. The automation of communications expressions is limited, and advertising in printed and other mass media is often used. Computerized support involves the communication form, for example the automatic design of the advertisement. Any possible effects of the advertising are measured via market research, sales statistics and market share; market research can also measure the top-of-mind position and the product's associations.

16.1.5 Applications of IT and the Internet

The application of IT is aimed at increasing efficiency and lowering costs. This fits within the value discipline of operational excellence. Naturally there is an overlap with product excellence, but from a marketing perspective this is minimal. Product innovations are prompted from the same efficiency aspiration as the application of IT. Product development is also a specific application, driven by innovation.

The application of IT within marketing is minimal; the application of the Internet will also be minimal. The Internet is regarded as a communication opportunity for the organization and the product. In the previous section we observed that the layout of the site would be efficient, and the information will be strongly sender-directed, including detailed information about results, the management and the mission statement. For products, the communication is also very sender-directed: plenty of information about product criteria, sales points and an FAQ. There is no opportunity for interaction, or at the very most an email address, but whether a reply will be sent is uncertain.

The Internet is regarded as an electronic brochure on which not too much money should be spent. The Internet budget is indeed often part of the marketing budget, and the execution and hosting lies with the IT department. Given the type of information which is provided, there is little need to modify the site regularly. In some cases there is an RSS feed with information about the organization or the product from other media.

This characterization of internal or product orientation is summarized in Table 16.1.

Table 16.1 Characterization of internal or product orientation

Internal or product orientation	Focus	IT and Internet support
Customer relations	Based on product characteristics and price	No direct technology application, sometimes only for customer relations programmes (savings programmes directed at transactions)
Product	Based on products and efficiency	None, or at best information about sales and product characteristics on the Internet
Distribution	Via indirect channels	Delivery terms and conditions, and delivery. By linking systems or tags, VMI-like propositions are also possible
Price	Fixed price based on cost price	Cost price calculations and profitability models
Communication	Mass communication	For laying out commercials and advertisements
Information	Market information, often via market research and sales data	Processing information for production and planning
Organization	Hierarchical, strongly financially driven	ERP and financial calculation models
IT/Internet	For Internet processes, for products and accounting. ERP is an important application. Internet-only information about the organization and product characteristics	Extremely limited for marketing. Sometimes a few supporting modules via one's own system (PC)
Sales process	Support for the distribution channel, highly transaction-orientated (and margin-orientated)	Pipeline management and scorecards for sales and planning

16.2 Market orientation: target group focus

A changing orientation is caused by different market conditions, the application of a CRM system and by a different value discipline (Figure 16.3).

With target group or market orientation, attention shifts from the management mainly out to the market position. In particular the relative position in a specific market segment is important. There is a clear focus on target groups, in other words on recognizing the wishes and desires occurring among target groups, and then on attuning the offer to those wishes and desires. Possible extra dimensions here are striving towards a competitive advantage within the target group, and inducing repeat transactions (repeat sales). In contrast to the internal orientation, more time is devoted to following the competition and the relative market position. A specific objective is to enhance the market share within the specific market segment. This focus is sometimes called 'competitor-centred', although this is not entirely appropriate because the relationship with the target group is just as important.

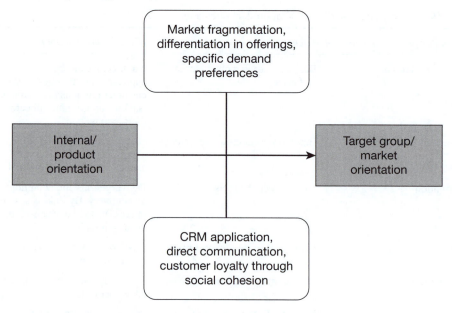

Figure 16.3 Changes in orientation, cause and consequences

The target group orientation equates to the classic market approach, but the market is more specified and smaller in scope. The problem is also different to that in a class market approach, namely in building a solid position in the market segment and enticing customers into repeat purchases. This means direct communication plays a more important role in this orientation. In the 1980s it was largely the direct marketing which determined the principles for the target group approach:

- Determine your target group and identify your customers.
- Communicate directly with the potential customers (identified relations).
- Measure the response of the actions.
- Record the purchases and use this information for new communication.

In particular, the direct distribution channel (webshop) and the focused communication to the target group are typical here (Figures 16.4 and 16.5).

It is precisely this target group approach and the application of direct marketing which were made possible by the application of IT. Databases enabled the address details of clients to be recorded. Through the link with customer cards or as part of the ordering process from mail-order companies and direct writers, it was possible to record the purchases. Segmentation and analysis, and the use of laser printers, made it possible to communicate personally.

IT is the basis for the current approach to the target group. The Internet has added a new dimension to this, namely personal communication that is interactive and focused. The Internet offers the following opportunities:

- direct communication through the Internet site, personally through the personal log-in facilities;

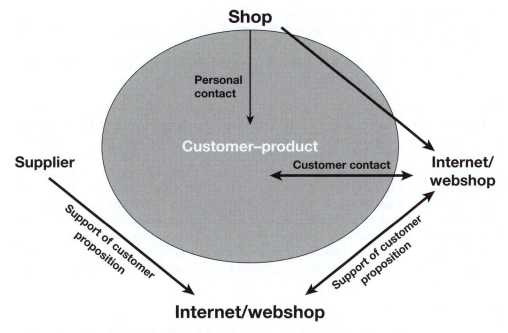

Figure 16.4 Focused marketing to a target group

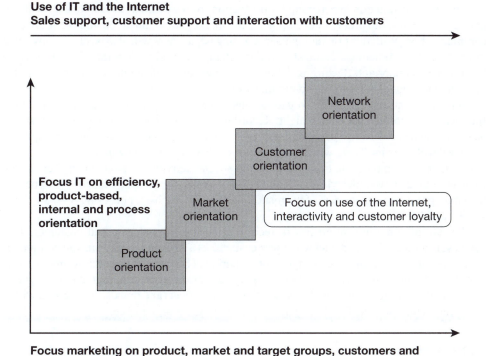

Figure 16.5 Target group orientation

- direct communication through email;
- continuous market research and market communication through blogs, social media and bulletin boards; and
- direct sales via the webshop, enabling automatic recording of purchases at the customer level.

Through the application of IT and the Internet, the target group orientation has gained significance. A focus on the competition and the target group is important to apply the Internet and IT in the right way, which should lead to a larger market share. If the competition has used the Internet differently, for example by selling direct, a dynamic arises in the market whereby the competitors must determine their own strategy and marketing orientation afresh. The continuous analysis of the target group and the customer leads to a rising significance of marketing in the decision making. Marketing also needs to adapt its activities to this orientation. The activities and instruments are determined on the basis of the wishes of the target group. Through continuous contact with the target group and a focus on this target group, changes in the market and customers' purchasing behaviour must be recognized quickly, so that the organization can modify its proposition as quickly as possible to stay ahead of the competition.

16.2.1 Product or service

The offer is attuned to the wishes and desires of the target group. This finds expression in product differentiation and offering a variety of products to a variety of market segments. The products must be distinguished from the competition, or the market approach must contribute to a distinction in perception. Information from a continuous relationship with the market determines the product development, the market communication and the individual communication. With this orientation the marketing department will also be closely involved in product development (in contrast to the internally focused orientation). The after-sales service is also important. Recording the purchasing details (with addresses) is important for the guarantee, but also for future communication.

To have this all run efficiently, organizations increasingly encourage registration via the Internet after a product has been bought. Recording purchases has thus become an automatic process. The details are also used for direct communication, such as keeping buyers updated on new developments. There will also be a degree of social cohesion within the target group. Companies can capitalize on this by organizing special activities to stimulate this cohesion, such as fashion shows, lifestyle shows and holiday expos. Sponsoring activities to appeal to the target group can also be part of the marketing strategy, such as sponsoring football clubs, skaters and F1 drivers.

The role of computerization lies in recording customers and potential customers (the database), in maintaining contact with these customers (CRM) and in carrying out continuous analysis of the market and the changes in the market. The Internet has an information role, but also a limited sales role. The Internet plays a major role in bringing about the social cohesion of the target group and the association with products and brands. A clear role within the social media, such as Facebook and Twitter, is of great importance.

16.2.2 Distribution

With distribution it is also important to reach the target group. There thus needs to be a clear location policy, in which the action radius of the intended target group is important. Location is also important for the desired attractive force on the target group. As we saw earlier, a distinction can be drawn between convenience shopping and luxury items, where there is a distinctive purchasing behaviour. In the target group orientation the image of the shop is extremely significant to support the desired positioning (you buy a Swatch wristwatch from a different shop than a Rolex). The position in the shop also plays a role: the shelf position and the shelf space. Important items have a greater shelf space and a conspicuous position on the shelf. The shopkeeper derives a specific status from being permitted to sell these items.

Alongside the indirect distribution there will also be limited direct distribution. These direct ways are a consequence of acceptance of the Internet as a distribution channel. Alongside the indirect distribution, manufacturers also develop the possibility of buying directly through the Internet. There are various reasons for this. Direct sales also furnish a direct insight into the target group, what is sold and what preferences exist in the market. Particularly with distinctive target groups and changes in the market, it is vital for a manufacturer to retain this feeling. In fashion, buying by the retail stores often needs to occur six months in advance. This causes a delay in signalling market changes. With direct sales the manufacturer is better able to assess the market and can work the market more effectively. Normally there is no price difference between the retail price and the price paid through the manufacturer's webshop. There are several reasons for this:

- Sales are not intended to increase the market share.
- The interests in existing retail are too great to bring about any change in this.
- Differing prices lead to a lack of clarity in the market and a loss of focus.
- The objective of the webshop is supportive of classic retail and is intended mainly to obtain direct contact with the customers, and thereby also to obtain information directly from 'the market'.

16.2.3 Price

The price utilized per target group may differ. This difference depends on the market circumstances (competition), the market position (market leader, follower or infiltrator) and the sales circumstances. A bottle of beer will be cheaper in the supermarket than in a restaurant or a disco. There are various target groups, various choices and various buying behaviours. The price will be determined by external (market) causes. The price strategy for a target group orientation is determined by the market and purchasing circumstances and not by the manufacturer's cost price. The (marketing) choice of a manufacturer is only whether they want to serve this target group. If the average price level lies below their own cost price, and if there is no possibility of dictating the price over time as a market leader, a different target group/market must be selected, with a higher price level.

16.2.4 Communication

Communication with the target group is through classic media, such as radio, television and print. But it is precisely for this target group orientation that direct communication is so important. Alongside creating a transaction, what is so typical with the internal orientation is that a relationship with the client is also envisaged, which should lead to repeat purchasing. Communication is important here. Direct communication by phone and letter were the classic media for direct marketing; currently communication more often occurs via the Internet and email. To achieve this, the link with a CRM system is important. With this orientation, two types of communication can be distinguished (Figure 16.6):

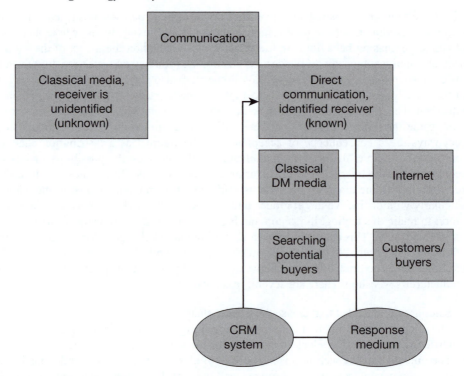

Figure 16.6 CRM system within the communications strategy

- classic communication to the target group; and
- communication to identified recipients.

The CRM system is the central system and is often part of an ERP (enterprise resource planning) system (see Chapter 8), so that direct advantage can be taken of demand changes. By also using the opportunities offered by campaign management, a continuous communication cycle can be created, stimulating repeat purchasing. For this, however, the contact details, the purchasing details and all direct communication expressions (and the response) must be kept updated.

16.2.5 Information

Market information is vital for a good target group approach. This information could be generic, such as the scope of the market, the competition and distribution points, but it could also be very specific. Market research is used for the generic information. This provides an insight into the market relationships, the trends and the market scope. Because of the dynamism in the market, these generic details need to be checked regularly. Continuous market research is then used.

An organization's own information supply can be used for specific information. The company's position in the market can be determined based on sales data. The role of retail can be determined through distribution point analysis, as can neighbourhood and city profiles. This enables developments to be tracked at the regional level, while determining the effectiveness

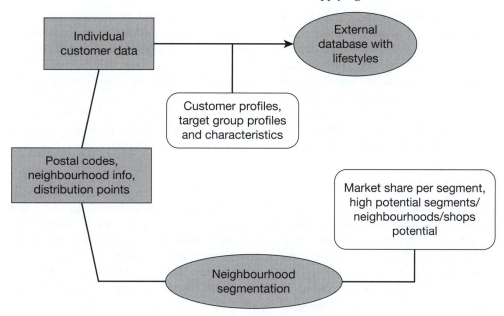

Figure 16.7 Customer data as the basis for target group profiling

of distribution points. Specific support for the distribution is then possible for manufacturers or purchasing combinations (or other collaborative ventures).

Recording sales data can also enable developments to be determined based on individual purchases and customers. This could lead to direct communication, as described above, but also to an analysis of target group profiles. By linking the individual customer criteria to external databases, customer profiles can be produced, and target group penetration can also be indicated at the segment level (Figure 16.7).

16.2.6 Organization

With this market orientation there is an organizational structure where the marketing activities are grouped around products and product groups based on product/market combinations. The organization will always have a top-down information provision, in common with the internal orientation. The marketing activities are aimed at the listed target groups. The organizational structure is adapted for this target group orientation. This could be through a matrix organizational form, where the external departments have a specific focus on a market segment and purchase the products internally for this. Unit managers enjoy a considerable degree of freedom in the products and services they want to sell to the listed market segment. Their success is determined on the basis of the success of the marketing activities (market share) and in terms of the yield from their activities. Internal tensions could arise between the tied purchasing and the possible fact that not all available products are offered to the market. Tensions between the units (internal and external) mean that this organizational form is less effective.

A different organizational form is the independently guided teams, as in a cluster organization. Here clusters have their own focus and objectives. The external clusters have a greater degree of freedom to buy in products and services and to then offer them to the target group. Internet facilities can often be used, such as F&A (financing), IT and human resource management (HRM) support. The clusters' considerable degree of freedom can also lead to their own brand being used, or a different company name. Strategic business units (SBUs) are then formed, with a considerable degree of authorization for the external activities. This can ultimately lead to independently operating companies within a holding. Each company has its own proposition for the market; however, information is often shared internally. These organizational forms do indeed have many characteristics of the internal orientation, such as strong financial control and financial objectives, aspirations for a high (acceptable) return and hierarchical control. Operational freedom is a freedom with strict restraints.

16.2.7 IT and Internet applications

Alongside systems orientated towards the internal processing of orders (from shops and distribution points), stock and invoicing, various systems are also used in support of the marketing. The administrative systems are part of an ERP platform. This platform is configured on the basis of the operational processes. Support is provided per independent unit for that unit's activities, and the necessary information is offered. The ERP platform is a combination of standardized information processes and departmental application support (based on action and function). Thus the invoicing department has its own application, based on the central information provision, and this also applies to production and management.

Marketing was an exception. The ERP platform did indeed offer support for marketing with reports and analyses based on turnover data, but this was not sufficient. Support mainly concerned the need for an internal orientation, such as sales figures, turnover analyses and yields figures. Because companies also wanted to update and manage individual relationships, a need arose for specific information. This information had to comprise address-related information, profiling of the type of contact and historical communication information. The first need here was felt by departments which had direct customer contact, namely the call centres. Customers called in, and the agent then needed to have immediate access to each customer's data. If this was not the case, direct support could not be offered to the caller. The information was thus a 'core requirement' for this department and thus for marketing with the target group orientation (and customer orientation as we will see later). Specific software was acquired to be able to monitor the telephone traffic and support the agent. The market leader in this field was Siebel Systems. But the call centre was not isolated in its information provision. Other systems needed to be used, such as sales systems, invoicing and accounts administration. The result was a multiplicity of interfaces with corresponding problems.

The need grew for an integrated system which supported CRM (customer relationship management). The CRM system was then linked directly to an ERP system, which led to integration of the Siebel system within Oracle. A CRM application was also developed within ERP systems, creating an integral system with the envisaged interfaces, as with SAP. Marketing thus became a direct component of the standard systems and the standard information provision. All the functions were available within the CRM system for information storage, analysis and use of the data for direct (telephone) communication and indirect communication by letter or email. This laid the foundation for the organization's enhanced customer orientation and for a switch in the marketing orientation from target group orientation to customer orientation.

16.2.8 Sales process

The sales process is aimed on the one hand at inducing a transaction, but also at getting the same customer to buy more. The RFM module is applied here, aiming at getting the customer to buy more frequently, though with more variety of items and a higher purchasing amount (basket value). In order to be able to achieve this good support is needed with IT and the Internet.

To bring about the transaction, the CRM system will also need to have a sales module. A pipeline (sales funnel) is defined within this module. A pipeline is a timeline from the first contact to the sale. Particularly with the more complicated products, a longer timeline and more intense salesperson support is needed. The timeline can indicate with precision which contacts are needed, how often and with what message. A calculation of chance must be provided continually to form the basis for production or supply.

A good pipeline management system leads to greater effectiveness of the sale and the salesperson and to effective communication with the right message. CRM systems do not of themselves lead to a change in market orientation, but a CRM system is indeed a basic precondition for customer orientation. Based on the CRM system's information at the individual level and the possibility of integrating communication and the Internet within such a system, a change in orientation is indeed enabled. This must always be matched with a change in value discipline (from product excellence to customer intimacy); a change in competition strategy and market share, a focus on competition to share or wallet, and a focus on individual customers.

Table 16.2 provides a summary of the contents of this section.

Table 16.2 Profiling target group or market orientation

Target group or market orientation	Focus	IT/Internet support
Product	On target group and market share and thus also on competition	Competition analysis, market research, profile analyses
Distribution	Via indirect channels. Limited direct sales (Internet and own outlets)	Analysis of distribution, stock levels, ERP systems, pipeline management, webshop and active in social media
Price	Differs according to target group. Market-related price policy	Yield analyses and price elasticity calculation
Communication	Classic mass media alongside direct communication	CRM, databases, response analyses. Active in social media, blogs. Internet as support before and after the sale
Information	Target group information, response information, market developments. Market share	ERP and CRM systems. Internal reports and analyses. Support for direct customer contact
Organization	Focused on target group, matrix, cluster or department based	Permanent support for basic processes. Specific applications per function
IT/Internet	For Internet processes, for linkage with suppliers (based on	Strongly aimed at efficiency in activity execution. Strongly

continued overleaf

Table 16.2 continued

Target group or market orientation	Focus	IT/Internet support
	EDI, VMI, RFID), for reporting and analysis	aimed at supporting direct communication
Sales process	Support for the distribution channel and points. Support for account management and salespeople	Pipeline management, information about target groups, profile analyses, RFM analyses

16.3 Customer orientation: relationship focus

In customer orientation it is not only the market position or competitors' activities which should be considered, but also the relationship with individual buyers (Figure 16.8). A strong relationship with individual buyers is the foundation for a strong competitive position. The organization focuses on buyers' individual wishes and needs. An important guiding element here is customer satisfaction and the number of contact moments. The more contact there is between a customer and an organization, the more intense the relationship will be. Intense, interactive contacts generally lead to a large degree of customer satisfaction. Interaction with customers is the basis for product development and offering personal facilities, such as services, information or an extra warranty. This demand orientation causes a change in focus, from transaction orientated (supply driven), which was the case with the internal/product

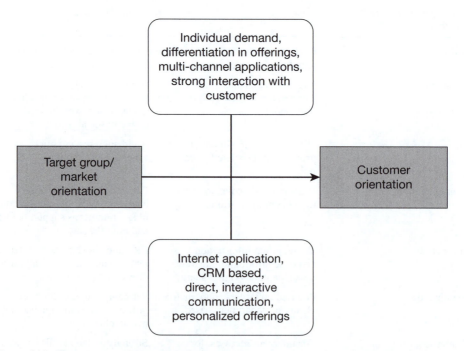

Figure 16.8 Change to customer orientation

orientation and target group/market orientation. Now there is a demand orientation (demand driven).

The orientation switch from market orientation to customer orientation is substantial (Figure 16.9). This switches the focus from marketing to identifiable relations (customers). The deployment of IT and the Internet will also change as a result. In target group orientation there was still a limited deployment of the Internet for sales, but with customer orientation the Internet becomes an integral part of marketing and sales. The Internet supports the sales process, maintains communications and is the means of building and maintaining relationships. There are also major changes for organizations, because the results of the actions are measured on the basis of customer-based yields.

Sales are no longer regarded as an occurrence at one moment with a one-sided influence from the supplier, but as an ongoing process of mutual influencing in a dual-sided relationship. There is a relation orientation rather than the transaction orientation of the previous orientations. The emphasis is clearly on the customer relationship and customer satisfaction, and on loyalty and interaction rather than market share. This could also be indicated as aiming for structurally sustainable relationships. The Internet has in fact become the basis for interaction and communication to achieve this. Purchasers are supported as fully as possible in their buying process (ORCA model).

As shown in Figure 16.10, marketing is focused on direct, interactive customer relations. Sales are also proactive on the basis of using the Internet and personal contacts. The role of the manufacturer changes through its own webshop.

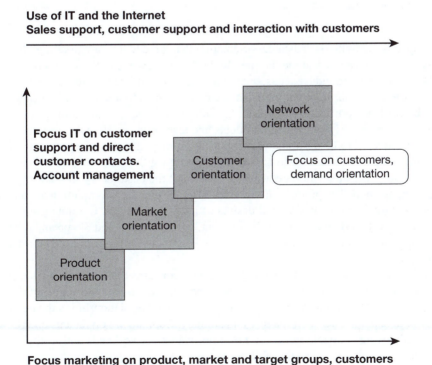

Figure 16.9 Changing orientation, cause and consequence

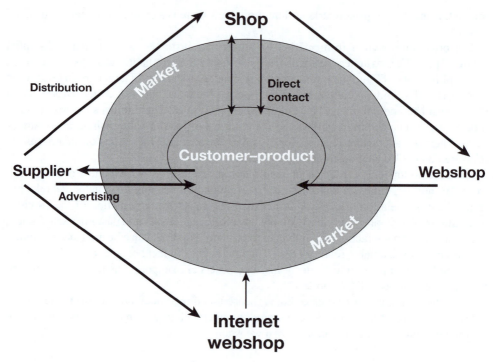

Figure 16.10 New market approach

It is specifically with this customer orientation that there will be e-marketing: direct marketing combined with IT and the Internet. In the first instance only limited account will still need to be taken of individual needs, but the organization will need to implement increasing numbers of adaptations to actually be able to capitalize on individual needs. Considered here could be further modifications to contacts with customers, an adaptation of the production process, modularly constructed products and also services. Here the customer decides what is considered to be desirable. An organization may also opt to appoint an individual account manager for each customer or for a limited group of customers. This enables optimization of the interaction between the wishes of the customers and their 'translation' by the organization. The product and services offer, pricing and distribution are adapted as closely as possible to the wishes and desires of individual buyers. Communication will be extremely direct, particularly using the Internet, both via email and Skype and other interactive opportunities (social networks, mobile). The focus shifts from a sales process to a buying process.

In this case the organization is strongly orientated towards the customer relationship and all marketing instruments and activities must be adapted to this end, but not only this: it must have penetrated through to management that the individual relationship is the determinant for the organization's decision-making and strategy. Capitalizing on the customer's wishes also entails being available when the customer wants, at weekends and in the evenings. Fortunately the Internet offers this ability.

16.3.1 Product or service

The products or services that are offered are adapted as far as possible to the individual wishes of customers. This applies both to the product in the narrow sense (the physical product) as well as to the product in a broader sense, the physical product augmented by the services. Trial subscriptions could serve as an example of pre-sales here, and maintenance as an example of after-sales service. Individualizing the services creates a customized product perception. But price, communication and distribution are also adapted to individual wishes. Examples of this are pricing based on historical buying conduct (the relationship) and 'time-based delivery', where the client determines the time at which the products can be delivered.

The production process is set up to meet individual wishes as fully as possible. Modular production and production on demand make this possible. It is also possible to individualize a standard product, for example to print a T-shirt with a specified name, or to have cufflinks engraved with a specified text. This semi-customization is initiated by the customer. A structural binding can be created, based on the knowledge of the individual wishes. The supplier understands the customer immediately. This could be extremely small-scale, by immediately stating the customer's account number and address when ordering, but tailor-made offers can also be provided such as music of your own preference, or selected books which meet your tastes precisely. The knowledge a company builds up of its customers must then be the basis for an individual offer and for personal communication.

An important component of customer orientation is services, because these services can be personal and precisely tailored. Based on the personal contacts, a company can react to a customer's wishes and needs. The contact individual has immediate access to the historical data which forms the foundation for the personal relationship. Part of this personal approach is also the proactive approach to customers about service intervals, product changes, stock clearances or other issues relevant to the customer. In all cases it is up to the provider to keep the relevant contact and profile information as updated as possible, and to use this in the relationship with the customer. IT, and particularly the CRM system, will form the basis, but it is the Internet in particular which gives shape to the customer orientation.

16.3.2 Distribution

The greatest possible flexibility is needed to meet the wishes of the individual buyer. This can occur through rapid delivery (a streamlined logistical process), through adequate stocks, through long opening hours and through extra support for purchasing. Here too the Internet offers many opportunities: by notifying customers of the precise stock, delivery times and the logistical process and by making purchasing suggestions. But this is possible not only by using the Internet as the distribution channel; the information can also be provided within the existing distribution network. An intensive information exchange between the supplier and the distribution is then vital. This information exchange is necessary to support the buying process: customers must be able to order immediately and must know whether certain items are in stock. A combination of Internet and distribution points is a development offering many opportunities for direct support. Customers order on the Internet: the product can be modified or simply despatched. Customers can also choose to collect the products from the supplier's distribution point (click and collect). This could be a branch of an associated company, a collection point or simply the supplier's shop.

Through this combination of online searching, ordering and buying, but also by simply collecting from the shop, there can be maximum capitalization on individual wishes. The

Internet supports the buying process, and the shop supports the after-sales. Information about the customer must be available online, but also at the collection point (in the shop). This enables shop staff to provide personal service, but also to offer associated products or furnish other advice.

A customer orientation is certainly not possible for all organizations and in all markets. It is particularly difficult in the FMG (food manufacturing group), where tailored operations are only possible if working with special theme packages, diet foods or food supplements. For all other products it is difficult, and there will in fact be an orientation towards target groups. Shifting production orientation to market orientation gives the maximum possible yield.

For service-providing companies customer orientation is ideally suited. After all the product is shaped for and with customers, and applying the Internet as a sales medium offers greater opportunities for applying a customer orientation. This is because physical products must always be awaited before they are delivered. This waiting period can also be used to adapt a product to individual wishes, so that semi-customization is possible.

16.3.3 Price

In customer orientation the price is not linked to a product, as was the case with the other two orientations, but it is linked to a relationship. This could be contractual pricing, where there has been a negotiating process between the principal and the supplier. It is also possible that a framework agreement has been agreed, in which a contract price depends on a certain calculation formula. It could comprise the order size each time, ordering in a specific time-frame or a specific product compilation (quality norms). The overall agreements and rules are then the individual price. A graduated scale is also sometimes used, where the client receives a discount for specific criteria, such as self-collection, ordering extra items or a discount on the next order. Another option for personal pricing is the possibility that the customers decide for themselves which components are desired. This is the opposite of the discount scale. A customer of Ryanair, for example, can decide whether to use priority board-ing or to take extra baggage for which he or she pays extra. With other airlines it is also possible to pay extra for business class or for a seat with extra legroom. By using a discount scale or a facilities scale, a personal price is created for the customer.

Price negotiation

The price of souvenirs is often negotiated on holiday. The seller assumes that tourists will offer a far lower price than is being asked. To accelerate this negotiating process, the tourist offers the price he or she thinks the souvenir is worth. If this price is above the seller's minimum price then the deal is rapidly sealed; if this price is below the minimum price, the seller knows immediately not to waste any further time here. A similar method is also used for business transactions, where buyer and seller consider together what a realistic market price would be, taking account of a realistic profit, to determine the selling price together. Here it is a challenge for the seller to actually be able to deliver profitably at this price, and for the buyer to achieve the market price.

16.3.4 Communication

With customer orientation a significant part of the communication will be direct, and where possible also interactive. This enables capitalizing on the client's wishes immediately. An inventory of the wishes is also needed to be able to make a personal offer. Sometimes the personal offer can also be a perception, as the previous example about price negotiation showed. But direct communication alone is not enough. An organization also needs to attract new clients. This is no longer possible by just actively seeking 'addresses' in the market; the opportunities for unsolicited mailing or emailing have been severely restricted by recent legislation. Customers need to be attracted spontaneously.

That the role of classic media has not yet gone for good is apparent from the following:

- Through the classic media the advantages of the structural relationships and the attractiveness of the offer can be communicated to the intended target group.
- By communicating the advantages of the 'customer intimacy' value discipline, customers can be attracted and distinguishing competitive advantages can be communicated.
- Because a structural relationship is sustainable, the organization must also be regarded as reliable, sound and honest: this is possible by communicating with the classic media.
- The classic media also offer opportunities for response. This can be done through a coupon or by listing a telephone number. It is better to list an Internet address, through which respondents can immediately arrive at the website.

A successful approach can be achieved by the combination of television and Internet. Brand awareness can be created by airing commercials on television and actions can be communicated quickly. The Internet address must be communicated immediately and very clearly, so that the response can be measured instantly. The television commercial is deployed for acquisition, while the Internet is for maintaining the contacts. In this orientation the classic media have acquired a different role from that in other orientations. This is, of course, logical, because they assume a market communication, while customer orientation and customer intimacy assume a personal relationship.

For customers it is important to be able to communicate immediately with an organization at one's own initiative (demand-driven communication). With the Internet the customer can communicate at any time by heading to the organization's website; they may be seeking a desired answer or information, but in doing so they also initiate a personal contact by sending a message through the contact section.

The role of IT and the Internet is crucial with this orientation; in fact the orientation is not really possible without IT or the Internet. The CRM system also keeps the data current and initiates the communication. The Internet is the most appropriate channel, followed by the telephone.

16.3.5 Information

For the customer-focused orientation it is necessary to have detailed customer information. This could be regular details (contact and profile information), but also communication and buying information. Regular research reveals whether the customer is satisfied and if specific changes may be necessary for better support of the buying process and the purchasing perception.

Customer satisfaction is also measured with this target group orientation, but here it is the satisfaction with the supplied product or service. The issue with this orientation is mainly to determine whether the target group is satisfied. Surveys are conducted randomly. With the customer-focused orientation, satisfaction assessment also encompasses aspects such as service provision, fulfilment of individual wishes, satisfaction with the direct communication and satisfaction on the handling of purchasing and complaints. Reactions to the website and to Internet conduct are also measured, such as navigation, product presentation and supplying the products.

For the distinction between good and less good customers, characteristics such as loyalty and value are used. Loyalty can be assessed on the basis of buying frequency and how wide a range of goods is bought (RFM). The value is the profit an organization has gained from a customer, based on the total duration of a relationship (lifetime value). For example, for a car dealer the value of a customer could be the number of vehicles that customer has bought from that dealership over his or her lifetime, but it could also be the maintenance services the garage carries out. Over the short term the return per vehicle sold could be regarded as a profit on this vehicle, in which the profit from services could be included. The total profit per customer is the value a customer represents. The value of an individual transaction, which determined the value in the internal orientation and the target group orientation, is now of secondary importance. Another example is baby nappies. It is not about the profit per transaction, but the profit for the term over which a baby uses nappies. For medicine suppliers it is clear that if medicines must be consumed for an entire life to treat a life-threatening illness they will have a real lifetime value.

On the basis of the 'value and loyalty' indicators, customer clusters can be produced which determine the service provided to the individual customers within a specific cluster. The profiles of the customers within a cluster can also determine the potential of a customer. If the profile of a certain relation matches the profile of customers in the golden cluster, more attention can be devoted to this customer to make him or her a golden customer. Of course the other way around is also possible. The profiles are built up using actual behaviour and characteristics and not assumptions. Cluster analyses and behaviour analyses (behavioural targeting) are used to encourage customers, but also to be able to predict the behaviour of individual customers. The role of automatic behaviour recording (which is so easy to do with the Internet) is the basis for this type of advanced analysis.

An important component of information provision in the customer-focused orientation is integrating information from various company operations and exchanging information with collaborative market parties (such as suppliers or shops). The basis must then be the individual customer. During the contacts all relevant details must be available, such as sales, payment discipline, stocks, delivery times and historical buying behaviour. This means not only an integrated information system, such as ERP linked to CRM, but also linking external systems with other market parties. The details must be shared with other company operations and other market parties if this is relevant for providing good service to the customer. The data must also be exchanged regularly to be able to harmonize production and logistical processes. There thus needs to be agreement on the method of recording and the use of standards for orders, products and names. Good inspection of the interfaces is necessary, as well as the same point of view for all parties, especially the customer!

16.3.6 Organization

When focusing on individual buyers it is no longer the products which are the starting point for an organizational structure, as with the internal and marketing orientation, but the customers, or in fact the needs of the customers. The organizational structure is attuned to the products from the range that is bought by the same customers (or groups). This requires the definition of a flexible division structure for customer groups and needs. There also needs to be a distinction in the distribution form. Classic distribution requires competences and skills other than direct distribution with the Internet. The organizational structure is aimed at achieving flexible integration concerning products, with an integration at the customer level. Work is done in multidisciplinary teams to enhance the service to customers; this function can also be fulfilled by the account manager.

For customers, this organizational form means there is just one point of contact within the organization. This contact point is fully informed and authorized to take decisions. A full insight into the customer, the history and the relevant operational function is needed for this. He or she will use the CRM application. Integrating information in this orientation is not restricted to the activities surrounding a product or a product/market combination, but reaches across all products that a customer or customer group buys. Strategic account managers are appointed for important customers, arranging all internal contacts. Those who are in touch with customers – the contact individual, the account manager or the strategic account manager – must be authorized to take all decisions relevant to the customer relationship, including delivery terms and conditions, pricing and returns.

The functions which the contact individuals have with customers guide the decision-making processes. These processes must be orientated towards customer contact. It must be an integrated approach for the entire operational process and not just for specific sub-processes or specific functions. This means there must be a process-orientated organizational form in which the processes are coordinated. The binding factor is customer information. Based on this information the operational activities are planned, results assessments are made and stock and production are determined. In this process-orientated organization, customers will also be involved directly or indirectly in drawing up product specifications. This can capitalize to the full on the wishes and needs of customers; greater customer loyalty is achieved and a better estimation of potential sales can be made.

In the functional configuration of activities there is optimization of parts of the operational process. If this is compared to the other two orientations, the instruments supporting the external activities in this orientation are determined more by individual customers. The marketing activities are no longer regarded as a separate operational process, apart from the other functions. For the customer-orientated organization it is important to regard the marketing activities, based on the individual customer relationship, as the basis for the internal structure, and to be integrated with the other operational functions. This enables a better and quicker anticipation of changes in the market and the wishes of individual customers.

The organizational structure is based on these customer wishes and the interaction with customers. This interaction in particular is important, because it enables important information to be obtained which is of interest for the marketing activities, but also for an organization's other operational functions. In the other two orientations there was clearly a product/market relationship, the classical marketing 'to market'. This is an inside-out approach. With customer orientation there is a dominant position of the wishes and needs of customers; these guide the product and services offering. Information collection and exchange, both within the organization and with external market parties, is essential. This is an outside-in approach where the external party, the customer, is the determinant for an organization's activities. For this reason the information will be based on the information from the customer, the behaviour of these customers and communication with the customers.

Alongside information systems the Internet is an integral component of this process. The organization's focus on customer contact makes it possible to apply a division in organizational components: customer contact, production and support. Customer contact is particularly important and determines profitability, while the other components are facilitative and can also be regarded separately from the organization. These components can be bought in from other organizations which have a different orientation. Construction companies, for example, use subcontractors and other service providers, allowing them to capitalize to the fullest on customer wishes, and enabling them to be flexible as organizations. Advertising agencies have also worked with subcontractors for decades. But with the opportunities offered by the Internet to maintain a direct relationship with these suppliers, this organizational form is occurring more often, and matches the increased focus on customer relations perfectly. The growth of sole traders, freelancers and small independent operators without staff can be partly attributed to this development.

16.3.7 *Application of IT and the Internet*

It will be clear from all this that IT is deployed to translate customer wishes into production. These wishes must be stored and form the basis for planning and developing new products and services. It is important here that all sales can be assigned to individual customers, and also to record all communication with these customers unequivocally. In particular, the combination of communication and sales is a good guide to the success of an organization. This enables a determination of who responds the best to which communications, when there is a response and what is bought. This interaction between marketing communication and sales is an indication of the success of the communication, but also of the offer.

By linking the individual details to profiles, potential customers can be identified. The market, as it is defined in the previous two orientations, is now the customer or the customer base. For marketing this switch means there no longer has to be a search for buyers for the products, but for products for the customers. These products are determined on the basis of customer wishes. The Internet plays a vital role in all facets – as support in the buying process (ORCA) for sales via the webshop, but also with social media. Bonding with the customer group is important. Within LinkedIn and Hyves there are separate customer sections for companies where customers exchange information about products and the organization. This creates a strong social bond (cohesion) between customers and exercises a stimulatory effect on an organization. There is a conscious choice for a social platform outside one's own website: to demonstrate the social cohesion but also to display an aura to the entire market. If there is only a blog on one's own website, the impact is clearly less. Often the website will refer to involvement in Facebook or LinkedIn. There is often also a reference to Twitter: 'Follow us on Twitter'. Particularly with Twitter, the initiative lies with the organization or the brand, and the social medium is used to communicate directly. With LinkedIn it is in fact the customers who discuss the organization or the brand, and who make up a sort of fan club.

With customer orientation, the role of IT and the Internet is vital for direct communication, direct contact and for directing marketing to other company disciplines. The Internet is more than a medium for information, sales or communication – the Internet application is the bond with the customers in every aspect.

Box 16.1 Air France-KLM enters the battle with price-cutters

DÜSSELDORF – Air France-KLM wants to use a new strategy to combat the competition from price-cutters. In an interview with the German weekly *Wirtschaftswoche*, to be published on Monday, CEO Pierre-Henri Gourgeon notes that the airline is already working on new operational models for air traffic within Europe.

'We are going to concentrate the service on what the customer wants, and will offer specific services to a limited degree, such as check-in at the counter,' says Gourgeon.

Source: Nu.nl, 21 March 2010

16.3.8 Sales process

Customer relations are important for sales. Sales needs to be less focused on acquiring and recruiting new customers, and more on maintaining the relationship with existing customers. The sales department will also often be divided according to the value of customers. This draws a distinction between the strategic account, the major companies, the middle segment and small customers. The medium deployed is also adapted in accordance with this accounts classification.

For strategic accounts all available media are deployed: personal contacts, their own page and log-in facilities on the Internet, and often a separate call number or special call routing with the call centre (priority routing). These customers have to feel special and important. Everything is facilitated by IT: routing, recording and CRM.

For the middle segment, an account manager is assigned to a number of accounts. Sometimes, if wished, a log-in code is created for the Internet and a separate telephone number is allocated to the call centre. A general number is also used, but a specific code can be given via the voice response system (customer number), which will acknowledge the 'value' of the customer.

Support for all other customers is provided via the Internet site. Answers are provided to the most frequently asked questions (FAQs). The account manager uses the analysis of purchasing and communication, which forms the basis for new communication with the customer. The sales costs can be determined per customer, where greater costs may be incurred for good, strategic relations than for other customers.

A CRM system is essential for this system; account records, pipeline records and customer analyses are needed. The customer pyramid is used, as well as potential analyses per customer. The potential analysis is based on the profile analysis of good customers compared with those of less good customers. Particularly for potentially important customers, intense communication can occur because the lifetime value is high. At regular intervals the efforts will be evaluated and the customer value will be assessed anew. In customer orientation the costs will be assigned to an account as far as possible, and the profit and yield per customer (account) will also be calculated.

Table 16.3 provides a summary of the information discussed in this section.

16.4 Network orientation: demand focus

With customer orientation there is capitalization on the needs of individual customers. Based on individual behavioural characteristics, individuals or organizations can be aggregated into clusters with identical needs and wishes. This enables sufficient economy of scale to also be able to produce efficiently. In some instances, however, the relationship between supplier and customer can go even further than just producing a customized product or service. In such an instance there is said to be active collaboration or participation between market parties (Figure 16.11). This collaboration can only occur at the individual level. Particularly in the business-to-business market this occurs more often, but the application of the Internet means

Table 16.3 Customer orientation categorization

Customer orientation	Focus	IT/Internet support
Product	Customers and potential customers (often called accounts)	CRM, purchasing and profile analyses, communication support
Distribution	Often direct sales or support	Analysis of logistical process, delivery, customer satisfaction
Price	Differs per target group and per customer. The basis is the costs and yield per customer, as well as relation-linked criteria	Yield analyses, account analyses and yield calculations
Communication	Direct personal communication by account manager. Telephone and Internet	CRM, databases, response analysis. Active in social media, blogs. Internet as support before and after the purchase. Active account support and relationship management
Information	Customer information about use, decision makers, organizational structure, market circumstances, customers, pipeline information	ERP and CRM systems. Internal reports and analyses. Support for direct customer contact. Strong communication support
Organization	Focused on individual customer relations, account management system, strategic business units	Permanent support with basic processes. Specific applications per function and information per business unit and per customer (account)
IT/Internet	For Internet processes, for links with suppliers (EDI, VMI, RFID-based), for reporting and analysis. Often also direct link possible with customers' systems	Strongly focused on effectiveness of the communication and the contacts. Strongly focused on supporting direct communication
Sales process	Support for account management. Focused on customer relations. Higher share of wallet, more sales per customer	Pipeline management, information about customers, profile analyses, RFM analysis

it is also occurring increasingly in the consumer market. The offer is then adapted to the individual needs of a customer, often tailor-made. In many instances the collaboration or participation will go so far that a mutual risk is also undertaken.

This collaboration occurs especially in the industrial sector, where products are produced to order for one or more customers. An example of this is the aircraft industry, where customers can suggest modifications on the basis of a prototype, after which the aircraft goes into production if there have been sufficient orders. A different participation model also occurs: the customer buys an aircraft, but marketing is carried out together on the basis of profit-sharing. This collaboration also occurs in the IT industry in the development of products or specific software. Customer and provider work on the product together and share the risk, the costs and the profits.

Figure 16.11 Changing orientation, cause and consequence

Here there can be two types of participation:

- communal product development as described earlier, a strategic partnership; or
- a process-orientated partnership in which a partner participates in a process, such as with VMI or in webshops where the logistical service provider also participates in the success of a webshop.

The collaboration between customer and supplier is relatively new, and really only reaches maturity if there is also an insight into both roles and into all processes (Figure 16.12). This is the reason that applying the Internet is essential to support this orientation, but also to develop new initiatives together on the basis of the Internet. This is currently also done frequently in a collaborative venture, such as when launching a CD, where the artist, the studio and fans together pay for a project and share the profits. The collaboration between a publisher and an author can also occur in this way, where the author also undertakes marketing and assumes a risk in the book project. This orientation has suddenly become possible as a result of the following factors:

- The progress of technology enables individualization and small-scale production.
- The investments needed to make a project or product successful are too large to be carried by one party (such as an aircraft or IT system).
- The changes in communication and contact brought about by the Internet have enabled a more intense relationship, and such initiatives can also be supported automatically.
- The dynamism in the market has increased marketing risks. Payback times are shorter, so that a 'launching customer' is a precondition for marketing success.

With a strategic partnership with buyers there is a focus on supporting individual buyers in their buying process, and production comes about in close collaboration. Compared with customer orientation, the collaboration leads to a greater harmonization of the product or services on offer with the wishes and desires of the individual customer. There is often also a sharing of the risk, which is important in product innovations and products with a major investment, such as machinery, aircraft or IT systems. This is why the manufacturers who first applied the participation model, such as IBM and Boeing, were in these industries.

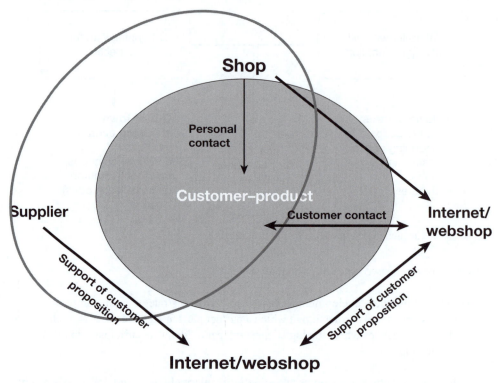

Figure 16.12 Close collaboration between customer, supplier and sales organization

A characteristic of this network orientation is sharing the risk or sharing in the result. The close harmonization of the products and services brings about a tighter relationship and greater customer satisfaction. Particularly given the dynamism of the market, this gives a strong competitive advantage. Naturally there are also disadvantages associated with this orientation:

- Interdependence is substantial. A purchaser cannot simply leave, and is bound for a considerable time to the supplier, while the supplier also cannot leave the purchaser.
- The results must be shared by the provider, and a purchaser often does not know exactly what the costs will be. The manageability of the investment is often a problem.
- Too strong a focus on a customer leads to a decline in focus on the market and on competitors.
- The tight relationship can cause laziness in innovation and can lead to less focus on market developments.

With the Internet the collaboration between web constructor, hosting partner, fulfilment partner and customer is an example of a multiparty collaboration. Depending on the arrangements, there is a customer versus supplier relationship or a partnership. In some instances these partners even set up a separate company for the customer, so as to be able to benefit from the success and share the risk. The separate company may be able to direct communally and be able to take responsibility with the marketing and market processing.

Other examples are portals, where a specific group is approached by suppliers who cooperate. Thus a youth portal could be produced by parties who have an offer for young people.

The participation is actually sought in the marketing (the portal) to be able to approach this target group. Youths will also feel a bond with a concept and not only with the individual providers.

16.4.1 Product or service

In network orientation the products and services offered to the buyer are better attuned to the wishes of the individual buyer. The production processes and the services offer are configured for customization. It is specifically this interplay between supplier and customer which is unique in this orientation. The close collaboration leads to more insight into each other's companies. The Internet facilitates the collaboration in every field. It is the Internet that is a basis for strategic collaboration because there are not yet any worn operational processes, the dynamism is very high and there are still different market relationships and market parties. With services the collaboration sometimes stretches so far that employees of a specific company also work on-site with the customer. These might be call centre agents, for example, or temporary employees and interim managers, but it could also be the staffing of an entire department. In reality this is insourcing by the recipient party.

The product or service is thus tailor-made, and the preconditions often differ depending on the costs model or the profit-sharing model, the location where the activities occur or the market risk.

16.4.2 Distribution

Distribution varies immensely. With customized work there is tight collaboration and a delivery date; sometimes there is an SLA (service level agreement) as a basis for delivery, but it is also possible that there is sharing within a proposition. A 'shop in a shop' concept in the retail outlet is an example, as is affiliate marketing. Here one party utilizes the attractiveness of another party to attract customers and sell more. It could even reach an extent where a shop-in-shop concept occurs on a website, where a shop also offers other shops (the click-through ratio is then the determinant for the billing model). Both instances concern a main party which is attractive in the market, so that other parties also wish to benefit from this.

16.4.3 Price

The price is often a combination of a fixed price and a variable part. This could be a bonus, a cost sharing or a profit-sharing agreement. A click-through ratio is also often used with affiliate marketing where a price is calculated for each customer who is linked through to the website of the other party. Constructions are sometimes created to share everything. Because of this variable pricing it is of course difficult and complicated to compare prices. Ultimately the added value which such an agreement has for one's own business model will be considered, as well as the market processing and the value for customers.

16.4.4 Communication

Communication in a network orientation will be continuous and tight. Often each other's systems are used. Sometimes employees do not even know that someone works for a different party (so-called insourcing). It is precisely this intense communication which is a strength of this concept. This enables optimum use to be made of each other's expertise. It is important to make the collaboration as transparent as possible and project members must strive towards the success of the project. There thus needs to be a communal goal to be able to carry out a collaboration successfully.

16.4.5 Market information

Although there is a strong focus on the relation and the provider, market developments will always be considered. In particular, developments among competitors (this applies to both parties) are important. If there are such collaborations, their risks must be considered.

Several important factors are:

- Time to market. The first mover has a competitive advantage over similar products.
- The market position of the collaborating parties. Major important organizations prefer to work with each other to gain more market strength. A smaller party can also collaborate with a larger party to extract more market strength for itself, while the larger party can access a niche, or can in fact become more flexible.
- There must be added value in the collaboration for both parties.
- There must be significant single-mindedness to make the product or service successful in the market.

16.4.6 Organization

Various organizational forms are possible in network orientation, ranging from a tight contractual collaboration with SLA agreements and penalty clauses, to setting up a combined company. The right form depends largely on the organizations, on their mutual trust and on the market position. There will often be a core organization, for example a project team, where the provider and the customer fulfil a communal role. This could in fact be part of a network organization where an organization has an increasing number of collaborative clusters with regularly changing parties, both for production and for customers. A network organization is a deeply implemented form of participation. The basis of the collaboration is the core competence of each organization, although huge investments are often required per project and various markets have to be served. To limit the financial risk a participation form can be sought. Collaboration with dominant customers in specific markets can also be the reason to form independent clusters – customer and market orientated. This produces a multiplicity of functionally separate clusters, which is in fact the network organization.

Table 16.4 provides a summary of what has been discussed in this section (see also Figure 16.13).

16.5 Applying the orientations

The marketing orientation is important for the way in which marketing instruments are applied and marketing activities are carried out. The marketing orientation is also important for the application of IT and the Internet. Differences can be noted according to orientation which can be traced back to an organization's degree of customer orientation. With an internal orientation there is a focus on products, operational excellence and on the distribution channel. With a market orientation there is a focus on the market or a sectional market. It is precisely here that market positioning is significant, as is the distinction in products (product excellence). With the customer orientation the individual, identified customer is at the core.

Table 16.4 Characterization of network and participation orientation

Network/participation orientation	Focus	IT/Internet support
Product	Collaboration, participation	Sharing systems and processes. Communal communication module
Distribution	Communal, or through participating with each other	Profit and cost reporting and analyses, insight into yields
Price	Determined mutually. Often a combination of fixed costs and a variable section. Comprises sharing costs or sharing yields	Financial model, ERP system, analysis and reporting software
Communication	Direct personal communication on a continuous basis at various levels. Both operational and project-related and strategic	Active reporting system. Project management report and financial reporting. Sharing ERP system
Information	Customer information, project information, information about decision-making, progress and planning	All processes are fully IT-driven and accessible to both parties
Organization	Sharing at a functional level, but also forming independent units between providers and customers. Network organization based on independent clusters	Independent financial system and reporting linked to systems of the participants
IT/Internet	For Internet processes, for linking with suppliers (EDI, VMI, RFID-based), for reporting and analysis. Often also direct links possible with participants' systems. Integral approach	Strongly focused on effectiveness of the communication and the contacts. Strongly focused on supporting direct activities, linked to participants
Sales process	Extremely specific client-orientated approach by dedicated sales team. Often long lead time. Significant management involvement	Opportunity management, information about customers, providers, market development and opportunities in the customer market

The individual needs are anticipated and the business model is based on a share of wallet rather than on transaction profit. With an orientation towards partners and participation there is close collaboration and often a shared risk. Operational functions are harmonized or are shared.

In these four cases e-marketing will differ markedly from support in communication and information provision (internal orientation), an after-sales support and information provision (market orientation) and an intense direct communication and sales (customer orientation) to sharing the infrastructure (participation orientation). The orientations determine the marketing instruments and activities, but also the role and function of marketing in an organization.

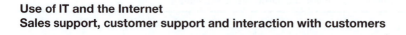

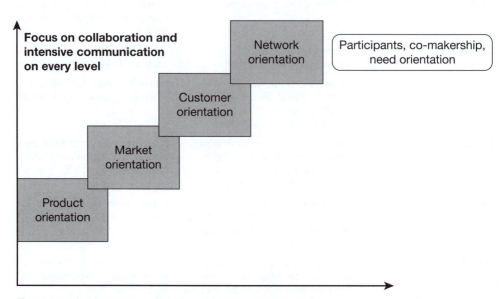

Figure 16.13 Changing orientation, network orientation

Summary

- Marketing orientations determine the position of marketing within an organization.
- Marketing orientations also determine the possibilities and the application of IT and the Internet within marketing.
- The strategic value of marketing within an organization depends on the external degree of focus and customer orientation of that organization.
- With a customer-focused orientation and even more so with an orientation towards customer participation, marketing is the basis of the entrepreneurial strategy.
- The increasing dynamism in markets means that applying e-marketing must be continually re-evaluated.

17 Changes and choices

An organization's market is restricted by the support needed for a product, both when purchasing and in its use. Market access is also restricted by customers' action radius for a sales outlet.

Distribution channels increased the number of sales outlets and arranged support for purchasing the product. This manufacturers' strategy led to the classic business model, where there was a sharing of tasks between producer, distribution, trade and shop. Trade's task was to bridge time, place and quantity and to mediate between manufacturer and sales outlet. Producers used the trade and a distribution network to get the products to the buyers. Producers focused on getting products and services to the market (classical marketing), while the retailers worked towards sales based on transactions. A producer's focus was thus on a good distribution network and good communication with the market. This classic model has come under pressure, however, because of the Internet. There is a trade-off between the richness of a product and the market reach (Figure 17.1).

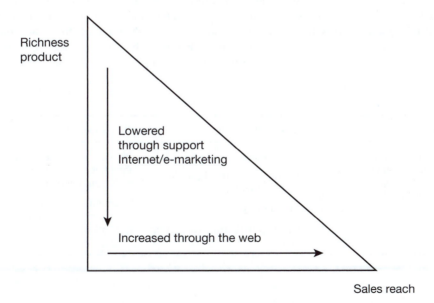

Figure 17.1 Relationship between market access and product complexity

Source: Based on Evans, P. and Wurster, T. (2000), *Blown to Bits*, Harvard Business School Press

17.1 Tension in the distribution channel

These days manufacturers can offer the products themselves on the Internet, while new webshops are constantly being created as well. This makes it necessary for manufacturers to determine their distribution policy afresh, and for shops to decide whether they only wish to sell through physical shops or also via the Internet.

Through the ability to buy both through the Internet and from a physical shop, a potential tension arises between the manufacturer and the distribution channel. Manufacturers want to sell directly via the Internet to capitalize on consumer demand. Shops also want to sell, but have to buy in from the manufacturer. Manufacturers can also in fact protect the distribution channel by not permitting Internet sales. Often a higher cost price is billed to webshops than to physical shops. This dual pricing strategy is intended to protect the existing distribution channel, but cannot be sustained for long. A quick decision needs to be taken on the marketing and distribution strategy to be followed.

A company such as Bose is very clear on this. Bose supplies high-quality audio equipment. You have to be able to hear it to be convinced. Selling via the Internet does not fit within this strategy. Bose uses the Internet for information and communicating with the market; but sales always occur through a shop. Shops may not sell via the Internet themselves – a requirement which is imposed in the contract.

If there are no clear reasons only to sell through a physical shop, the Internet can be developed as a separate channel. Here new webshops can claim a role in the distribution chain, but this role is also important for the existing shops. Because the costs of selling via the Internet do not need to be lower, a dual price strategy cannot be used. Given the current focus of manufacturers – the creation of products and sales via a distribution channel – the supporting marketing orientation is generally an internal orientation and sometimes a market orientation (towards sub-markets). In both instances the focus is on producing products and selling them. Customer support requires a different approach and a different marketing orientation. This is outsourced to the distribution channel and it also has to occur with the Internet. Manufacturers will use the Internet to provide product and company information. Sales occur through the shops and the webshops that place the customer at the core in their choice process. These shops will support the customers in purchasing (Table 17.1).

Table 17.1 Impact of the Internet on the marketing model

Reducing richness	*Increasing reach*	*Dual strategy*
Giving buyers a say by providing information through the Internet, applying interactive media, social media and weblogs, customer support	Webshops Linking with other busy sites (affiliate marketing) Multilingual Open more shops, create service points	Physical shops are service points for advice, viewing products and collecting Internet orders Internet for information, communication and ordering (if wished)

17.2 Choosing the Internet

Choosing the Internet is supported by the following arguments (see also Table 17.2):

- *Power of the distribution channel*: The stronger a channel is, the fewer opportunities there are for manufacturers to start selling online themselves.
- *Power of the manufacturer and the product*: Powerful manufacturers and market leaders can also be dominant; the distribution channel is already satisfied if the products are able to be sold.
- *Buyers' wishes*: Is there a bond with a shop or with a product, and do customers want advice or do they have a strong buying preference?

The cost components for the existing channel comprise distribution costs, stock costs and sales costs. In particular, stock costs and sales costs differ per channel. With a physical channel stock costs and distribution costs will be made up of the costs of distribution partners, such as wholesalers, logistical service providers, distributors, resellers and other service providers. The costs of the sales points comprise location costs (shop and warehouse), stock costs and staffing costs. Sales costs are also incurred for advertising costs and campaigns. The difference between all the costs and the turnover is the ultimate profit.

With webshops the cost components differ, giving rise to the idea that a webshop can deliver more cheaply and thus can exercise unfair competition over physical shops. Webshops have the same cost prices, but can save on location costs: cheaper accommodation, cheaper warehouse space and perhaps less stock through quick deliveries from suppliers (there is a timespan between sales and delivery). But against these cost savings there are other costs:

- Article returns (with the home-shopping guarantee hallmark, items may be returned within 14 days with a money-back guarantee). These items have to be examined to be able to be resold. The returns percentage ranges between 3 per cent on books and CDs to up to 50 per cent in fashion.
- IT costs for the CRM system, direct communication, the website, website content, photography, design and perhaps also videos for the product pages.
- Online advertising, perhaps with banners or AdWords and registration with comparison sites.
- Offline advertising for brand awareness.

Table 17.2 Applying the Internet choice based on strength in the market

Powerplay	Choice of channel	Internet role
Powerful product/manufacturer	With manufacturer, following distribution channel, own sales opportunities possible via the Internet	Webshops, 'me-too' sales, manufacturer sells directly. Internet for information, communication and sales
Powerful retailer	With retailer, manufacturer will follow the wishes of the distribution channel	Multichannel through retailer. Internet supports buying process
Customer wishes	Following manufacturer and distribution	Depending on the customer's wishes

Table 17.3 Strategy differences between physical location and the Internet

Marketing strategy objective	Physical location	Internet
To be found	Location with plenty of traffic, advertising and local awareness	Via Google ranking, AdWords with Google and, among others, Marktplaats, via comparison sites, banners, affiliate marketing and viral marketing
Contact	In the shop, presence of sales staff and products, sometimes via email or letter	Via the website, current content, email, social media
Repeats	Via local awareness and location	Through ongoing communication and top-of-mind position
Profit margin	Clear costs based on location and cost price	Profit based on conversion ratio (visitors–buyers) and customer value. Objective is often also to acquire a market position

The costs of online advertising should not be underestimated. This is significantly important in order to be found and to acquire traffic to your site and sometimes also to your shop. Taking these cost estimates into consideration, the costs of webshops will often not be lower. There is a highly competitive market on the Internet, and everything online can be compared at home and abroad. The strategy differences between physical location and the Internet are compared in Table 17.3.

A price comparison can easily be made by Internet users. In competitive markets there will always be pressure on prices and margins. This certainly also applies to the Internet. Given the cost structure a web retailer will always opt for high turnover and small transaction margins to keep the prices down. This produces the illusion that a web retailer can sell more cheaply, but often this is achieved through carefully controlling costs and a low margin. A web retailer will achieve a profit through a strong market position and by achieving a large number of transactions. Start-up webshops often do not incorporate all the costs, because they often work from home and their own (salary) costs are often not included (Figure 17.2).

The relationship between product manufacturers and shops used to consist of a mutual interdependence: one made products and ensured that these were attractive to a target group, while the other sold these products to consumers, often alongside many other products. The Internet has put this interdependence under pressure through independent consumers seeking information on the Internet and by webshops offering on the Internet. Shops and manufacturers deliberate on their role: to sell on the Internet or not.

17.3 e-Marketing application opportunities

Based on the ORCA sales model, three main activities can be distinguished:

1. searching;
2. considering; and
3. buying (Figure 17.3).

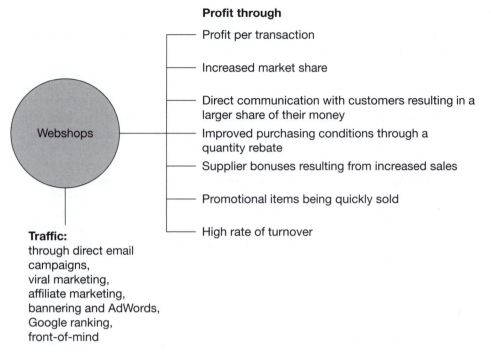

Figure 17.2 Commercial domain of a webshop

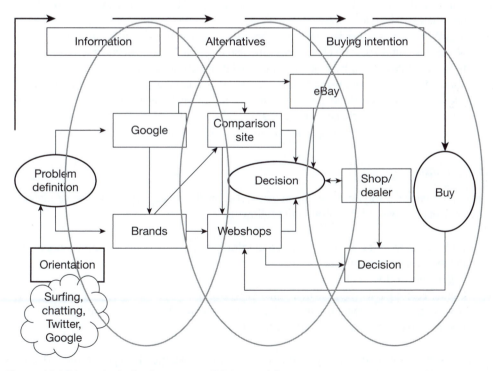

Figure 17.3 Phases in the buying process (ORCA model)

17.3.1 Searching

For the providers, the main 'searching' activity means that they need to be found. There are any number of possibilities here:

- A well-known website (a logical or a known name). A logical name is the name of a physical product and an existing shop. The shortage of domain names means that an increasing number of websites have a descriptive name, such as 'only for women' or 'the best videos'. The intention is to create a top-of-mind position, so that the site can be found quickly and soon reaches the top in a search key.
- High ranking by Google through a good description of the website, plenty of tags and plenty of traffic. It is also possible to buy a position via AdWords, or advertising with a tag or general advertising. The same is possible through trading sites such as eBay.
- Affiliates, through linkage with heavily visited sites. This could be achieved through an advertisement, or by hyperlinks in the text. It is also possible that a visitor considers buying a product via this site, where the processing actually occurs through a different provider. Sites with plenty of traffic play an important role here. In the future there will be a rising number of such sites which are dominant in a specific area, and which refer to other sites (and ask for payment in return); these could be providers who refer to manufacturers who supply directly for example, but also theme portals, social media or news sites.
- Emails. Under the many current legislation emails may only be sent to existing relations. By making these intensive and to the point, increasing traffic can be directed to your site.
- Other media. Advertisements in the printed press and particularly TV advertising, leads traffic to the site, certainly if there is a possibility of buying or if extra information is provided via the site.
- Mouth-to-mouth advertising where other users discuss the site. In its modern form this occurs through blogs and chat rooms, but also through Twitter. Because a hypertext link is provided directly, others can be taken to the site immediately.
- Viral marketing. A viral marketing campaign is a campaign that is so attractive that people look at it and attract other people to it by sending links or emails. To be successful if should be funny, offensive, rude or sexy, which will enourage people to share it with others. The campaign thus gets attention, creating awareness of the product or the site.

17.3.2 Considering

During the consideration process the buyer seeks out references and comparative material. The provider can assist here through the following:

- Links to the manufacturer where product information can be found (one must not be able to buy directly here of course).
- A guestbook/blog or chat room.
- Online customer service, via mail, chat or webcam.
- Notification at comparison sites. Comparison occurs by product, but can be linked instantly to a shop (physical and online) (Table 17.4).

Comparison sites provide a comparison of products and specifications per product. Because they attract many visitors, they also feature advertisements for other products and services.

Table 17.4 Top 15 comparison sites, November 2010

1	NexTag
2	BizRate
3	shopLocal
4	slickdeals
5	woot
6	GroupOn
7	coupons
8	pronto
9	shopzilla
10	ShopAtHome
11	smarter
12	PriceGrabber
13	fatwallet
14	DealTime
15	Become

Source: http://www.ebizmba.com/articles/shopping-websites

Customers search for comparison products, and for specific details based on a product. If the customer wants to buy these products, he or she can go to the shop or buy online. To make it easy to buy online, webshop links are provided. Nevertheless many buyers print out the information and take it to a physical shop.

Buyers can also search on trading sites. This gives them an idea of the market for used articles and prices.

All these details make for a well-considered decision before it is decided to buy. This process occurs at home or at work, in all comfort without any pressure to buy. Once the choice has been made, a decision must follow as to where to buy: on the Internet or from a shop.

17.3.3 Buying

The choice between buying on the Internet or from a shop is a personal one, and depends on several criteria, such as:

- the presence of a local shop which has the items in stock;
- trust in the shop and the bond with the shop (or the retailer);
- confidence in one's own choice and the correctness of the choice;
- the ease of buying online;
- the necessity or desire to see the articles, to touch them and take them away;
- confidence in Internet buying and confidence in the webshop; and
- the emotional bond with a product.

Despite the Internet being a worldwide platform, 80 per cent of European buyers prefer a national company, 15 per cent buy elsewhere in Europe or America, and only 5 per cent search shops outside this region (Asia or Oceania).

In choosing a webshop, buyers take into consideration its familiarity, range, email response speed, navigation ease and colour combination. The number of payment possibilities is also considered (including post-payment) and the home-shopping guarantee hallmark. In particular this hallmark induces considerable trust because there are identical rules in the interests of the buyer.

Alongside these objective comparative criteria, delivery is also taken into account. Many products advertise delivery within 24 hours or 24 hours after payment. The buyer only accepts a longer delivery time if the products still have to be produced or modified. In all instances the delivery time must be stated clearly in advance so that incorrect expectations are not raised.

But not everyone buys on the Internet, and not every time. Physical shops have the advantage of trust (you can see and touch and take away the item). Nevertheless physical shops also have to take the new customer into account. This customer is now better informed (through the Internet) than previously. The questions asked are extremely specific and tailored. The sales staff thus need to be expert in their field to be able to answer these questions. The advice function of sales staff will become increasingly important in the future. If this advice matches the image of the customer, a relationship of trust will be created. It is precisely for this reason that retailers must capitalize on customer wishes, must listen to these wishes and must provide good advice. Shops also have to be pleasant and must capitalize on experience. The shop must not compete on the basis of rationale, because this can be done far better by a webshop. The shop must compete with personal advice, a personal relationship and experience. Shops must be attractive and nice. It is precisely when the buying threshold is lowered as a result and trust has been built up, that the customer will prefer the physical shop. Customers have acquired enormous choice through the Internet, but also plenty of information about the product, prices and conditions. The retailer needs to understand this and motivate the customer to purchase in the shop nonetheless.

Although physical sales will certainly continue to occupy an important position, the role of Internet sales will increase strongly. It is also important to remember that the influence of the Internet on buying is powerful because 80 per cent of people use the Internet to obtain information before deciding to buy. Internet sales will grow still further in the years ahead. It is expected that by 2015 sales will be around 30 per cent of the total non-food sales in most western countries. This is not because of the market growth, but through a market shift from offline to online. This means existing shops need to develop a clear strategy towards the Internet.

One possibility is for shops to set up their own Internet sites where customers can buy. This does, however, require a very special approach to this medium. Rushing ahead may lead to disruption in the shop, because less attention is devoted to the shop, and may also lead to disruption in the online sales. Customers expect prompt deliveries, quick processing of emails and complaints, and an insight into stock levels. If a shop opts for the Internet, it immediately opts for a dual strategy: shop versus online. To enable these two channels to operate independently, a separate strategy is needed which capitalizes on the buying process and the expectations of buyers.

Sometimes a separate name is chosen for the Internet shop. The new department may use different systems, like a CRM system, a webshop system and separate stock to make it immediately visible on the Internet. Nothing is more frustrating for a buyer than to receive an email several hours after the online purchase stating that the article is sold out.

Separate channels will mean that a separate pricing strategy can also be followed, and possibly a different range can also be offered. The choice for what a shop represents is then between the following options:

- The shop is only a physical player and the Internet is used to provide information about the range and the products. The shop must be set up in such a way that it capitalizes on the physical process when the customer enters.

• The shop is only there to be an Internet player, a so-called pure player, where it can capitalize to the fullest on the wishes of the online buyer.

But there is also a third possibility: cross-retailing. Here both channels are supportive of each other. The customer can search and view on the Internet, but can also go to the shop. The shop uses the same name on the Internet. The Internet refers to the shop, the opening hours and the range. On the basis of the customer buying process, with the product choice it can be indicated whether this product is in stock, and at which shop. In addition, the opportunity to buy on the Internet but to collect the articles in the shop is an interesting development. The shop will have traffic without extra stock or promotions. On websites the 'click and collect' proposition is offered. The customer chooses a shop or location in the neighbourhood to collect the shopping. Although a pick-up place is possible, more interesting is of course a pick-up place in the shop or another shop. Extra sales can be made but it is also a good place to return the articles, if needed. This enables the customer to decide for him- or herself whether to buy the item online and have it delivered at home, or whether to go to the shop for a demonstration. There the customer can either buy the item immediately and take it away, or have it delivered at home.

This cross-retailing system takes maximum advantage of the new buying behaviour of customers and optimizes the buying process. There is no waiting period for the customer, and the shop gains a visitor with the attendant chance of 'incidental purchases'. Through the ability to collect items from a shop or service outlet, the items can be viewed and, if necessary, can be tried or exchanged. The irritation of 'not being at home' for delivery is thus no longer an issue.

For the retailer this is also an opportunity to capitalize on. The retailer can open smaller outlets with a limited range and stock, and customers can buy the other items on the Internet and collect them in the shop. This means retailers can open shops closer to the customers, and can thus return to residential areas rather than large and expensive shopping centres and shopping precincts. This makes optimum use of both channels: of the buying process of customers but also of the power of the nearby physical shop and the presence of goods.

17.4 The challenge for marketing and distribution

The Internet is becoming increasingly integrated within customers' buying processes. This means companies have to look afresh at their own distribution and their own proposition, and they need to capitalize on the wishes of customers. The Internet can be deployed in sectional areas: for information and to compare and buy. The shop adapts itself to this buying process. Providers can focus on their own strengths: manufacturers support the distribution, but disseminate information through internal channels and any possible services and supplies. For the sales there will be purer players, who utilize the virtual channel and who will seek out shops for a cross-functionality that matches the concept. Shops will also be adapted to the physical moment, for experience and trust, and they will come closer to residential concentrations. Location was and still is extremely important for shops.

For organizations this means a conscious choice must be made and that the marketing orientation must be adapted to this end, including the organizational structure. This also means that e-marketing must be applied in the right way, as described in this book.

Summary

- Shops need to adapt to market changes. The ultimate decision and buying moment is changing constantly because of the Internet.
- The relationship between shops and manufacturers must become tighter, with more interdependence.
- Alongside rationale there is a strong emotion with buying – this is the power of physical shops and the physical presence of products.
- e-Marketing must be an integral part of every marketing strategy irrespective of the marketing orientation.

18 New developments in marketing

The application of the Internet is leading to new developments in marketing, in relation to both suppliers and customers. A major development is the change from supply driven to demand driven. No longer is the major focus to make a transaction (deal), but to create an individual relationship. Part of the changed focus is the involvement of supplier and buyer in the buying process as described earlier, the different forms of relationship in the supply chain and with suppliers, and finally the interaction and communication with customers.

18.1 Changes in the role of suppliers

The relationship with suppliers will change in a business-to-business environment (Figure 18.1). The dependency on each other will grow, but will also make the relationship closer. The market is agile and dynamic, market changes are rapid and the loyalty of customers is

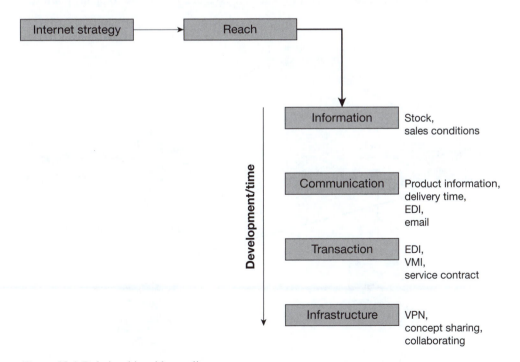

Figure 18.1 Relationship with suppliers

diminishing. This will lead to a more flexible approach to the market. The standard supply chain will lead to inflexibility because of the different roles of supplier, wholesaler, logistic service supplier and retailer, but also because of the 'buffer stock' in the supply chain. There will be a need for less stock in the total chain, which will lead to a 'single stock location' approach. But there is also a need for more interaction based on information sharing and a single financial responsibility for all supplies. In this new relationship suppliers will be responsible for production, delivery and stock levels. New concepts such as VMI (vendor-managed inventories) and EDI (electronic data interchange) will make this possible if they are applied in an integrated way.

18.1.1 Focus of retailers

Retailers will focus on the customers and will communicate with the final customer, delivery of services will be done by the retailer, but delivery of articles can be done out of stock in the shop or on delivery when the articles are bought on the Internet. This is a new concept, where the central stock can be used for home delivery and the stock in the shop for immediate delivery. In this concept the retailer will receive a bonus for home deliveries and a margin for sales out of the stock. In both cases it is a bonus for customer contact (Figure 18.2).

The relationship with suppliers will no longer only be based on a transaction relationship where one party delivers the goods and another party sells the goods or in a business-to-business environment where one salesperson sells to the buyer of another company. The relationship will be closer and based more on partnership and cooperation. The focus of the relationship will evolve from information gathering and sharing to communication. This communication will be through static means such as websites, newsletters and email, but also interactive through webcams (like Skype), instant messaging, interactive company platforms

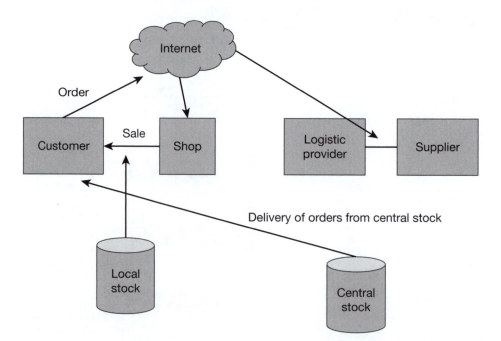

Figure 18.2 Sales and delivery process retailers

and teleconferencing. The personal interaction is important for decision-making and relationships.

A next step will be the automatic buying process based upon minimum stock levels or other triggers. Based on contracts, the individual transactions are generated automatically or the order is placed by operational staff without further involvement. The last phase is the deployment of the Internet as a facility platform. Tracking and tracing is an example where physical processes are integrated into virtual information processes. The customer (company) can control the flow of goods and always knows where articles, cars, lorries or other physical things are. In all cases and for all processes the business-to-business relationship between suppliers will change the market structure. In retail the change will also take place in the delivery of goods. If an article cannot be taken directly home by the customer there is no need for a retailer to have it in stock. Suppliers or central warehouses can stock the shop but also deliver directly to the customer at home!

18.2 Changes in the role of and communication with customers

In the future contacts with customers will also change (Figure 18.3). The customer is no longer an unknown buyer of goods and services – a lucky passerby walking past the shop – but an identified person. Because the identification is important it can also be the basis for

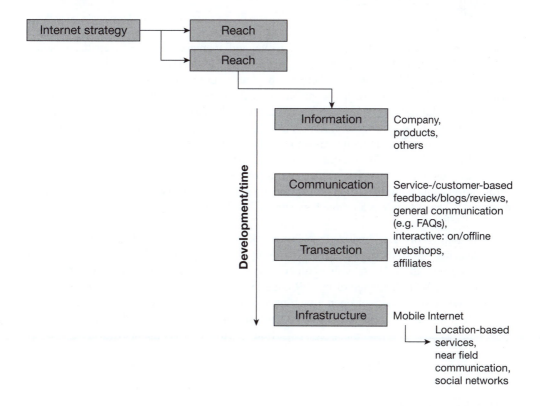

Figure 18.3 Relationship with retailers and customers

communication, information-based interaction and in some cases the reason for new business concepts involving the customer. In the future the challenge will no longer be to find customers for your products, but to find products for your customers. In other words, it is the individual need of the customer that will lead the service offered.

To know and understand the needs of the individual customer's interaction with the service is a primary activity of every business. The Internet as a platform will make this possible. The important steps that need to be taken to involve the customer in this process are shown in Figure 18.3. Information gathering is the first step. This includes identity (name, address), information about the person, about his or her behaviour and finally information about the purchases. This information is needed for direct communication and personal messages based on the behaviour and expected needs (behavioural communication). The communication should lead to feedback and response analyses but a company should also facilitate direct communication efficiently. A step-by-step approach is best and should include:

- information on the website;
- frequently asked questions (FAQs);
- interaction in social media (user-generated content);
- email requests and responses;
- chatting, microblogging; and
- a call centre.

The level of interaction and customer involvement will increase with every step, the personal contact will be intensified with every step, but so also will the costs involved.

The last step will be integration between physical and virtual contacts. The customer is always connected with his or her smartphone or iPad and will combine physical presence with online information or messages. Augmented reality, location-based services and near field communication are examples of this. The customer is known and approachable. Companies will need to integrate this opportunity in their contact scheme.

Another possibility is QR, the quick response code. This code, which looks like a barcode, is a small program. With a photo on a smartphone this program can be activated to provide information about a product, shop or location, a video about the use of the product or how to buy direct. The QR code is a bridge between physical and virtual.

> QR codes storing addresses and Uniform Resource Locators (URLs) may appear in magazines, on signs, buses, business cards, or almost any object about which users might need information. Users with a camera phone equipped with the correct reader application can scan the image of the QR code to display text, contact information, connect to a wireless network or open a web page in the phone's browser. This act of linking from physical world objects is termed hardlinking or object hyperlinking.
>
> Source: http://en.wikipedia.org/wiki/QR_Code

A QR code is shown in Figure 18.4.

18.2.1 Social media[1]

Social media is the collective creation of content on online platforms by users with little or no intervention by a professional editor. Also, there is interaction and dialogue between the

Figure 18.4 QR, quick response code

Source: http://www.bengfort.com/benjamin/quick-response-qr-codes-are-awesome/

users themselves. Every Internet user is a communicator and reporter in creating and delivering information to family, friends and colleagues. An example is Wikipedia, where articles are formed by multiple editors.

Wikipedia articles are based on user-generated content and not always reliable, although an editorial staff monitor the content. Studies show that the reliability of information in Wikipedia might be close to that of the well-established traditional encyclopaedias The rise of social media (and Wikipedia) serves a different purpose. The estimated monthly visitors of 350 million worldwide use Wikipedia's platform to gain a broad variety of information with great ease. The information is mostly up to date. It seems to serve their purpose of being a good starting point and is more than sufficient and is therefore accepted as reliable enough.

Communities

People still organize in groups. In the past these groups were static, nowadays they are much more mobile. The consumer lives in a changing social structure, which influences his or her social behaviour. Individualization and the need for social contacts cause consumers to move, searching for the same kind of people or people with the same interests or needs. Individual consumers have the need 'to belong somewhere' and therefore search for formal and informal 'clubs' where they feel they belong. An important difference with the standard social contacts of the past is that consumers now choose the nature of their groups whereas before society or friends were dominant. Consumers participate in multiple groups of interest using the Internet as a platform. Online networking opened up possibilities for people to communicate with anyone in the world, at any time, which was previously more difficult because of geographical boundaries.

Social media are driven by the interaction within groups consisting of members. An online community is a virtual community that exists online. Its members enable its existence through taking part in the rules of the community and behaviour of the group. These groups share a concern or a passion for something they do and learn how to do it better as they interact regularly. The group has something in common that makes them a group. It might be an interest, a problem or a love for a brand. This common interest is the magnet. The stronger the magnet, the more members in the group. With respect to differences in online and offline communities, it is obvious that online communities are more based on shared interests, while real-life communities and networks depend rather more on place (neighbourhood or village) or shared ancestry/family ties. Furthermore, there seems to be a difference in the value of online and offline communities. In order to become a truly valuable link, interaction must occur offline as well as online.

18.2.2 Types of social media

Social networking

A social network service is an online service, platform or site that focuses on building and reflecting social networks or social relations among people (for example, people who share interests and/or activities). A social network service essentially consists of a representation of each user (often a profile), his or her social links and a variety of additional services.

Collaborative user-generated content

On some platforms professional or non-professional users give a substantive contribution to an online medium. This collaborative user-generated content is created via multiple entries. Wikipedia is an example of this.

Blogs

A blog (a blend of the term 'web log') is a type of website or part of a website. Blogs are usually maintained by an individual with regular entries of commentary, descriptions of events, or other material such as graphics or video. Entries are commonly displayed in reverse-chronological order. The author, also known as a blogger, provides a log of information that he or she wants to share with an audience, visitors to the blog.

Microblogs

Microblogging is a broadcast medium in the form of blogging. A microblog differs from a traditional blog in that its content is typically much smaller, in both actual size and aggregate file size. A microblog entry could consist of nothing but a short sentence fragment, an image or embedded video. There are many microblog platforms, but by far the most notable is Twitter.

Media sharing

Media sharing is a comprehensive platform and diversified interfaces to aggregate, upload, compress, host and distribute images, text, applications, videos, audio, games and new media. YouTube is an example of this. Media sharing is also widely done via peer2peer networks.

Social news sites

These are websites where users submit and vote on news stories or other links, thus determining which links are presented. Popular examples are Digg and Reddit.

Social bookmarking

Social bookmarking is a method for Internet users to organize, store, manage and search for bookmarks of resources online. Unlike file sharing, the resources themselves are not shared, merely bookmarks that reference them. Delicious is a well-accepted social bookmarking platform.

Ratings and reviews

Sites on which reviews can be posted about people, businesses, products or services may use Web 2.0 techniques to gather reviews from site users or may employ professional writers to author reviews on the topic of concern for the site. Ratings and reviews features are often embedded in webshops. Examples are Amazon and the various comparison sites.

Forums

An Internet forum is an online discussion site where people can hold conversations in the form of posted messages. Depending on the access level of a user and/or the forum set-up, a posted message might need to be approved by a moderator before it becomes visible. A forum is hierarchical or tree-like in structure: forum – sub-forum – topic – thread – reply.

Virtual worlds

A virtual world is a type of online community that often takes the form of a computer-based simulated environment through which users can interact with one another and use and create objects. Virtual worlds are intended for their users to inhabit and interact, and the term today has become largely synonymous with interactive 3D virtual environments, where users take the form of avatars visible to others graphically. Second Life is a popular example.

18.2.3 Users of social media

Social media is seen as the new way of sharing and interacting via Internet platforms and from a business perspective doing business with customers. Although social media is widely accepted by a large number of people, it is mainly used by specific groups in society.

Developments in the use of media by the elderly and youth are very heterogeneous. Where older generations do not abandon their media use patterns, on the other side of the age spectrum is a continuously growing 'digital generation' without nostalgia for established institutions such as the newspaper and public broadcasting. Young people embrace new media and abandon the old much more quickly than do older people. Older people are more likely to want to see first what the benefit is compared with existing media or behaviour. The online computer is to this generation all in one: not just a mass medium, but also an interaction medium. Those possibilities are also often used simultaneously.

18.2.4 Categorization of users

Social media has been adopted rapidly by large groups of users. These users do not approach social media equally and can be categorized as follows:

- *Active users for connections and networking:* This group is present on social media sites and have their own page with a profile and photos. They check 'friends' in their network, update their profiles but are not actively communicating (the so-called joiners).
- *Active communicators:* These users use social media for active communications. They give their opinions about things but also use the medium for active communication with other users. Active communicators with knowledge are active based upon their knowledge. Sometimes they are experts in a certain field and like to discuss topics with people who are also experts or will use them as an expert, like a specialist on software, devices or holiday places or hobbies.
- *Passive users:* These users are only on those sites to observe and to see what other people have to say about certain products or activities.
- *Creative users:* These users make blogs, write active reviews and respond to other users.

Acceptance and commercial opportunities

The acceptance and use of social media depend on personal situations. People who are active on the Internet are mostly also active on social media sites. People with a passion or active hobby like to share this activity on social media. And young people are more active than older people. It is a need for social contact and a need to share that is the main motivating force. It may also be a frustration that is the driving force but mostly this is of short duration.

The commercial opportunities of a social media are based on the common interest of the users. This common interest can be the basis for commercial offerings, active or passive via AdWords or banners. A fee may also be charged for participating, newsletters, tickets or whatever. Companies should be careful about being too commercial, which may be counterproductive. Participation in a site should be based on knowledge, not on giving a different view on problems. Using tags (top words) certain names, problems or messages can be seen or followed. In Twitter it is possible to tag names, which will lead to an alert. In this way a direct response is possible to the user of the word. The developments of social media are still at a very early stage. The idea is that it will lead to a further progress of sharing information and combining people with the same interest. A target group in classical marketing was a predefined target group based upon objective criteria. This target group is a post-defined target group where members actively form a group. The impact is mostly stronger!

18.3 The difference between Web 2.0 and social media

The terms Web 2.0 and social media are often used interchangeably because the functionalities of Web 2.0 are often intertwined with social media. Yet there are clear differences between Web 2.0 and social media. Social media are employed for social interaction, using highly accessible and scalable publishing techniques. Social media use Web-based technologies to transform and broadcast media monologues into social media dialogues content.

Web 2.0 refers to renewed attention to both the usefulness and also the underlying technology of web services. Social media existed before this development. Examples include the introduction of the Internet message boards before Internet outside military and academic circles was used, a forerunner of the current forums. New (Web 2.0) technology enabled social media to mature into a stage where it is adopted rapidly by a fast growing constituency.

18.3.1 The 'social' in social media

The growing accessibility of information technologies puts the tools required to collaborate, create value and compete at everybody's fingertips. This liberates people to participate in innovation and wealth creation within every sector of the economy. It is nothing new; social media has existed for decades (for example, bulletin boards) but it is only through advances in infrastructure (increasing bandwidth and fixed/wireless infrastructure) that its popularity has been able to expand rapidly. The infrastructure can therefore be seen as the enabler of change.

User-generated media is at the heart of social media. With a snap of the fingers, ordinary citizens are transformed into citizen journalists – writers, radio broadcasters and film-makers. Ordinary people have power like they never have had before.

Traditionally, advertising was created by organizations and consumed by consumers. The intentions of the advertiser have thus always been clear: messages were used to inform, persuade or remind. Consumers, on the other hand, have always been passive recipients of communication. Times have changed, and the creation of advertisements is no longer the prerogative of the organization. Consumers now have a whole toolbox of instruments available to them with an unprecedented speed and scope through which to share their brand experiences and opinions. Never before have they been exposed to such a wide range of opinions and recommendations of many different people. Where once they could share ideas and experiences with their peers at work, school or in the family, now their networks can extend well beyond the immediate social group, even globally.

Consumers now have at their disposal a highly effective instrument by which to share their brand experiences and opinions, whether positive or negative, regarding any product or service. As major companies are increasingly coming to realize, these consumer voices can wield enormous influence in shaping the opinions of other consumers – and, ultimately, their brand loyalties and purchase decisions.

What has not changed is the fact that the brand experiences, recommendations and opinions of some are more influential than those of others.

Word of mouth

Word of mouth is always an important factor in the formation of opinions. Word of mouth publicity is not a new phenomenon. Word of mouth influence includes direct effects on the behaviour (and thus the factors that determine the behaviour, such as needs and attitudes) of a consumer through informal interpersonal contact with another consumer. Because there is no intervention of a marketer in word of mouth influencing, the influencer is more reliable. He or she has no commercial interest in giving either positive or negative information about a product; and because of this, the adviser will give exposure to both the negative and positive aspects of the subject of the advice. This makes the word of mouth adviser more credible than most advisers.

18.4 Changes for marketing

Marketers are being challenged to shift their focus from traditional supply controlled marketing to a demand orientation, where they seem to have less control. Generating positive word of mouth among consumers therefore is an important tool for marketers, and this is particularly true for the digital media. Consumer-generated content can be seen as very similar to word of mouth communication, as both are created and maintained by consumers and not by organizations; but the impact is greater because of the number of users of the social media.

18.4.1 Social media within marketing

It is clear that organizations should shift from trying to control customer behaviour; they should enforce a social media marketing strategy which enables the support of consumers' and customers' (word of mouth) conversations about their brand, product or services.

Word of mouth, especially the online variety that in part gives rise to social media, emphasizes the relationship that has long existed – more or less invisibly – between promise and delivery. The social feedback cycle is set in motion by a post-purchase opinion that forms based on the relationship between the expectations set and the actual performance of the product or service. This opinion drives word of mouth, and word of mouth ultimately feeds back into the purchase funnel in the consideration phase.

Building a social media strategy

A good strategy should be based on customer needs. This strategy cannot be isolated from the organizational strategy, marketing and sales strategy and the IT strategy.

Marketers often approach communication as if it is an objective in itself, and seem to forget that it should be a part of the corporate strategy and marketing strategy to reach the objectives. The problem is that companies tend to go about their strategy backwards. It is more productive to approach social media from a traditional communications standpoint and consider each tool and social network in the context of whether it is the right medium for the audience, the message, the budget and the company's objectives.

When the organization and business objectives are clear, the primary social media objectives should be used to support the main goals. A strategy is concerned with the actions and resources needed to achieve specific long-term objectives. A one-size-fits-all strategy to engage in social media should not be developed, in part because businesses and their needs and objectives vary. Nevertheless, a comprehensive roadmap that organizations can use as guidance for the preparation of a social media strategy can be formulated. While research and strategy continue to be essential for successful social media programmes, flexibility and improvisation are equally important.

Defining a strategy starts with the question: how should we engage our customers and how will that engagement grow over time? The missing ingredient in most social media strategies is actual strategy. Organizations should outline exactly how their approach in their social strategy will bridge the gap between customer/stakeholder needs, existing online conversations and the company's positioning. Many firms fail to establish a connection between their strategy planning processes and the processes they use to identify, select, implement and deploy individual projects. An effective Internet marketing strategy should therefore be aligned with a business strategy, with specific annual business priorities and initiatives, and should recognize that a social media initiative does not operate in isolation but must be integrated with other parts of the organization and its operational structure.

Social media should therefore be seen as a part of the whole, and so a holistic approach is needed.

Summary

- Social media is based on a group of coherent users with a common interest.
- Social media is based upon user-generated content.
- Social media is a perfect target group for companies to listen, learn from users and to act accordingly.
- Social media uses 'word of mouth' with considerable impact.
- Social media is an example of the change from a supply-driven to a demand-driven approach, involving a change from focusing on unidentified customers to a focus on identified and known customers.

Note

1 Part of this research was conducted by Mark de Loose, student at Rotterdam School of Management in 2010.

Index